Fictitious Capital

Fictitious Capital

SILK, COTTON, AND THE RISE OF THE ARABIC NOVEL

Elizabeth M. Holt

FORDHAM UNIVERSITY PRESS *New York* 2017

the modern language initiative

THIS BOOK IS MADE POSSIBLE BY A COLLABORATIVE GRANT FROM THE ANDREW W. MELLON FOUNDATION.

Fordham University Press also publishes its books in a variety of electronic formats. Some content that appears in print may not be available in electronic books.

Visit us online at www.fordhampress.com.

Library of Congress Cataloging-in-Publication Data

Names: Holt, Elizabeth M. author.
Title: Fictitious capital : silk, cotton, and the rise of the Arabic novel / Elizabeth M. Holt.
Description: First edition. | New York : Fordham University Press, 2017. | Includes bibliographical references and index.
Identifiers: LCCN 2016058727 | ISBN 9780823276028 (cloth : alk. paper) | ISBN 9780823276035 (pbk. : alk. paper)
Subjects: LCSH: Serialized fiction—Lebanon—History and criticism. | Serialized fiction—Egypt—History and criticism. | Arabic fiction—19th century—History and criticism. | Literature publishing—Economic aspects—Lebanon—History—19th century. | Literature publishing—Economic aspects—Egypt—History—19th century.
Classification: LCC PJ8082 .H65 2017 | DDC 892.7/3509—dc23
LC record available at https://lccn.loc.gov/2016058727

Printed in the United States of America

19 18 17   5 4 3 2 1

First edition

For Hadley and Sasha,
and for Jason

CONTENTS

ACKNOWLEDGMENTS

Many institutions, colleagues, friends, and loving family members have been instrumental in the process of bringing this book to publication.

I am grateful to Bard College for its generous support of my research since I joined its faculty in 2008. I thank the National Endowment for the Humanities for funding research for chapters 4 and 5 while I was a fellow at the American Research Center in Egypt. The American University of Beirut's Center for Arab and Middle East Studies graciously hosted me while I was researching the earlier chapters of the book. I first discovered the journal *Al-Jinān* at the heart of this manuscript while I was in Cairo on a Fulbright IIE grant, and for that I am also grateful.

At Fordham University Press, I am especially appreciative of everything Tom Lay, Tim Roberts, Susan Murray, and Katie Sweeney have done to produce this book.

Earlier versions of work included in *Fictitious Capital* were presented at several Middle East Studies Association conferences, annual meetings of the American Comparative Literature Association, the Tufts Seeds of Revolution Symposium, the American University of Beirut's 150 Years conference, the Westfälische Wilhelms-Universität Münster conference on Arab Media, the Columbia Arabic Studies Seminar, the Teaching Arab Intellectual Thought conference at Columbia University, the Migration, Diaspora, Exile, and Estrangement conference at Columbia University, the speaker series of the Department of Near Eastern Studies at Cornell, and the American Research Center in Egypt.

Portions of chapters 1, 2, and 5 appeared in an earlier form in "From Gardens of Knowledge to Ezbekiyya after Midnight: The Novel and the Arabic Press from Beirut to Cairo, 1870–1892"; in "Authoring the *Nahḍa*: Writing the Arabic 19th Century," a special issue of

Middle Eastern Literatures 16, no. 3 (December 2013); and as "Narrative and the Reading Public in 1870s Beirut," *Journal of Arabic Literature* 40, no. 1 (2009). Part of chapter 6 appeared as "Speculating in Egypt: Yaʿqūb Ṣarrūf's 1905 Novel *Fatāt Miṣr*," Abhath (2016). I am grateful to those journals for allowing me to republish portions of those articles here.

The archive of *Fictitious Capital* spans more than fifty years of the Arabic press and could not have been assembled without the librarians and archivists of the American University of Beirut, Université St.-Joseph, the American University in Cairo, Dār al-Hilāl, the United States Library of Congress, Harvard, Columbia, Princeton, New York University, the New York Public Library main branch, Brooklyn College, and the French archives in Nantes and Aix-en-Provence. I wish to also thank Ḥilmī al-Namnam at Dār al-Hilāl in Cairo for thoughtful comments on the legacy of Salīm al-Bustānī.

Without my advisor, Muhsin al-Musawi, or my teachers, Nadia Harb, Muhammad Siddiq, William Granara, Gayatri Spivak, Noha Radwan, Madeleine Dobie, and Joseph Massad, I could not have read this archive or written this book. I owe them all a debt of gratitude.

Fictitious Capital benefited tremendously from the careful eye and ear of Mike Allan, Roger Allen, Walter Armbrust, Nadia Bagdadi, Omar Cheta, Elliott Colla, Tarek El-Ariss, Dahlia Gubara, Cole Heinowitz, Aaron Jakes, Rashid Khalidi, Hoyt Long, Timothy Mitchell, Muhsin al-Musawi, Bilal Orfali, Kamran Rastegar, Dwight Reynolds, Bruce Robbins, Lucie Ryzova, Jeff Sacks, Stephen Sheehi, Shaden Tageldin, Shawkat Toorawa, Ali Wick, and Barbara Winckler. I wish to thank all of them, and Roger Berkowitz, too.

Without the hospitality in New York, Beirut, and Cairo of Walter Armbrust, Anna and Beau Bothwell, Jason Broome, Christine Boustany, Nora Boustany, Tarek El-Ariss, Jenny Gootman, Dahlia Gubara, Cole Heinowitz, Elizabeth Johnston, Sabina Kerimovic, Sonya Meyerson-Knox, Lucas van Lenten, Muhsin al-Musawi, Tsolin Nalbantian, Mariano Paniello, Dina Ramadan, Kamran Rastegar, Lucie Ryzova, Sophia Stamatopoulou-Robbins, Mary and Nader Sadek, Stacey Sperling, Trish Stegner, Daniel Weintraub, and Ali Wick, this would have been a far lonelier undertaking.

Without Sadie Moss Jones and Allan Warshowsky, I fear *Fictitious Capital* may never have seen completion. I thank them for their loving care.

While on the way from the French archives in Nantes to those held in Aix-en-Provence, I had the great good fortune to stop for lunch with my aunt Anne Marie and her family. She has since passed away, and I deeply regret that she will never see the book I told her about that afternoon, even as I remain grateful it occassioned those moments together.

My father-in-law, Morris—who taught me the ins and outs of day-trading one Florida afternoon, cautioning me that "the market has more pain than one person can absorb"—also did not live to see this book in print. I hope it is in some way a testament to his memory.

I thank my dear sister, Julie, and brother, Stephen, for their love, and my mother-in-law, June, for hers. My parents, Philip and Kathy, have been a constant source of sustenance. I love them, and thank them for being the first and most enduring supporters of my education (and novel reading!).

I began writing this book when my daughter, Hadley, was in the womb—she has lent me much creative energy over the years. I am so thankful to have her in my life, and for the transformations and joy my son, Sasha, has since brought to our home.

It is to them, and to my husband, Jason Frydman—whose generous critique, years of thoughtful conversation, nourishing cooking, and boundless, humbling love sustain and inspire me—that, in deepest love and gratitude, I dedicate this book.

NOTE ON TRANSLITERATION

Fictitious Capital follows the transliteration conventions of the *Journal of Arabic Literature*, maintaining diacritical marks for Arabic words and names of authors writing in Arabic. Cities go by their most common English spelling (so Beirut, not Bayrūt).

Fictitious Capital

Introduction

This is a book about the history of the Arabic novel, but it will not be a tale so much of nation as of capital—finance capital in particular—in an age, much like our own, of speculation and empire; and while *Fictitious Capital* ends in Egypt, the history it charts does not begin there, but in Ottoman Syria. For a curiously long time, Egyptian lawyer Muḥammad Ḥusayn Haykal's 1914 novel *Zaynab* marked the beginning of the Arabic novel. That narrative was consolidated in ʿAbd al-Muḥsin Ṭāhā Badr's canon-forming *Taṭawwur al-riwāyah al-ʿarabiyyah al-ḥadīthah fī Miṣr (1860–1938)* (The development of the modern Arabic novel in Egypt, 1860–1938) at the moment, Elliott Colla reminds us, that Egypt was decolonizing under Nasser, an Egypt for Egyptians.[1] *Fictitious Capital* reads from the extensive, disremembered archive of the early Arabic press, a prehistory of *Zaynab*, a time when the Arabic novel as a serialized form provided the narrative technology for imagining a new kind of future, one founded in the speculative habits of finance capital remaking Arab cities of the Eastern Mediterranean from at least 1860.

The novels serialized in Arabic at a moment so often heralded as one of *Nahḍah*, of rise and renaissance, limned in form and plot what Giovanni Arrighi reminds us is a "hidden abode": the realm of finance, "the real home of capitalism."[2] "Hard to see because of the actual invisibility or the complexity of the activities that constitute it," Arrighi writes, it is a realm of capital where profits are made off the "monetary illusions" of others.[3] *Fictitious Capital* reads serialized Arabic novels in the late nineteenth and early twentieth centuries alongside a persistent critique of practices of financial speculation in first the Beirut press and later that of Cairo and Alexandria. Novels by Khalīl al-Khūrī, Salīm al-Bustānī, Yūsuf al-Shalfūn, Jurjī Zaydān, and Yaʿqūb Ṣarrūf inscribe the monetary illusions colonizing the silk and cotton markets of Syria and Egypt. Giving form week after week, month after month, and year after year to the complex speculative practices attending the global rise of finance capital, the serialized novel in Arabic as elsewhere asked readers to wait, ever-attentive to the future, for "the remainder was to come."

There is a conspicuous density of historical scholarship and literary criticism available in English on turn-of-the-twentieth-century Egypt.[4] While *Zaynab* no longer stands at the beginning of the history of the Arabic novel, little attention is given to the Beirut journals of the 1870s and 1880s,[5] which had wide circulation in Syria, Egypt, and far beyond.[6] In their pages, as in the Egyptian press at the turn of the century, time itself was being reconfigured in Arabic by finance capital and fiction, and had been since at least the 1860s. This "hidden abode" of speculation and its momentary collapse in 1907, however, has proven in retrospect to indeed be "hard to see": it barely registers in the work of Middle East historians, while it has met with silence in the work of their colleagues in Arabic literature. On Barak's recent *On Time: Technology and Temporality in Modern Egypt* speaks of cotton, the Cairo Bourse, the telegraph, and debt repayment, and yet *On Time* never attends to what these new technologies of time enabled, namely speculative financial practices and trades in mortgage-backed securities on a simultaneous, global scale, premised on hopes and fears for a future ever tilted out of Arabic's favor and pitched to crash. Timothy Mitchell's acclaimed *Rule of Experts* notes that the Egyptian stock market, "by the early twentieth century . . . was one of the three or four most active stock exchanges in the world,"[7] but it oddly neglects to mention that this very stock market disastrously fell into ruins in 1907, a year to which *Rule of Experts* returns repeatedly in an extended discussion of the regime of calculability ushered in by the British. Reading from the Egyptian press, Aaron Jakes has begun a history of Egypt that insists on the centrality of this forgotten financial crisis, arguing that "an early generation of economic nationalists railed most of all against the ephemeral and immaterial character of the fictitious value that had exploded under the auspices of colonial rule."[8] *Fictitious Capital* reads the archive of these fictions of capital, cultivated from Syrian mulberry orchards and Egyptian cotton fields, in colonial archives, the pages of the Arabic press, and in particular in the tenor of suspense subtending and habituated by the serialized Arabic novel form as it mimed and undermined the impossible *telos* of a dream of *Nahḍah.*

Beginning in 1859, on the eve of a bloody civil war that would decisively change the cultural, financial, and industrial geography of Syria, Khalīl al-Khūrī serialized a novel, a *riwāyah*, as he termed it, in his Beirut-based journal *Ḥadīqat al-Akhbār.* Entitled *Way—idhan lastu bi-ifranjī* (Alas, I am not a foreigner), its serialization both presaged the path the novel form would take in Arabic over the course of the late nineteenth century and into the twentieth and got its geography wrong. At the threshold of Arabic's first age of finance capital, al-Khūrī foretells an Aleppo that would soon "be among the first to respond to the voice of the age that calls us to literary and material progress [*al-taqaddum al-adabī wa-l-māddī*]."[9] Like many of the serialized novels that would instead be published in 1870s and 1880s Beirut, and in considerable number in the Cairo and Alexandria press beginning in the 1890s, al-Khūrī's novel invited readers to speculate about the future of the region, to hope even as they feared it.

Aleppo, Beirut, Alexandria, and Cairo were all nineteenth-century cities enframed in gardens, idyllic spaces that met the changes apace in agriculture and industry with dreams of cultivating in Arabic a modernity of progress: a *nahḍah* that did indeed usher in highly unruly modes of not only literary but also financial speculation. Writing in *Ḥadīqat al-Akhbār* (The garden of news), al-Khūrī tells of an 1859 Aleppo whose inhabitants find that "the aspirations of the world leave time in which to benefit from that which restores *al-nafs* (the soul or self) . . . their gatherings and delights abound in their free time, such that their gardens [*janāʾinuhum*] have nearly taken the place of public spaces in the civilized countries."[10] Readers of the weekly *Ḥadīqat al-Akhbār*, a Garden of News, here find themselves doubly immersed in a garden. This space of the garden is the founding fiction of the Arabic press. It was a place apart, a utopia of paradise that, like Eden, was ever threatened with the promise of a fall. Hopeful, tentative, contingent gardens of the future will proliferate as the Arabic press flourishes in Beirut and the Nile Valley, serving as sites of mediation from which to speculate as to what the future will bring.

Those 1859 readers of al-Khūrī's novel, awaiting its next installment as they looked to the future, could not know the nightmare of

1860 that awaited the region, or the course their literary and material affairs would take over the coming decades. The French became increasingly invested in industrializing the region's silk cultivation in the decade following the 1860 civil war, which engulfed the silk harvest in flames. A city of refugees, merchants, new banks, and soon a spate of new Arabic newspapers and journals, Beirut emerged as the definitive center of Syria's hopes for literary and material progress. Subtending it all was a great deal of credit and debt, much of it financed through French and Ottoman banks and enabled in part by the telegraph, the private press, and its narrative genre par excellence: the serialized Arabic novel.

Beirut's rise was discernible even before the war. Al-Khūrī writes of an Aleppo whose trade, in the 1860 bound-book version of his novel, "resembles Beirut's, in some respects, though it falls short [*taqṣur ʿanhā*] due to a lack of a system for monetary pursuits, considering the behavior of its money changers, and its being devoid of banks. It has begun to not insignificantly progress in the realms of industry, resulting in great success, for various regions have become filled with its cotton and silk and brocade textiles, and it would keep pace with the greatest of cities, were it aided by the hand of steam and the inventions of minds."[11] The speculative conditions of late nineteenth-century Arabic fiction are laid before the readers of one of the earliest Arabic novels: with a pace meted out and measured "by the hand of steam and the inventions of minds," the dream of the future will be one of finance and textiles. As though indexing the radical contingency of the moment, however, there is a curious slip between the 1860 bound-book version of this passage just cited—in which Aleppo's trade "falls short of [*taqṣur ʿan*]" Beirut's "due to a lack of a system for monetary pursuits"—and the one that the reader of *Ḥadīqat al-Akhbār* encountered in 1859 in this early installment of al-Khūrī's serialized novel. On the eve of war, readers of *Ḥadīqat al-Akhbār* were invited to speculate each week about a future that would not be, a time in which Aleppo's trade might in fact "*exceed* [Beirut's] [*tazīd ʿanhā*]," and it would have been that city's insularity from the unruly economic practices afoot in Beirut, its "system for monetary pursuits[,] . . . the behavior of its money changers, and its . . . banks," that held the promise of future material progress. Attending to this skid in the archive, between the serialized novel and the bound book it would later become, 1860 marks the rise of finance capital,[12] when the Arabic novel syncopated with a mode of financial speculation that engendered an anxious, hopeful habit of looking to the future, ever wondering what was to come.

It would not be only Syria's silk industry but also Egypt's cotton economy, its long-stapled fibers fitted to the mechanized needs of the factories of England,[13] that plotted the region's future. Here again, al-Khūrī's novel proves prescient; *Way—idhan lastu bi-ifranjī* is a novel that conceives of texts, of textuality, through the materiality of textiles: "translation," al-Khūrī writes, "in relation to the original, is like the back of the cloth to its face."[14] The moment in which the region's textiles trade is being reconfigured as part of a capitalist world market enabled by an intricate web of finance and centering on Paris and London, is the moment of the emergence of a certain kind of textuality, taking form in the private Arabic press and the serialized novel form.

In our own present moment, both within and beyond the academy, there is a persistent will to read Arabic literature and the press for renaissance, for revival, for a hopeful progress. Scholars such as Stephen Sheehi[15] observe the lineaments of a field called *Nahḍah* studies coming into view, as a generation of historians and literary critics turn to the puzzlingly neglected archives and libraries of nineteenth- and early twentieth-century Arabic with an ear to Arabic narratives of rise. The *Nahḍah*, so often heralded as a renaissance of wakeful modernity, indexes too a moment when European imperialism proliferated in the Arab world, securing its future in cities like Beirut and Cairo through a network of finance destined to repeatedly crash at Arabic's expense. The stuff of paradox, of hope against fear, this speculative rejoinder that would read *Nahḍah* in the archive is jammed then as now by financial ruses that meet culture and a dream of progress with the promise of creative destruction. It is a story that Arabic's early serialized novels came to know well.

While *Fictitious Capital* draws in inspiration and critical insight from the rich body of Marxist literary criticism surrounding Victorian England and the Black Atlantic, looking to the recent work of scholars such as Ian Baucom and Anna Kornbluh, as well as an earlier generation (including Raymond Williams, Bruce Robbins, Linda Hughes, Michael Lund, and Caroline Levine), it also departs from that body of work, and necessarily so. The growing scholarly interest in the intersection of finance and the novel has taken the English department as its center of gravity, much as Marx's three volumes of *Capital* return again and again to the factory floors of the British textiles industry. *Fictitious Capital* argues, though, that the late nineteenth- and early twentieth-century rise of the serialized Arabic novel, emerging at the very moment that finance capital was reconfiguring global trade and the region's silk, cotton, real estate, and futures markets, was uniquely poised to elaborate finance and the novel's mutually constitutive practices, and to recognize in them older tales of risk at sea, the likes of *Sindbad* and sometimes *A Thousand and One Nights.*

The new global economic order upending Arabic from at least 1860 was still only coming into focus in the wake of the 1907 stock market crash in Egypt, even as its serialized novels had long borne it out. Writing from Cairo in 1897 in his journal *Al-Hilāl*, the editor-novelist-*litterateur* and immigrant from Beirut Jurjī Zaydān introduces his readers to a field of thought and inquiry with a robust history in the land of Egypt's occupiers, namely that of "political economy," *al-iqtiṣād al-siyāsī*, which enabled those inducted into its perspective on the world economy to "remov[e] the veil from the border between the ruler and the ruled." It was almost the twentieth century, Egypt was fifteen years under British occupation, and Beirut had felt the pressures of French capital even longer; it would hardly seem an accident that Arabic had been left with "a great need for books on this subject as what has been translated into our language is very little."[16] *Fictitious Capital: Silk, Cotton, and the Rise of the Arabic Novel* speaks to a critical opacity that persists to our day, to something that has been "hard to see," showing that it was the very financialized fictitiousness of the long-neglected Arabic novels of this period that enabled them to inscribe in both form and content the practices of speculation that were colonizing Arabic.

In the early 1870s, the French general consul of Beirut, one M. Roustan le Gerant, stood poised to record an encounter between empires, charting the general tenor of the Beirut economy. While these are the years that so many read as a moment when the *Nahḍah,* inspired by the likes of Khalīl al-Khūrī, began to found in Beirut cultural institutions of the literary future, including the private Arabic press and the Arabic novel, for those looking with an eye to the region's silk harvest, these were times of economic uncertainty and change. Ottoman bankruptcy was imminent, as French capital industrialized the region's silk trade, its cocoons and thread destined for export, to be finished for Parisian department stores in factories in the South of

France. Debt was rampant, silk harvests were unstable, and returns were falling, yet on the horizon of the future was always the hope for material progress.

In 1871, the Ottomans stoked something of a crisis in Beirut's silk industry, threatening the city's newly burgeoning wealth. The French consul wrote to the French ambassador in Istanbul of "the most scandalous frauds,"[17] of "intrigues,"[18] of a sense of being "left in suspense,"[19] of a pervasive fear of "the most unrealistic pretexts"[20] on the part of the Ottomans, of the knowledge that "three-quarters of the cultivated land is dissimulated [*dissimulés*]"[21] by its local proprietors, and of a "certain agitation produced by the raising of hopes, unconfessed but poorly disguised"[22] at a moment when "no one is sure of his tomorrow and confidence is lacking."[23] Suspense born of unconfessed hopes, of scandal, intrigue, and deception at the intersection of empires—this was the stuff of both finance and fiction in Arabic in the late nineteenth century and its culture of speculation.[24]

When the Ottomans announced intentions that year to slow down the arrival of silk cocoons to the region's filatures, claiming the need to weigh in order to later levy taxes on this fragile, perhaps ephemeral commodity, Beirutis and French alike were asked to imagine a nightmare: broken silk thread of little to no value on the weigh station floor, so many yet unsteamed chrysalises yielding to the heat of day, as moths within them rent their cocoons and took flight. Beirut was left in suspense, hanging upon threads of silk whose future integrity depended on hurried night journeys across the distance that industrialization placed between the mulberry orchards and the steam chambers of the filatures. The Ottomans were looking to check the dizzying speed with which Beirut was being incorporated into a capitalist world economy. Their tactic: the threat of *papillonnage*.[25] The fear that the cocoons would be rendered incontrovertible into the long silk threads they had just promised to become, that they had just seemed to be, took form in an immanent cloud of silk moths looming at the future's horizon in late nineteenth-century Beirut.[26]

In an essay entitled "Culture and Finance Capital," Fredric Jameson begins what he terms a "history of perception,"[27] considering in particular how literary and financial habits of speculation accompany what Ian Baucom, following Jameson and Arrighi, terms the "serial appearances of finance capital."[28] A vertiginous sense of impending capital flight is finance capital's augury, a sign of its accumulation.

Jameson will insist that "the term is literal," but he will invoke it through a simile:

> It was cotton money, or wheat money, textile money, railroad money, and the like. Now, like the butterfly stirring within the chrysalis, it separates itself from that concrete breeding ground and prepares to take flight. We know today only too well (but Arrighi shows us that this contemporary knowledge of ours only replicates the bitter experience of the dead, of disemployed workers in the older moments of capitalism, of local merchants and dying cities as well) that *the term is literal*. We know that there exists such a thing as capital flight: the disinvestment, the pondered or hasty moving on to the greener pastures of higher rates of investment return and cheaper labor.[29]

"It was cotton money, . . . textile money, . . . and the like. Now, like the butterfly stirring within the chrysalis"—what is to be made of Jameson's "and the like. Now, like" if "the term is literal"? It is a question that Arabic's dream of *Nahḍah* can begin to answer. The fear being speculatively staged in early 1870s Beirut as silk industrialized and empires overlapped, of a butterfly stirring in its chrysalis was at once a literal simile and a material sign of capital flight

Jameson's broken chrysalis finds an antecedent in Arabic in 1897, in the Cairo-based *Al-Mushīr*, a sometimes satirical newspaper edited by the Syrian émigré S.[alīm] Sarkīs, who ran a story entitled "The Migration of the Silkworm" ("Muhājirat dūd al-qazz"). Mindful of the newspaper's audience, accustomed as they were to serialized narratives, anecdotes of everyday life, and literary and trade-related news items perhaps only partially true, "The Migration of the Silkworm" acknowledges that "at first the reader might wonder at the presence in the newspaper *Al-Mushīr* of this title, as its subject is the province of scientific and agricultural journals."[30] *Al-Mushīr* can explain: "The silkworm holds high importance for Egypt today, for after residing a long time in Syria and Lebanon benefiting its people and increasing the Sublime Porte's receipts, it has migrated today . . . to free states. Just as the Syrian could not endure the repression and oppression of Ottoman rule [*ḍaghṭ al-ḥukūmah al-ʿuthmāniyyah wa-ẓulmahā*] and so migrated to America and Egypt fleeing its despotism [*jawrihā*], the silkworm appears similarly inclined, migrating to America, Brazil and Egypt."[31] In the 1890s Arabic press, in a newspaper publishing in a "free" British-occupied Cairo by an émigré from Beirut, Ottoman despotism has left such a storied trail of here specifically economic oppression that the Syrian, figured as an agent of restive capital, reads the leaves of mulberry orchards left behind: "the little silkworm, its appetite gave out, unable to endure the oppression [*al-dhill*]."[32]

These stories of migrating silk speculators and their attendant silkworms are, for Sarkīs, "the strangest we have heard up to now about the wisdom of animals."[33] Placing the silk moth among the fabled likes of *Kalīlah wa-Dimnah*—that most famous Arabic collection of strange stories of the wisdom of animals, Sarkīs locates his critique of Ottoman despotism at the intersection of literature and empire. The moments where this article stages the old Arabic narrative posture of *taʿajjub*, of receiving strange tales with a sense of wonder[34]—the animal tale of silk moth wisdom received as "among the strangest heard," under a title heading that seems to have wondrously strayed from "the province of scientific and agricultural journals"—are precisely the points where the leaves of mulberry trees and the migration patterns of the silk moth are read literarily for auguries of the economic and political future of Syria and Egypt. The "little silkworm" from Mount Lebanon makes the Cairo papers not just because it is not eating its mulberry leaves but also because it marks the persistent imbrication of the literary and economic: strictly "scientific and agricultural journals" are ill-positioned to see the wondrously simultaneous literary and economic signs stitched into this literal simile of capital migration. To read the rapid shifts in the economy, to speculate as to what the future holds, is for Sarkīs to read the leaves (*awrāq*) of mulberry trees and the pages (*awrāq*) of the Arabic financial press literarily in a posture of wonder.

Though *Fictitious Capital*'s debt to the recent wave of *Nahḍah* scholarship will be evident to readers of that growing corpus,[35] this book also seeks to redress a critical tendency to take those heralding a *Nahḍah* at their most literal word, particularly as that particular word does not appear much until Jurjī Zaydān starts writing a series of histories of *nahḍāt*—of rises or renaissances—in *Al-Hilāl* at the turn of the twentieth century. *Fictitious Capital* underscores instead a sense of anxiety, one Joseph Massad, too, has noted, and locates it at the troubled intersection of fiction and finance capital.[36] And while this book draws upon philological studies of this period,[37] from the rich archival research entailed in Stephen Sheehi's *Foundations of Modern Arab Identity*,[38] and from Samah Selim's, Kamran Rastegar's,[39] and Muhsin al-Musawi's[40] thoughtful work on popular fiction and its changing forms and audiences, *Fictitious Capital* at the same time breaks with all these studies and others on the *Nahḍah* even as it learns from earlier histories of the Arabic novel by scholars such as Roger Allen, Sabry Hafez, ʿAbd al-Muḥsin Ṭāhā Badr, ʿAbd al-Raḥmān Yāghī, Ibrāhīm al-Saʿāfīn, Muḥammad Yūsuf Najm, and Matti Moosa.[41]

Fictitious Capital argues that the history of the early Arabic novel is that of the rise of finance capital in the Eastern Mediterranean; the illusions subtending finance capital find their form in the serialized installments of the fictions published in the journals of Beirut and Cairo, in the colonial metropoles (as Victorianists have compellingly shown), and no doubt elsewhere. *Fictitious Capital* is not an argument about how capital shapes the novels that can be written any more than it is a history of how fiction begets the financial practices that tear its dreams asunder. The Arabic dream of *Nahḍah*, of a reunion of lovers in the next installment of a novel, of financial markets that will never crash, is one and the same; and though they are fictions, one need only read the many bankruptcy announcements from these decades of the Arabic press to know that in all their immateriality, they are in the end material. Where Rastegar draws from the work of Pierre Bourdieu to argue for the emergence of a literary field that is an "entirely self-sufficient system of values and legitimization," relying on the economic as only a metaphor for literary belief ("to subscribe to its value and to have faith in it much as economic markets are said to rise and fall on faith in their integrity and promise"),[42] *Fictitious Capital* reads from fifty years of the Arabic press and its reprints (with a particular eye to the business practices of the novelist-journalist-turned-media-mogul Jurjī Zaydān) to show that this was always a ruse.

Raymond Williams, in his seminal *Marxism and Literature*, urges critics to "look at our actual productive activities without assuming in advance that only some of them are material."[43] He is arguing against a "self-subsistent order" and against notions of the autonomy of the literary, or any other aesthetic sphere; it is, for Williams, precisely this notion of self-subsistence that papers over and "suppresses the material character of the productive forces which produce such a version of production."[44] *Fictitious Capital* begins to redress Arabic literary historiography's persistent neglect of the materiality of Arabic literary production in the late nineteenth century—a time of speculation, economic as well as literary—in order to read the twin tale of the early serialized Arabic novel and finance capital. In this,

Fictitious Capital is also responding to recent calls in the field of Arabic literature, as in a special roundtable section of the *International Journal of Middle Eastern Studies* in 2011 on "Theory and Arabic Literature in the United States." In a contribution to the roundtable, Colla lamented that "many of the primary sources of the modern period (first editions, literary journals, letters, diaries) have yet to be read by scholars,"[45] while Selim entreated "that there is a vast archive of 19th- and 20th-century texts, critical debates and institutional struggles, and material circuits of production and dissemination that requires urgent attention."[46] *Fictitious Capital* takes up the novels of the late nineteenth- and early twentieth-century Arabic press of Beirut and Cairo, looking in particular at how novels were serialized, advertised, and offered for sale in first, second, and subsequent editions. In so doing, *Fictitious Capital*, again following Williams, "develop[s a] mode of analysis which instead of reducing works to finished products, and activities in fixed positions," can "discern . . . the finite but significant openness of many actual initiatives and contributions."[47] Reading serialization, advertising, and the bound-book volume (as a process of becoming) through the pages of journals such as *Ḥadīqat al-Akhbār, Al-Jinān, Al-Zahrah, Al-Muqtaṭaf,* and *Al-Hilāl* allows for just this sense of "openness" to the historical juncture. In turn, *Fictitious Capital* can then read the "material character of the productive forces which produce such a version of production" to see that finance and fiction are mutually imbricated and deeply material, even—or perhaps, especially—at the moment they seem to take distance from one another.

This is a book about the Arabic novel, "to be specific, about the novel's quantitative rise," something Clifford Siskin dates for the English novel to the late eighteenth century, "precisely when the audience of its close ally—the periodical—began . . . to fracture."[48] That fracture and the novel's attendant rise in Arabic were wrought of economically turbulent times, migrations from Beirut to Cairo and beyond, and the proliferation of the number of privately owned journals (and the number of novels being published) that made 1890s Egypt and especially Cairo a far more fractured place than 1870s Beirut had been, even as the nightmare of 1860 echoed from the Mountain. Siskin closely connects the very notion of the novel's ascendency with "'rise' narratives," placing the history of what he calls "novelism" at a moment when "Neo-Classical tales of imitative decline from past masters give way to Romantic tales of developmental innovation."[49] *Fictitious Capital* argues that this narrative of "rise"—the story the *Nahḍah* (especially at the hands of Jurjī Zaydān) tells of itself, and so many literary and intellectual historians have repeated in its wake—is not the same in Arabic, in cities like Beirut and Cairo, as it is in English, from the colonial metropole of London. Melancholically caught like so many other colonized languages, Arabic and its novels would ever aim at shaking "tales of imitative decline," only to find the "tales of developmental innovation," its speculative hope for progress in a material and a literary register, threatened by a sense of belatedness and debt: master tropes of the financial machinations subtending empire.

While Sarkīs's 1897 Cairo was speculating as to what kind of investment Egypt's mulberry orchards of the future would yield when the trees reached maturity, leaves of cotton could be read for a state of the contemporary textile industry: for a moment free of cotton worms, child labor was proving cost-effective in picking over the rows of high-quality cotton, sent as exactly-long-enough staple to British textile factories.[50] These were boom times in Egypt, an Egypt to which many Syrians, disappointed by dashed futures and diminishing returns in Beirut, had migrated along with Sarkīs's wondrous silkworms. Egypt was witnessing a wave of speculation in stocks, commodities, real estate, and agricultural land, enabled by newly available financial tools that once again Jameson can help us understand; "it was not just cotton money now":

> This free-floating capital, in its frantic search for more profitable investments . . . will begin to live its life in a new context: no longer in the factories and the spaces of extraction and production, but on the floor of the stock market, jostling for more intense profitability. But it won't be as one industry competing with another branch, nor even one productive technology against another more advanced one in the same line of manufacturing, but rather in the form of speculation itself: specters of value, as Derrida might put it, vying against each other in a vast, worldwide, disembodied phantasmagoria.[51]

Speculation—spectral value, ever looking to the future, the "butterfly stirring within the chrysalis." In this "worldwide, disembodied phantasmagoria," no amount of hope or belief in progress and its fictions could provide a hedge against the capital flight apace. Beirut and Cairo, even as they exulted in luxury goods from Paris, even as new villas and parks lined the streets, and their bourgeoisies, ensconced in gardens, founded journals of culture and hope, were filling coffers in British and French factories and banks.

Despite all the dream of progress, these were anxious times: the early 1870s repeatedly disappointed those invested in the sericulture of Mount Lebanon and Beirut; 1875 witnessed the bankruptcy of the Ottoman Empire; the 1882 bombardment of Alexandria by the British is said to be the first time that bankers called for war; and 1907 would see a collapse of property value in Egypt following a speculative boom and stock market crash.[52] The *Nahḍah* that Zaydān and countless others were charting was playing itself out against a nineteenth century that Walter Benjamin has memorably related as a time of speculation, illusion, and utopia: "Every epoch not only dreams the next, but while dreaming it impels it toward wakefulness. It bears its end within itself, and reveals it—as Hegel already recognized—by a ruse. With the upheaval of the market economy, we begin to recognize the monuments of the bourgeoisie as ruins even before they have crumbled."[53] Among the conceits of *Fictitious Capital* is that one of the monuments of the bourgeoisie that is already in ruins in Arabic in the late nineteenth and all the more so the early twentieth century, already shown to be so by the "upheaval of the market economy" in Cairo as in Beirut, as "by a ruse," is the *Nahḍah*. The *Nahḍah* dreams its own wakefulness, dreams of future prosperity and progress, of renaissance, of Baghdad before the fall; and yet it has escaped many that the *Nahḍah* so often celebrated "b[ore] its end within itself." The *Nahḍah* was a dream culminating in the "wakefulness" toward which it impelled the epoch: as if "by a ruse," it is the melancholia of a *Nahḍah* that perpetually lay in the realm of future speculation, and from which many had all too abruptly, all too materially already been awoken.[54]

Chapter 1, entitled "In the Garden: Serialized Arabic Fiction and Its Reading Public—Beirut, 1870," centers on the numerous new periodicals that joined Beirut's lone newspaper *Ḥadīqat al-Akhbār* (The garden of news) beginning in 1870. After a decade of increasing returns from silk, readers were invited to imagine Beirut and its new journals as so many gardens of culture, economics, and useful news: the gardens of *Al-Jinān,* the Paradise-like *Al-Jannah*, or the smaller still garden of *Al-Junaynah*; the flower of *Al-Zahrah*; the bee of *Al-Naḥlah*; joined later in the decade by the choice clippings of *Al-Muqtaṭaf*, and the fruitful arts of *Thamarāt al-Funūn*. Reworking a far older *adab* and poetic tradition of figuring knowledge as the product of idyllic gardens, the editors and authors of the Beirut press cultivated a utopian fiction of the garden as site of what Zaydān would later call the *Nahḍah.*

As in Eden, the garden is always threatened with a fall, and both Salīm al-Bustānī's novel *al-Huyām fī jinān al-Shām* (Love in the gardens of Damascus) and Yūsuf al-Shalfūn's novel *al-Shābb al-maghrūr* (The conceited or tempted youth), serialized simultaneously over the course of 1870 in *Al-Jinān* and *Al-Zahrah,* respectively, deliver that story. In one, the beloved is imprisoned and ransomed; in the other, she is shown to be a whore to material goods, leaving behind her a trail of debt and lies. With the promise of the next installment—"the remainder is to come"—serialized Arabic novels of 1870s Beirut acculturated their audiences to the practice of speculation, of waiting, looking to the horizon of the future, in both hope and fear, as narrative and financial investments hang in the balance, the subject of chapter 2.

Chapter 2, "Like a Butterfly Stirring within a Chrysalis: Salīm al-Bustānī, Yūsuf al-Shalfūn, and the Remainder to Come," argues that finance begot fiction, just as fiction enabled readers of the Arabic press to apprehend the dangerous and deceptive fictitiousness underwriting a financialized society. With the rise of a credit economy in Beirut, transactions textualized in the form of ledgers, receipts, checks, promissory notes, and mortgages were securing the economy, but the very immateriality of these exchanges introduced a new kind of risk and uncertainty. Fiction loomed within finance and threatened dreams of progress; speculating in Arabic became the province of novelists and financiers alike. Merchants and brokers became stock protagonists of novels, as readers imagined what might happen in the next installment; financial fates turned on the ability to speculate in the rise and fall of the markets; and news from the financial sections of journals punctuated installments of novels serialized in the same issue.

The textualization of money in the form of credit fueled extensive transformations in Beirut. Chapter 2 analyzes how journals documented, participated in, and commented on this intersection of literacy and credit, and the changes it effected in the marketplace, between classes, and in the home. Enabled by the telegraph, a new sense of speed and simultaneity emerged: merchants, brokers, traders, and financiers relied on the press for the latest shipping news and commodity prices; a single year's silk harvests could make or break fortunes; and imported fashions changed so fast, as one printed anecdote had it, that a wife's hat could go out of style before her husband even made it home from the shop. Ultimately, a sense of anxiety pervaded the Beirut press over the costs of keeping pace with the flows and imbalances of a global order of finance capital.

From the 1870s, Beirut's reading public intensely debated the future of its speculative economy in the journals now proliferating in the city. Chapter 3, "Fictions of Capital in 1870s and 1880s Beirut," reveals how readers struggled to negotiate the contradictions of their position in the world economy: Beirut was at once a peripheral hub of speculation, a market for finished French textiles, and an industrializing source of the unrefined silk off which French factory and department store owners profited. While *Al-Muqtaṭaf*, founded in 1876, was averse (at least in its Beirut years) to speculation and instead championed the local production of commodities in all their materiality, Salīm al-Bustānī's serialized fiction offered late nineteenth-century Beirut and more generally readers of Arabic lessons in how the credit-driven consumption of material goods allowed the keeping up of appearances, those unreliable indexes of financial well-being. Al-Bustānī's 1872 serialized novel *Budūr* trained its audience to read financial documents and serialized fiction alike for deception and ambiguity, as laborers were allegorized as servants, and the silk industry flickered through Umayyad palace gardens and a trail of jewels. The early 1880s serialization of *Sāmiyyah* staged the Beirut economy's dependence on labor and speculation in considerably more direct terms; read alongside his short 1875 serialized novel *Bint al-ʿaṣr* (Daughter of the age), a critique of the fictions inherent in the financial (and labor) practices animating the markets of Beirut in an age of global capitalism comes into view.

Chapter 4, "Mourning the *Nahḍah*: From Beirut to Cairo, after Midnight," contends that the 1880s, witnessing disappointing returns on silk in Syria, Salīm al-Bustānī's far too early death in 1884, the increasing censure of the Sublime Porte, and the emigration to Cairo of Jurjī Zaydān, Fāris Nimr, and Yaʿqūb Ṣarrūf—fleeing the collapse of the Syrian Protestant College intellectual community—disillusioned the dreams of material and intellectual progress that fueled the rise of the private Arabic press and the serialized Arabic novel in 1860s and 1870s Beirut. In spite of this disillusionment, Nimr and Ṣarrūf's *Al-Muqtaṭaf* and Zaydān's journal *Al-Hilāl* nevertheless invested in the markets of British-occupied Egypt, reencoding the tenuous contingencies that made the Edenic imaginary of 1870s Beirut and its reading public historically possible.

It is a macabre, melancholic turn for the Arabic novel, haunted by Salīm al-Bustānī, whose novels lie buried, Zaydān tells us, "in the pages of *Al-Jinān*." Zaydān's early 1892 novel *Asīr al-Mutamahdī* (Captive of the self-made or would-be Mahdi) emblematically pivots around a bloody lock of hair locked in a box in Cairo since the novel's protagonist fled 1860 Mount Lebanon, allegorizing even as it obscures the worrisome implications of Beirut's experience of French-financed *Nahḍah*. In Egypt, debts to British and French banks simultaneously funded the speculative irrigation of cotton land as well as the transformation of Cairo's city center, sedimented in the public garden of Ezbekiyya. In the not too distant future, bookstalls would take the place of cabarets and their attendant nightlife. Before then, though, the addictive, illicit, nocturnal pleasures of Ezbekiyya would cast an anxious pall over its Edenic grounding of Egypt's own *Nahḍah*, if only readers would decode its specious, speculative foundations.

Jurjī Zaydān, by capitalizing on the novel form as a commodity that could both edify and entertain, secured his own posthumous legacy as well as that of the *Nahḍah*. Chapter 5, "Of Literary Supplements, Second Editions, and the Lottery: The Rise of Jurjī Zaydān," reads from the archive of first and second editions of his novels alongside reprintings of *Al-Hilāl*, as traces of the process by which novels were imagined as commodities in book form gleam through. While Zaydān serialized novels in early issues of *Al-Hilāl*, which began publishing in September 1892, installments of future novels staged a gradual migration, from the center of each issue, to the end of the issue, to become a stand-alone supplement, and later sold as a bound book (in multiple editions and to our present day). In many reprints of back issues of the early years of *Al-Hilāl*—offered in Zaydān's time as the bound volumes that now comprise our library archives—Zaydān's novels are nowhere to be found. While a number of scholars of Arabic literature have been left befuddled by this archive's literary poverty, this chapter argues that by carefully attending to these palimpsestic traces of serialization, a history of the Arabic novel comes into view: these early editions reveal to us the historical moment of which they were a product, bearing the mark of a contingent mode of speculation, and of the threatening porosity of fiction and finance.

This market-savvy turn to the book form shaped the library of the *Nahḍah* that subsequent authors such as Ṭāhā Ḥusayn and many a scholar have relied upon for the story they would tell about the early Arabic novel. Zaydān built a reading room with books available for purchase, issued an annual book catalogue, advertised his novels and the novels of others in the pages of *Al-Hilāl*, and even held a lottery for subscribers—to the winner went Zaydān's complete works, gilded and bound in leather. Salīm al-Bustānī, on the other hand, wrote his novel installments for that issue of *Al-Jinān*. Uncollected, unbound (except for a single novel published in late nineteenth-century New York), al-Bustānī's novelistic oeuvre could be relegated to a mere spectral presence haunting Cairo's literary production.

Chapter 6, "It Was Cotton Money Now: Novel Material in Yaʿqūb Ṣarrūf's Turn-of-the-Twentieth-Century Cairo," observes that while *Al-Muqtaṭaf* had long hesitated over the merits of the novel form, by the early twentieth century, the journal's editor, Ṣarrūf, could be counted among Cairo's novelists. His first foray in the genre, *Fatāt Miṣr* (The girl of Egypt) was serialized as a literary supplement to *Al-Muqtaṭaf* over the course of 1905. A tale of finance capital's restless wandering in Egyptian cotton fields, Cairo apartment buildings, Japanese war bonds, and the stock markets of the world—from London, to St. Petersburg, Tokyo, and back to Cairo—*Fatāt Miṣr* met with critical praise upon its initial publication. Soon forgotten, the novel has been left unread by Arabic literary critics, despite the prescient augury it held for how a culture of speculation in Arabic would culminate in Egypt less than two years later in the stock and real estate crash of 1907.

Ṣarrūf's *Fatāt Miṣr* is a novel that, like several of al-Bustānī's earlier works, is deeply invested in the ruses of the marketplace, finding in finance capital the plotlines that could capture an audience of Arabic fiction. And yet despite any critique these novels might offer of the market's tendency to meet hope with ruin, novelists, particularly in serialized format, were speculators. Indeed, the plot of *Fatāt Miṣr* owes much to Ṣarrūf's own personal financial speculation in Egyptian land. The mode of speculation fostered by the literary genealogy that *Fictitious Capital* traces from Beirut to Cairo was complicit with the rise of imperial finance capital—and its corollary, capital flight—even as these speculative narrative forms posed as edifying and entertaining hedges against the depredations of finance capital in an age dreaming of rise and renaissance, of *Nahḍah*.

CHAPTER I

In the Garden

Serialized Arabic Fiction and Its Reading Public—Beirut, 1870

In early 1870, the private Arabic press in Beirut encountered a time of telegraph-enabled global simultaneity, its immanent future of unfettered progress punctuated weekly and fortnightly by serialized novels: *riwāyāt*.[1] That year, early installments of both Salīm al-Bustānī's *al-Huyām fī jinān al-Shām* and Yūsuf al-Shalfūn's *al-Shābb al-maghrūr* unfurled in the gardens of Damascus. The Arabic press and its novels renegotiated the classical anthology's trope of the garden as well as the tenor of merchant capital-infused suspense of *A Thousand and One Nights* and *Sindbad* as they confronted the industrializing mulberry orchards of Mount Lebanon. Readers, men and women alike, were invited into gardens of culture and useful news, the stuff, they were told, of literary and material progress, gardens that could trump the ruses and risks of the card table, and the meddlings of merchants, bankers, and brokers that ever threatened this fragile idyll with a fall. Yearning to belatedly be one with the bourgeoisie of Europe through a new culture of reading, the early 1870s Beirut press adopted a posture of briefly unbridled hope that the *Nahḍah* and its critics would ever seek to recover. And yet the novels serialized in the pages of the Arabic press, though they might begin as romances set in a garden, were from the very beginning not tales of *nahḍah*. Rather, they recognized in the persistent sense of uncertainty and suspense at the convergence of competing empires, the simultaneous, coterminous, and deeply implicated rise of finance and the novel in Arabic.

There was something of a botanical obsession animating the early 1870s Arabic press in Beirut,[2] a city, like Damascus and Aleppo, that was once renowned for its gardens: there were the gardens of *Al-Jinān*, the paradise-like garden of *Al-Jannah*, the little garden of *Al-Junaynah*, all curated by their gardeners, the Bustānī father and son, having joined *Hadīqat al-Akhbār*, that official garden of Ottoman news, and publishing alongside the flower of *Al-Zahrah*, and joined later that decade in the fertile Arabic press by the bee of *Al-Naḥlah*, and those fruitful arts and choice clippings discussed in *Thamarāt al-Funūn* and *Al-Muqtaṭaf*. Reviving a long tradition of figuring compendia of literature and knowledge as so many gardens,[3] the serialization of *riwāyāt* in the pages of the press further annexed irrigation to the gardens cultivated in late nineteenth-century Arabic. As Roger Allen once noted in passing: "The Arabic word *riwāya* is . . . an etymon with a very ancient history. The primary meaning of this root is 'to convey water.'"[4] As irrigation, sea travel, and the 1869 opening of the Suez Canal were remaking the region's economies, increasingly monocultures[5]—Beirut's of silk, Cairo's of cotton—in the pages of the burgeoning Arabic press ran *riwāyāt*.

Riwāyah was the term used in Beirut, Cairo, and beyond in this period for Arabic prose narrative and plays, regardless of length, and was generally followed by qualifying adjectives: *tārīkhiyyah* pointing to the historical; *gharāmiyyah* to the romantic; *tashkhīṣiyyah* to the theater; with *adabiyyah* delineating proper comportment, ethics, and increasingly a sense of our own contemporary connotations of "literary."[6] In 1859, al-Khūrī deemed *Way—idhan lastu bi-ifranjī* a *riwāyah*; and in 1870 Beirut, it was *riwāyāt* that were published in Buṭrus al-Bustānī and his son Salīm's journal *Al-Jinān*, as well as Yūsuf al-Shalfūn's short-lived *Al-Zahrah*, and the Jesuit journal *Al-Bashīr*. Later in 1890s Cairo, Jurjī Zaydān, Yaʿqūb Ṣarrūf, and so many others would go on to inherit this literary project, deeming their novels *riwāyāt*. The term *riwāyah* incorporated the orality of narration into an older etymology of irrigation, such that the novels serialized in a growing number of Arabic journals could be imagined as textualized wellsprings of narrative flowing through gardens of knowledge.

In 1870, Salīm's sister Adelaide al-Bustānī serialized a short two-part *riwāyah* entitled "Hanrī wa-Amīliyā" in the family's *Al-Jinān*,[7] heralding the gardens to come in its final coda: "If there are some ladies joining the gentlemen in reading *Al-Jinān* [The gardens], the gentlemen deserve to have something of the fine, fair pen of the ladies and—ha—the gate of al-Jinān is opened to the ladies."[8] A few issues later, Marianah Marrāsh, sister of the acclaimed *adīb* and proto-novelist Fransīs Marrāsh, seconded Adelaide al-Bustānī's invitation to enter the garden gates, writing: "Let us then gird ourselves with wisdom and understanding, and robe ourselves with true politeness and meakness, and be crowned with the flowers of the 'jenan'"—the garden—"of knowledge now open to us."[9]

The sense that writing in the new journals of the early Arabic press was something like being in a garden was a notion that Adelaide and Salīm's father, Buṭrus al-Bustānī, had pursued several months earlier in the initial announcement for the new journal *Al-Jinān*. The announcement was circulated in late 1869 and bound as the first page of the first year of *Al-Jinān*, articulating sentiments of both belatedness and hope, the early affective architecture of the *Nahḍah*, though fear hovered at the horizon. In 1869, Buṭrus bemoaned the unidyllic state of Arabic:

> Our language remains without a medium among the great media to spread general knowledge, which includes scientific, literary [*adabiyyah*], historical, industrial, commercial and civil [knowledge], in addition to literary pieces and anecdotes, as takes place in foreign countries. Its uses for all [*li-l-khāṣṣ wa-l-ʿāmm*] are evident due to its being a means to encourage general knowledge and strengthen its support among the public [*al-jumhūr*]. . . . Among these gates [*abwāb*] we open a gate [*bāb*] to the possessors of knowledge and a space in which the pen of the skillful among possessors of the pen might circulate.
>
> We have decided to place our trust in God to bring the aforementioned goal into being by publishing a newspaper in the Arabic language entitled *Al-Jinān* (the plural of *jannah*) encompassing the stated benefits, [flowing] from our pen as well as the pens of those who wish to present us with precious selections original or translated in the fields previously mentioned.[10]

This garden trope, aside of course from the inspired accident of the Bustānī family name (said to derive from a fertile Syrian garden [*bustān*] the family once cultivated), indexes a utopian imagining of what the Arabic press and its readers could be that was deeply constitutive of the early years of the *Nahḍah*. When the Christian-Druze war and ensuing massacres of 1860 had receded to become an earlier generation's nightmare, and before the silk industry had repeatedly disappointed Syrians, before the British had bombarded Alexandria and then occupied Cairo, before the Ottoman Empire and the Khedival state had gone bankrupt, indeed before the contradictions of finance capital and industrialized textile production became manifestly legible as empire, there was a moment when the Arabic press in Beirut was flooded with hope and idealism, in a sense a mark of everything yet to be negotiated by authors, editors, and their readers. In this Edenic early moment of Beirut's press, the gates of the gardens stood open to readers who wished to pick up the pen.

Buṭrus's announcement for *Al-Jinān*, motivated by a pedagogical felt-need to spread knowledge *li-l-khāṣṣ wa-l-ʿāmm*, accumulates accretions of definitions of what kind of knowledge is useful. For if this appeal was to a need, "as takes place in foreign countries" for more scientific, industrial, and commercial knowledge, something that print capitalism's newspapers were seen as uniquely poised to provide to a general audience seeking knowledge, it simultaneously pledged to also provide this emerging reading public—not just *al-khāṣṣ* but also *al-ʿāmm*—with the sorts of knowledge that might be found in the long tradition of Arabic *adab* anthologies, with their emphasis on organizing selections of poetry and prose based on categories that corresponded to the social contexts and topics of discussion and composition in which they would be put to use. *Adab* in 1870 Beirut contained both the broader, older sense of edified, courtly comportment that persists today mainly in colloquial expressions like *(q)alīl al-adab,* as well as our present, narrower use of *adab* to mean literature.

Indeed, the tradition of *adab* anthologies is doubly relevant here: from its first page, *Al-Jinān* emphasized the practical use of knowledge in a manner akin to the *adab* anthology; while its very name could be read as continuous with the titles of many *adab* anthologies with their play on the garden of knowledge and its fruits. One could look as well to the poets or the Sufis or the long history of pining after the lost gardens of al-Andalus in tracing the multiple genealogies of these *nahḍawī* gardens.[11] Consider the work of Abū Manṣūr ʿAbd al-Malik b. Muḥammad b. Ismāʿīl al-Thaʿālibī, an anthologist, critic, and author writing in the shadow of Arabic prose's ascendancy in the tenth century. The *adab* anthologies *Tatimmat al-Yatīmah* and *Thimār al-qulūb fī-l-muḍāf wa-l-mansūb* attest two examples of not just an interest in gardens on a descriptive level (which abounds in classical Arabic works of poetry and prose) but of the garden and its fruits as a trope for literary production. In the former, something of a sequel to his anthology *Yatīmat al-dahr,* al-Thaʿālibī justifies his continuation of *al-Yatīmah*, announcing in the preface to *Tatimmah* that it "comprises witty, rare coinings and anecdotes, more pleasurable than the early basil and fresh aromatic flowers."[12] In *Thimār al-qulūb*, as Bilal Orfali notes, al-Thaʿālibī borrows from his friend, the poet Abū al-Fatḥ al-Bustī, in a self-deprecating "presentation of a supposedly inferior book":[13]

> Do not condemn [me] when I present to you the choicest from your [own]
> venerable sciences or bits from your [own] literary arts
>
> Indeed, the gardener presents to the owner the precious produce from his
> [own] garden by virtue of his service.[14]

Al-Khūrī, the Bustānīs, Nimr, Ṣarrūf, and many other *nahḍawī* editors would continue in this metaphor, playing the role of "the gardener," offering Arabic readers of the late nineteenth century and into the twentieth "the choicest from your venerable sciences" and "bits from your literary arts."

Of course, there is a much older tradition of the garden at work here as well, one that resonated both in the singular *jannah* as well as in Buṭrus's pluralization of it into *jinān*. Not only does this evoke notions of *al-jannah* as paradise—be it one of Eden or the afterlife—but in Buṭrus's compulsion in 1869, on the eve of a proliferation of gardens of the Arabic press, to tether *al-jinān* to this particular singular noun *al-jannah*, an anxiety is betrayed as to the other meanings lurking in the root, which elicits not only idyllic gardens but also affairs of the heart, rapture, madness, and the *jinn*.

One of the primary meanings of the root *j-n-n* is to cover, hide, or make dark, and it is to that sense that Buṭrus turns in the sixth volume of his encyclopedia *Dāʾirat al-maʿārif*. The entry for the fully voweled *jannah* begins: "*al-jannah* in language is the garden [*al-ḥadīqah*] containing palms, trees and plantings [*bustān*] and it is called that because it shades or covers the land with its shadow."[15] Moving from these earthly shadows, Buṭrus next turns to "earthly paradise" [*al-firdaws al-arḍī*], or the Garden of Eden, inviting his audience to read more about Eden under the letter *ʿayn*. Buṭrus composed this encyclopedia, beginning with *alif* and dying in 1883 while at work on the seventh volume, well before reaching the letter *ʿayn* (nevermind the *nūn* of *Nahḍah*). Neither would his son Salīm live to see the Eden of *Dāʿirat al-maʿārif*, dying the next year at the young age of thirty-seven while at work on the eighth volume, as his brothers Najīb and Nasīb, and their cousin Sulaymān inherited the earthly responsibility of transcribing Eden. By 1898, nearly finished with the letter *ṣadd,* Sulaymān had finally found a publisher for the still incomplete, still Eden-less encyclopedia, announced for purchase through Jurjī Zaydān's Maktabat al-Hilāl, then located in Cairo in al-Faggālah, just across from the train station.[16]

After Eden, Buṭrus continued in the entry on *al-jannah* to note that "in all religions" *al-jannah* is the paradise that awaits the righteous after death. He goes on to describe both the "spiritual, mental" conception of paradise among Christians, as well as the more material, sensory garden awaiting Muslims.[17] This sense of *al-jannah* as a paradise to be pluralized is likewise suggested by the only word in this entry written in Latin letters—"paradis-e"—with its curiously hyphenated final letter "e" straddling French and English. Naming his new journal *Al-Jinān*, already a plural, alongside his other newspapers *Al-Jannah* and *Al-Junaynah*, Buṭrus invited a disparate readership to imagine the garden as a plural, heterogeneous space, as the necessity for the individual reader of staking a claim to a particular vision of the garden was momentarily elided. Staged in its multiplicity, the gardens of the early Beirut press interpolated a readership comprised of readers perhaps partial to quite different notions of what *al-jannah* could be, offering the plural as, I am arguing, in the end a rather fragile, ephemeral figuring of the early private Arabic press, containing within itself the inevitability of a fall, and the specter of death in the plural that haunted the *Nahḍah* from its fraught beginnings.

In his 1859 lecture "Khuṭbah fī ādāb al-ʿarab" (A lecture on the culture of the Arabs) on the eve of civil war,[18] Buṭrus al-Bustānī heralded the founding of al-Khūrī's Garden of News, *Ḥadīqat al-Akhbār*, noting that its printing press al-Maṭbaʿah al-Sūriyyah was "the first Arabic press specializing in journals," which he hopes "will become stronger" with time.[19] Al-Bustānī's aspirations for the future of the periodical press in Beirut are in keeping with his conviction, articulated in this seminal *khuṭbah*, that "there is no doubt that journals [*jurnālāt*] are among the greatest means to civilize people and to increase the number of readers if they are used properly."[20] Indeed, the Bustānīs would found their own journals, playing upon their family name and al-Khūrī's precedent, being joined in 1871 by the newly established American Protestant Arabic weekly *Al-Nashrah al-Usbūʿiyyah* in investing journals with a hope that they would be "among the greatest means of success" and would "spread . . . civilization and knowledge." *Al-Nashrah al-Usbūʿiyyah* would go so far as to include a chart listing the ratio of citizens per journal in a number of countries, with the Ottoman Empire coming in second-to-last after Russia. America, France, and England were held out as examples of salutary citizen to journal ratios, emblems of a dream of civilizational progress.[21]

In the wake of the civil war of 1860, Beirut witnessed the founding of several institutions of learning and scholarship that would increase the number of readers who could be welcomed into the Arabic press's gardens of the future. New schools opened their doors, including the preparatory institution al-Madrasah al-Waṭaniyyah or the National School founded by Buṭrus al-Bustānī in 1863, and the Syrian Protestant College (later to become the American University of Beirut in 1920) founded by American Presbyterian missionaries beginning in 1866, while an 1869 Ottoman law called for the construction of an imperial lycée, which would be known as al-Madrasah al-Sulṭāniyyah, or the Sultanate School.[22] Al-Jamʿiyyah al-ʿIlmiyyah al-Sūriyyah (the Syrian Scientific Society) was founded in 1868 and was partly modeled on the earlier al-Jamʿiyyah al-Sūriyyah li-l-ʿUlūm wa-l-Funūn, or Syrian Society for the Sciences and Arts, which met from 1848 through 1852 and had itself been modeled on an earlier society known as Majmaʿ al-Tahdhīb, which loosely translates as the Assembly of Culture or Refinement, founded in 1847.[23]

This chain of learned societies played a decisive role in cultivating an educated bourgeoisie, but by 1869, there was a sense of an imminent collapse. As Salīm Farīj, a member of the Syrian Scientific Society, noted at what would be the group's final meeting: "We see that a large number of societies . . . have fallen. For it is easy for all of us to meet at the beginning of the matter, but we find it less easy to keep the obligations of these meetings. . . . I hope that this society's path will not be like those earlier ones that have fallen."[24] Though later many other Arabic learned societies and salons would emerge in not only Beirut but also Cairo and other Arab cities, the imminent fall of the Syrian Scientific Society permeated the cultural scene amid calls for a shift to the periodical form. The journals that would begin to emerge the next year felt this sense of contingent fragility, and yet there was a persistent will to find in the "gardens of knowledge" being dreamed in the Arabic press a promise of "useful" material, to be located in more stable institutions that could secure a future of not just literary but also, and often especially, material progress imagined in capitalist terms.

In 1870, its first year of publication, *Al-Jinān* ran a story entitled "Time Is Gold" in which its author, ʿAbd al-Qādir, underscores the value of the readership's time. Over the course of this essay, the acquisition of knowledge through the consumption of literature and the press ensures the sort of economic progress readers imagine to be apace in Europe. Citing a line of verse—"if your life were capital be warned against squandering it on what is not necessary"[25]— al-Qādir notes that "some people ignore this matter and thus waste their time on entertainment [*malāhī*] and playing backgammon and cards and the like and sitting around coffeeshops in which there is no use." To squander time is to gamble with it, to play games of risk, and it would remain a persistent trope of the *Nahḍah*, troubling its gardens of knowledge. The economy of reading for al-Qādir works otherwise: imagined through European gatherings, al-Qādir tells of a scene in which a member would "ask those seated one by one about what they have read in the way of books and newspapers and what they benefited from that day,"[26] a model of reading adopted by the Syrian Scientific Society in 1868 and 1869. Readers of *Al-Jinān*, already invited into the gates of the gardens of knowledge, are invited into an economy not of risk, chance, and entertainment—the stuff of "playing backgammon and cards"—but of a utopia of knowledge underwritten by the secure distribution of capital through the investment of time in reading books and newspapers.

Guarding against a vision of the future governed by the unruly workings of the card table (and the perhaps still unrulier practices of the brokers and merchants in the markets of Beirut, many of whom were also reading Beirut's early Arabic journals for trade-related information, and maybe its novels, too), "Time Is Gold" is followed in the pages of *Al-Jinān* by another brief essay expounding upon, as its title states, "The Usefulness of Reading." Ilyās Ḥabālīn observes that "it is said of us [Syrians] that we are rarely interested in anything other than the material aspect," and that what is generally considered useful is that which "is a means to amass much money quickly."[27] He points out the need among Syrians to instead invest "interest in eloquent books and refined newspapers which improve the value of pens," citing *Al-Jinān* as a prime example of this sort of edifying material. Gardens of knowledge are held out to readers in 1870 Beirut, readers perhaps more familiar with the ruses of the market than the order of knowledge subtending this vision of idyllic progress. Reading appears simultaneously as a refuge from risk, and a path to the "literary and material progress" al-Khūrī had envisioned for the region eleven years earlier: "Literary [*adabī*] reform gives rise to material progress. . . . [T]he people who are the most prosperous in terms of wealth and progress in [acquiring] material luxuries are those who have reached the highest rungs of the intellectual ladder for they, due to the pleasure [they take in] dwelling upon essential events and scientific secrets, have produced from the reading of newspapers important material and financial results."[28] The idealism flooding the early years of the Arabic private press is hard to miss here, as, too, is its vision of material progress with its imperative to invest capital in institutions of learning before it is squandered through gambling. In 1870, to a reading public dwelling in the gardens of the Arabic press, it seemed for a moment that all one needed was to take pleasure in that experience, and one could match step, through a dreamy alchemy of reading, with "the most prosperous in terms of wealth and progress." Like Buṭrus al-Bustānī, Ḥabālīn was worried, though, about a problem of keeping pace, a sense of belatedness founded in "our lack of speed in [acquiring the habit] of reading periodicals [*al-manshūrat al-durriyyah*]."[29] Not only is there much left unreconciled in Ḥabālīn's vision of the ledgers of progress, but the spelling is off: periodicals are not *durriyyah* but rather *dawriyyah* in Arabic, further underscoring the radical newness of this reading enterprise in 1870 Beirut, and the correctives that awaited it.[30]

As 1870 came to a close, *Al-Jinān* invited readers to imagine the contours of the gardens of literature to come. An announcement read:

> It is by His great might and the protection of those overseeing important matters that *Al-Jinān*'s first year nears its end. We have attained much more than we had foreseen in terms of achievement and success, and that is the greatest proof of the progress of the Arab nation [*al-ummah al-ʿarabiyyah*], under the protection of the Sublime Porte, ever advancing to a fine stage in the stages of the age of civilization and knowledge, for many have entered the gardens of literature [*jinān al-adab*] and useful news by spending glittering gold and the essence of precious time in reading newspapers and writings built upon the foundations of truth and integrity and a lack of bias. Due to that, and to it being evident that those seeking *Al-Jinān* are many and that the majority of this year's subscribers will be renewing their subscriptions, we have decided to continue to send *Al-Jinān* this coming year to all those who do not request that we stop doing so. That is to say that we are not requiring those who wish to renew their subscriptions

> to request that in writing or orally, but rather ask those who do not wish to renew their subscriptions to be so kind as to let it be known so that we can sunder them from *Al-Jinān*. And we request those who wish to subscribe for the coming year among those who have not subscribed this year to be so kind as to let that be known before we enter our second year in order that we may be informed as to how many copies to print each time. And finally we ask God to grant them health and success and a long life of many years for He sees and hears and His response is just.[31]

There are two ways, then, that one can be sundered from the hopeful gardens of *Al-Jinān*: one can inform the editors of a desire to no longer subscribe, to no longer participate in spending "glittering gold and the essence of precious time in reading newspapers and writings"; or one can be sundered from these earthly gardens of the future by death (even as issues of *Al-Jinān* continued to arrive in the departed's mail), by the hope of a "long life of many years" being thwarted by the divine, in an eerie augury of the far too early death of Salīm in 1884, whose hand may well have penned these lines. Annexing the gardens of paradise, of the afterlife, to the earthly gardens frequented by subscribers to the newly established Beirut periodicals, for a moment the Arabic press sustained competing imaginings of the garden and its connotations.

Gardens abounded in a bourgeois vision of late nineteenth-century Beirut, as the social historians Nada Sehnaoui and Leila Tarazi Fawaz chart in their studies of the city.[32] The bourgeoisie, many of whom comprised the audience for journals such as *Al-Jinān*, were increasingly looking to Europe, building homes modeled on the Italian villa, with large picture windows surrounded by gardens. The whole idea was predicated on seeing and being seen, and in this sense was a radical departure from the courtyard-centered style of building traditionally favored in the region. The vision of the garden offered in the Arabic press was one of knowledge, of paradise, of a world apart from which to dream of the future, posit alchemical economies, or critique the present; it could be that secluded space of the courtyard and its orange trees and fountain, or that very public garden that surrounded the bourgeois homes being built in not only Beirut's Zuqāq al-Blaṭ, but also other Arab cities of the region, including Cairo's new quarters, with carriages and their passengers rolling by and taking in the view. Or, yet again, it could be the public parks appearing in cities throughout the region, joining more informal spaces on the edges of cities such as Beirut, Damascus, and Cairo, where families, friends, and would-be lovers might while away their days and later evenings, and where Salīm set an early scene in his first serialized novel, *al-Huyām fī jinān al-Shām* (Love in the gardens of Damascus).

In its first installment, Salīm writes his character Wardah, with a book in one hand and a namesake rose in the other, into these eponymous gardens of Damascus with a group of female friends in 1868. While Wardah wishes her friends could enjoy their "free time reading useful, literary [*adabiyyah*] books concerned with promoting the causes of civilization and knowledge and improving morals and strengthening the mind,"[33] we as readers are left to wonder if this novel we've just begun, or for that matter the journal in which it is serialized, is the sort of writing Wardah has in mind. For our entire vantage point on this scene is through the gaze of our male narrator, Sulaymān, who, having already followed these women to the gardens at the edge of the city of Damascus, wanted at the beginning of the second installment, published in mid-January 1870, to get closer still, so as to better hear one of their voices. "And yet," he said to himself: "I was afraid that they would become aware of me, and so would run away from me and leave this garden [*ḥadīqah*]. . . . [T]hen I saw a grove of young trees behind which I could hide from their sight even as I could both hear and see them. So I advanced to a place behind that grove, and, using its branches to hide me from their eyes, I sat on the ground. My heart was beating like one fearful the sky would fall upon him."[34] As Salīm al-Bustānī enframes it, our perspective on this scene of women whom we can "both hear and see" (even as the narrator is, like Arrighi's finance capital, "hard to see") is enabled by the shading branches of this "grove of young trees": we are in the garden again, and yet already the novel, a *riwāyah* in *Al-Jinān*'s gardens of knowledge, through its very enframing, unsettles the idyll; our narrator, a fearful eavesdropper ensconced in this shading grove, confesses: "I felt as though I was in the Garden of Eden." Shrouded in darkness, conjuring matters of the heart, while Buṭrus had so labored to tether a pluarlity of gardens of *al-jannah*, of paradise, to his family's *Al-Jinān*, in this novel, *Al-Jinān* strays into the word's other senses of love, rapture, and shadows, staging these reverberations of *jinān* as the very conditions for the act of narration. Afraid lest he sunder the novel from the garden, hidden in a shady grove in a garden in Damascus, "hard to see," here we find the throbbing heart of the narrator of this novel in *Al-Jinān*.

The young women are discussing how best to spend their money and their time. As Wardah praises "useful, literary [*adabiyyah*] books," Ḥawāʾ, a fallen Eve in the Bustānī gardens, is revealed, despite her father's wealth, to be not only illiterate but far too fond of both alcohol and makeup. Not much better in Wardah's estimation is her friend Suʿdā, an avid smoker[35] and a rebellious reader interested only in being entertained by the likes of Abū Nuwās, and who, if "she had thought a given book would be of true use" or benefit to her, "would not have allowed herself to read it."[36] The garden is from the beginning then figured as containing both idyllic and yet also surprisingly hazy and intoxicating scenes, a tale of desire in Stephen Sheehi's reading,[37] abetted by the shade of trees not unlike those that would appear in the *jannah* of *Dāʾirat al-maʿārif.* While these young women are briefly returned to a utopian vision of the garden and the press when the gardener [*al-bustānī*] presents them with its fruits, which they ate and then "rose [*nahaḍna*] and went for a walk in the garden [*al-bustān*]," our male narrator's "gaze never wandered from Wardah."[38] A utopic garden into which readers were invited to bring their pens is already and perhaps always troubled, and with the passage of time it appears only more so.

It is not just the scene that unfolds before the narrator and his audience's eyes but also the manner in which it is enframed that begins to trouble the gardens being propounded in articles and announcements in the pages of *Al-Jinān.* While *al-Huyām fī jinān al-Shām* labors to annex gardens of reading and useful knowledge to its plot—holding out Wardah as the readerly ideal; staging scenes of the story's protagonist, Sulaymān, "reading some books and newspapers (*jarāʾid*)"[39] with a group of French women in a Syrian hotel—unruly readers like Suʿdā in her love of the infamously ribald poet Abū Nuwās (so beloved for his eighth- and ninth-century poems of wine and licentious living that he even appears as a character in *A Thousand and One Nights*) vex the alchemy of reading suggested by the likes of Ḥabalīn, elaborating a smoky, shady garden of wine, lewd poetry, and seduction, where narrators lurk in shady groves.

After the narrator Sulaymān falls in love with Wardah in the eponymous scene in the gardens of Damascus, he meets her again on a sightseeing excursion to Tadmur (the ancient city of Palmyra recently leveled by ISIS). Later in the novel, the two have just managed to escape from the Bedouin tribe that captured them near Tadmur when Wardah is captured again, this time by a band of robbers, and then taken aboard a pirate ship, such that the audience of this adventure novel never quite knows what will happen next. The narrator learns of these and other events when he meets Sulaymān one day on Mount Lebanon, from which point this becomes an epistolary novel: Sulaymān sends a series of letters to the novel's narrator updating him on his progress, with the last letter arriving from Italy, where Sulaymān and Wardah finally marry

Al-Shalfūn's *Al-Shābb al-maghrūr*, too, figures pivotal scenes of letter reading, without which the plot cannot proceed, suggesting that the sometimes epistolary mode of these two novels, serialized simultaneously over the course of 1870, can shed light on this emergent genre in an age of *nahḍah*. The epistolary nature of these novels focalizes the formal similarity between an installment of a novel and a letter, both of which might arrive in the same post, both written by someone who is "hard to see."[40] The anticipation familiar to readers from sending and receiving letters via the post reverberates with that experienced as one awaits the next issue of *Al-Zahrah* or *Al-Jinān*, and the novel installment each promised to contain. In *al-Huyām fī jinān al-Shām*, written correspondence is the very means by which the plot is sustained after the narrator and protagonist part following their meeting, in issue 16, beneath a cedar on Mount Lebanon overlooking the Mediterranean. The two exchange not only letters, by means of the French and Austrian mail, but also telegrams, as Sulaymān's travels take him in the direction of Izmir, then on to Crete and finally Naples. It is through his signature at the end of a letter that we discover that the narrator of *al-Huyām fī jinān al-Shām* is none other than one Salīm al-Bustānī; and, in the final installment, that the protagonist who has up to this point remained nameless is Sulaymān Khālid. Letters and telegrams not only communicate Sulaymān's travels during his search for his beloved Wardah but also enable Sulaymān to conduct economic transactions while far from the financial institutions of Beirut. Their correspondence is staged as allowing the tale to continue, as Salīm sends Sulaymān funds, and Sulaymān sends Salīm, and thus *Al-Jinān*'s expectant readership, the latest news of his adventures in pursuit of Wardah. Like the storyteller, the editors of *Al-Jinān*, the novel seems to be reminding us, must be paid.

At one point in the nineteenth installment of *al-Huyām fī jinān al-Shām*, Salīm has not heard from Sulaymān for three months, despite the many letters Salīm has sent to every port in which he can imagine his friend may have arrived. Salīm begins to fear for his friend's fate, and the story *Al-Jinān*'s readership has been following threatens to come to an unresolved end. Finally, Salīm happens upon a group of sailors on the shore of the Mediterranean just north of Beirut and discovers that they were on a ship with Sulaymān—the narrative continues. The narrative threat represented by a suspension of news via letter or telegram reappears in the novel's final installment. *Al-Jinān*'s readership is reminded that they, along with their narrator, were awaiting news of the tale's conclusion. To read a novel is, then, to wait in suspense. Salīm explains that "the beauty of a novel is in the quality of its ending. After thinking about that for a long time I was determined not to publish this novel" without news of how Sulaymān's search for Wardah finally concluded.[41] The update comes once again in a letter from Sulaymān and Wardah, the final installment in their epistolary correspondence reaching Salīm from the distant shores of Naples, and the remaining loose narrative strands are woven together. Letters and telegrams in the pages of *Al-Huyām fī jinān al-Shām* allow Salīm al-Bustānī to metafictionally stage the relationship between reader and text, down to the material question of how texts circulate, using familiar epistolary models as a pedagogy for readers and potential future writers. Using an old narrative ruse borrowed from the storytelling for which the region is famous, the novel, like the frame tale of *A Thousand and One Nights*, is a technology of suspense.

While in the pages of *Al-Jinān* the reading of books and journals is figured as a useful means of edification and proper bourgeois comportment, in *Al-Zahrah*'s 1870 serialized novel *al-Shābb al-maghrūr* (The conceited or tempted youth), reading is a more private activity, connected to affairs of the bedroom and offered as a mode of entertainment and relaxation. Indicative of the uncertain status of bourgeois reading habits, while also indexing the disruptive seductions through which suspense can operate, an illicit, clandestine aspect haunts the entertaining and relaxing side of reading in *al-Shābb al-maghrūr*, exposing an anxiety in and about this new Arabic press and its novels, one that remembers not just the dream of paradise but also the story of the fall from Eden.

The readers of *Al-Zahrah*'s 1870 novel *al-Shābb al-maghrūr* are introduced in its first installment to an unnamed narrator who travels in June 1866 from Beirut to Damascus, where, like Sulaymān, he stays in a hotel and wanders the city's infamous gardens. It is there in the gardens of Damascus that the narrator meets his protagonist, Khalīl, and much of the novel is his narration of Khalīl's tale to a fellow traveler on the return trip from Damascus to Beirut. This very traveler turns out to be Faḍlū, whose fiancée, Anīsah, is a character in the tale the narrator has just told him: despite Anīsah's protestations, Khalīl leaves Damascus to travel around Syria before returning to Damascus with a woman he has fallen for named Ghirrah and her mother, Fitnah, women he should have known better than to trust as soon as he learned their portentous names. The novel is the story of the narrator's attempts to help bail Khalīl, the conceited, tempted youth of the novel's title, out of the debts he has incurred as a result of Ghirrah and her mother's penchant for extravagance, which turns out to be his undoing. He is left bankrupt and wandering the streets of Damascus in the penultimate installment of *al-Shābb al-maghrūr* in the fall of 1870. Though he came from a wealthy family living in Beirut, the speed with which Khalīl falls into debt and ill repute stands as a striking warning to readers of the vulnerable, fragile position of a tempted bourgeois youth faced with the seductions and deceptions of late nineteenth-century Syria.

Reading in this novel is not so much a path to material and literary progress as an invitation to entertainment and the bedroom. After meeting Khalīl—his protagonist destined to fall into bankruptcy and disrepute—in that hopeful space of the garden, the narrator returns to his hotel room and begins to change his clothes, narrating: "I turned to my bed, and it appeared as if it were saying to me, 'Come here, delight in the relaxation of sleep and the pleasure of dreams.' There was, furthermore, beside the bed a book containing some literary stories [*qiṣaṣ adabiyyah*], which I heard calling to me as if its pages were saying 'Here is calmness and pleasurable reading [*muṭālaʿah*].'"[42] He undresses and crawls into bed with the book and must beg his new friend's forgiveness when the latter comes knocking a few moments later: reading is a distraction, it is a private affair, it is performed in one's underclothes; reading is so seductive it threatens to overwhelm the very narrative possibility of the novel upon which we have only just embarked. Later, in the thirteenth issue of *al-Shābb al-maghrūr*, the unnamed narrator of the second issue has faded from view and follows along with us the first-person narrative of Khalīl. His neighbor Anīsah (the young fiancée of Faḍlū, the story's enframed recipient who hears this tale on the return trip from Damascus to Beirut) has just let herself into Khalīl's hotel room in Damascus in the middle of the night; when he awakes, he finds her by his bed, reading by candlelight. She explains: "In order to entertain myself I picked up this book to read [*uṭāliʿa*]." She knew the way to his room from an earlier scene, when she had asked Khalīl to borrow something with which to relight her fire, which had died out.

During a conversation that stretches across several installments of the novel, Khalīl repeatedly thinks Anīsah is about to bring up a lost letter, creating an air of suspense and seduction around the mysterious circumstances of its reappearance. Finally, in the tenth issue, she does. Swearing that she never read it, Anīsah explains that she was interested in it because she thought it might be "the writings of a woman."[43] He insists that she must have read it, citing the changed seal; she laughs, telling him that she did that so that he would come and speak to her. Far from the edifying nature of reading championed in the pages of *al-Huyām fī jinān al-Shām*, reading here becomes a clandestine activity, staged by the engaged Anīsah to lure another man's attention, and communicated via a coded language of seals.[44] Reading in this novel entails seduction, not only of the characters within the novel's frame but of the very audience that *Al-Zahrah* was beginning to attract as subscribers in 1870.

Al-Shābb al-maghrūr makes this air of seduction as a narrative device explicit, laying it before the reader as Khalīl warns the already engaged Anīsah, in a story readers will be asked later to imagine from the perspective of her fiancé, that "this sort of entertainment (*tasliyah*) might give birth to thinking on my part of which you are unaware."[45] She replies that this is not a fear, and they discuss what might happen if it does become an issue, to which she responds that they will have to then refrain from their evening chats. He decides that it would be better for him to travel as planned, and she says: "If you do, I will be encompassed by intense boredom."[46] This conversation extends over several issues, punctuated both by weekly breaks and the looming mystery of the changed seal, creating an accumulating sense of illicit romantic tension that leaves the reader uncertain yet anticipating what will happen next. The novel's readership is implicitly asked to imagine a situation in which Khalīl does not travel as planned, and as the possibility is left suspensefully hanging over four issues, *Al-Zahrah*'s readers would have spent nearly a month speculating, perhaps hoping, perhaps fearing, what was to come of this affair.

Al-Shābb al-maghrūr's narrative investment in suspense becomes palpably acute when Khalīl's tale breaks off in the seventeenth installment and the narrator of the novel's early installments is left with a sense that Khalīl "was hiding something."[47] He sets out in search of Khalīl, a narrator in search of a narrative, trailing *Al-Zahrah*'s readers along with him. In the nineteenth installment, the narrator's search delivers him to Khalīl's door, where he asks after Isṭafān,

Khalīl's servant, who is said to know where Khalīl is. The woman who answers the door tells him that she cannot disclose Isṭafān's location, as everyone is afraid of him. The narrator responds, "You have made me long [*shawwaqtīnī*] to see him even more, so where is he?"[48] The woman directs the narrator to a coffeeshop, famous for the heavy drinking (not of coffee) that takes place there. When the narrator gets to the coffeeshop, he asks someone sitting by the door, "Is there a man by the name of Isṭafān here?"[49] The next line of text reads, "and he said to me," only to be followed by the weekly coda: "the remainder is to come."[50] The serialized form of the novel leaves the narrator, along with his readers, at the threshold, wondering even as they feared if their narrator has at last picked up the plot again and located the elusive Isṭafān in a narrative turn that duplicates and so reiterates at the level of form the sense of suspense—in Arabic, *tashwīq*, from the same root and form as the narrator's "*shawwaqtīnī*"—produced by the novel's plot.

The first installment of *al-Huyām fī jinān al-Shām*, too, formally relies on suspense, cutting off a character and leaving readers of *Al-Jinān* to wait and wonder for two weeks as to what a female voice in a Damascus park might possibly have to say that is more beautiful than anything the protagonist has heard in all his travels through Europe. Later in the novel, Salīm, the narrator, tells his protagonist, Sulaymān, that "if you spoke to me for a year of your strange tales, boredom would not afflict me. For they take a person from one situation to the next as he awaits the outcome."[51] Suspense again trumps boredom five issues later, when Salīm recounts a conversation with Sulaymān: "Perhaps you are bored of hearing my story[, Sulayman said.] And I told him no, and grabbed him . . . as one grabbing a bird that almost escaped from between his hands."[52] Both *al-Shābb al-maghrūr* and *al-Huyām fī jinān al-Shām* keep audience boredom at bay by sustaining an atmosphere of suspense over the course of the year 1870, a suspense propelled by the enframed structure of the two novels, enframed both within their pages by a frame tale and its narrator as well as within the pages of *Al-Zahrah* and *Al-Jinān*, respectively, as each installment of the novels occupies the final section of an issue, inviting readers to await the remainder—not only of the novel and the journal but of the path to progress they are led to hope is unfolding—that is to come. Over and over again, installments end with a character in midsentence, or a dramatic scene is played out over the course of a number of issues.

Linda K. Hughes and Michael Lund limn the "delight in 'more to come'" that readers of the Victorian serial encountered at the end of each installment.[53] Their study links this delight to a nineteenth-century confidence in progress, in Arabic *taqaddum*, a word for which *Al-Jinān* in 1870 shares *Ḥadīqat al-Akhbār*'s hopeful affection in 1859.[54] Building off the work of N. N. Feltes in his *Modes of Production of Victorian Novels*, Hughes and Lund insist that the serial form "harmonized in several respects with capitalist ideology," not least of all in the "assumption of continuing growth."[55] Their observations are pertinent to the utopian gardens of Beirut in early 1870, when the silk trade was still booming, banks and schools were flourishing, novel ideas of bourgeois life were filling the public sphere with hope, and the ruses of this first age of finance capital remained relatively opaque, "hard to see."

In her book *The Serious Pleasures of Suspense: Victorian Realism and Narrative Doubt*, however, Caroline Levine renders the nineteenth-century debate around suspense among Victorian authors and thinkers otherwise, and her argument holds an augury for what was to come in Arabic. In a survey of previous theorizations of suspense, Levine explains: "It has become something of a commonplace to presume that suspense fiction reinforces stability, activating anxiety about the social world only in order to repress that anxiety in favor of unambiguous disclosures and soothing restorations of the status quo. But it was not always so. This book makes the case that Victorian writers and readers understood suspenseful narrative as a stimulus to active speculation."[56] While the regular repetition of the coda "the remainder is to come" at the end of each installment of a serialized novel such as *al-Shābb al-maghrūr* or *al-Huyām fī jinān al-Shām* may well have resonated with comforting notions of progress and continuing economic growth in the 1870 Beirut where they were published, readers, too, may have begun to find in the suspenseful tactics of the serialized novel the stuff of hope's *doppelgänger*, a fear of what the future—rendered newly uncertain through a new mode of capitalist speculation and industry—would bring.

Suspense, of course, was not at all new to Arabic. Ibrāhīm al-Saʿāfīn, in his study of the Syrian novel, argues that the early Arabic novelist "knew with certainty that his audience's taste had been raised on popular literature going back for generations," and that this audience had a unique "connection . . . with this narrative heritage."[57] Not just Victorian England can lend insight into the formal investments of the serialized Arabic novel but also, and far more familiarly for its 1870 audience, the popular Arabic narrative tradition, particularly works such as the story of ʿAntar and *Alf laylah wa-laylah* (*A Thousand and One Nights*).[58] As 1870 Beirut dreamt of idyllic gardens of knowledge, the serialized *riwāyāt* that coursed through the press intimated in their form and in their frame tales the suspense inherited from an earlier mode of Arabic storytelling. The frame tale of *A Thousand and One Nights*, as well as many of the stories contained within the collection, bore traces of centuries of merchant capital and its techniques of deferral, opening onto a hope for a limitless future of trade and the gradual accumulation of profit, addled by the fear inherent in games of risk and wager. Nevertheless, for the Arabic press in early 1870, the figure of the gardens, paved with the glittering gold of a newly emerging reading public, for a moment held out a path of material and literary progress.

In 1870, *Al-Zahrah* wove this narrative heritage into an anecdote precisely about its audience's acute awareness of the workings of suspense. The anecdote tells of a man who attended a storyteller's circle every night to listen to the story of ʿAntar. One evening, "the storyteller read until ʿAntar was captured by the Persians who imprisoned him and bound his legs and there he stopped speaking."[59] The man who had been listening to the story "went home sad and depressed,"[60] eventually beating his wife out of frustration. Later that night he wandered in the markets trying to decide what to do, and finally it occurred to him to go to the home of the storyteller. There he begs the storyteller to get ʿAntar out of prison, telling him that he will pay him as much as he regularly collects from an evening's audience "for I am unable to sleep."[61] The storyteller agrees, "taking the book and reading him the rest."[62] The circulation and commodification of the story of ʿAntar, like the serialized novel *al-Shābb al-maghrūr* that appears at the end of the issue, hinges on a form of narrative suspense that has a long history in the region (as does this penchant for begging storytellers for a further installment),[63] one with deep connections to merchants and the workings of merchant capital. It is the very economic system being eclipsed by European industrialization in the late nineteenth century, such that when finance and the serialized novel emerged simultaneously in Arabic, it was into a narrative tradition well versed in stories of capital, risk, and empire.

A Thousand and One Nights, *Sindbad*, and similar collections of popular tales repeatedly appear in late nineteenth-century Beirut. In

1859, Buṭrus al-Bustānī painted a portrait of the storyteller who frequented Beirut's coffeeshops, "one with a hoarse voice and a good memory who has memorized some of the tales from the stories of Sindbad the sailor and Banī Hilāl and what is most similar to those among the stories present in the book *A Thousand and One Nights*."[64] New Arabic editions of the collection also appeared over the course of this period and were advertised on the back page of *Al-Jannah*, a trade journal founded in 1870 by Buṭrus al-Bustānī and available in joint subscription with *Al-Jinān* as well as Khalīl Sarkīs's *Lisān al-Ḥāl* upon its founding in 1877. The printed copies of *A Thousand and One Nights* circulating among storytellers and the periodical reading class alike suggest that the collection felt relevant not only to its traditional audiences at the edges of Beirut's markets but also to the growing reading public of serialized fiction as well.

In her book-length study of *A Thousand and One Nights*, Ferial Ghazoul points out that Shahrazad, the infamous female narrator of this collection of tales, "is simply awarded a privilege that can be withdrawn at any moment, and it is precisely the feeling that she may not manage to please her audience—and, therefore, the hovering possibility of her condemnation [to death]—that makes *The Arabian Nights* a suspense story throughout its course."[65] There is a burden upon Shahrazad, night after night, to "please her audience." In Husain Haddawy's translation of *A Thousand and One Nights*, based on the text of the fourteenth-century Syrian manuscript edited in 1984 by Muḥsin Mahdī, the first night ends with Shahrazad in midstory, "leaving the King Shahrayar burning with curiosity to hear the rest of the story."[66] Salīm al-Bustānī left his readers in suspense from the first issue of *Al-Jinān*, inviting them to pass through the gates of the gardens and echoing Shahrazad's concern with "pleasing her audience" as he repeated every fortnight that "the remainder will come" until his untimely death in 1884. Nearly every issue of *Al-Jinān* contained a new installment of a serialized novel, each issue asking readers to speculate as to what would happen next.

While *Al-Jinān* went on to publish for more than a decade, *Al-Zahrah* was a short-lived venture. Perhaps with the serialized novel al-Shalfūn had not played his cards quite right, perhaps printing too much in the way of seduction, showing too much of the darker, more illicit side of what the garden held for late nineteenth-century Arabic. In an announcement at the end of *al-Shābb al-maghrūr*, al-Shalfūn wrote:

> Given that the novel *al-Shābb al-maghrūr* has come to an end, and many asked that we include a useful history in serialized form, from this point forward we will run the history of the war of the kings of *al-Tabābaʿah* in Yemen before Islam, taken from the book *Jamharat al-ʿArab* [The Arab populace], as it is likely that it will appeal to our esteemed subscribers. We likewise advise them that we will change the form of this our newspaper at the beginning of the New Year by including useful foreign and local news that it will appeal to the reader to peruse, in accordance with what space will allow for, as we seek to spread public benefits to the audience.[67]

It was the end for the novel in the pages of the journal. Indeed, *Al-Zahrah* never did see the New Year, like a Shahrazad who had run out of stories, meeting with its own "condemnation to death."

Al-Shalfūn joined forces with Luwīs Ṣābūnjī, whose 1870 journal *Al-Naḥlah* (The bee) had likewise proved itself an unviable enterprise, unable to pollinate the gardens of knowledge being cultivated in the Beirut press. The two published together a new journal entitled *Al-Najāḥ* (Success), but it, too, was short-lived, a recurrent theme in Ṣābūnjī's publishing career. In August 1871, Ṣābūnjī, himself a Catholic priest, published the following announcement in the Jesuit journal *Al-Bashīr*:

> We inform the dear audience that from the date of the first of this present month of August we have completely quit work on the journal [*jurnāl*] *Al-Najāḥ*. And we have desisted entirely from involvement in its publication. . . . [F]rom now on we will not pen a line or write an article in it. And we will not ever publish a political summary in it as we did previously. And we will not translate the novel [*The Count of*] *Monte Cristo*, which we had taken upon ourselves the responsibility of translating from French to Arabic while correcting those impolitenesses transgressing religion. In order to lift all responsibility from ourselves for the journal *Al-Najāḥ* as well as responsibility for the impolite language in the novel *Monte Cristo*, the reading of which is forbidden to all Catholics by Rome due to its excessive crudeness against religion, we have issued this announcement without delay, written the 16th of August in the year 1871.[68]

Like *Al-Zahrah* and *Al-Naḥlah* before it, *Al-Najāḥ* had failed to fulfill its readership's (or at least the Catholic Church's) emergent narrative desires for Arabic.

The critic ʿAbd al-Raḥmān Yāghī points out that *Al-Jinān*'s inclusion of serialized fiction set a precedent that, through its popularity, created a demand for *riwāyāt* among Arabic journal readers.[69] "The press," Ami Ayalon notes, "like other commercial areas, involved competing for a limited market."[70] Caught between a dream of a garden of knowledge, fed by the waters of the *riwāyāt* serialized in its pages, and the demands and seductions of the commercial market for periodicals and fiction, the novels of early 1870s Beirut, both formally and in the stories they could and could not tell, left a deep and telling trace in the archive. They foretold a mode of anxious speculation just beginning to be articulated in Arabic, one that would perpetually suspend the *Nahḍah*'s dream of literary and material progress between an alchemy of hope, and the fear looming at the horizon of the gardens of the future.

CHAPTER 2

Like a Butterfly Stirring within a Chrysalis

Salīm al-Bustānī, Yūsuf al-Shalfūn, and the Remainder to Come

If Beirut's Arabic press could be figured in 1870 as an Eden of material and literary progress, a refuge of hope, it also registered a sense of anxiety. Silk was industrializing, French networks of credit were eclipsing Ottoman taxation practices, and the future of sericulture was anything but certain. Two 1870 serialized Arabic novels (*riwāyāt*) discussed in chapter 1—Salīm al-Bustānī's *al-Huyām fī jinān al-Shām* (Love in the gardens of Damascus), unfolding in fortnightly installments in his family's journal, *Al-Jinān*; and Yūsuf al-Shalfūn's *al-Shābb al-maghrūr* (The conceited or tempted youth), appearing simultaneously in al-Shalfūn's short-lived satirical journal *Al-Zahrah*—published springtime scenes in the gardens of Damascus, love stories in the making. By the early summer of 1870, however, these hopeful plotlines were undermined by the suspense charted not only at the level of form, each serialized installment ever asking readers to wait: the remainder was yet to come, but also by the historical conjuncture, a moment when the very unruliness of global—here especially French—capital was profiting at a quickening pace off the risks entailed in financing and speculating in silk moths and mulberry orchards.

The fall was foretold: woven of clouds of locusts and the proliferation of unpayable debts, the serialized *riwāyāt* coursing through the Arabic press in 1870 decisively registered the fragile vulnerability of Beirut's economy. The stuff of contradiction, Eden's demise all over again, the local Beirut bourgeoisie, even as they dreamed for themselves gardens of progress, were bankrupting the mulberry orchards of the future. The balance of trade stacked the bourgeoisie's importation of the latest French finished silk textiles and their subscriptions to the rather expensive journals of the *Nahḍah*, against the commodification of local silk cocoons and fibers as an industrialized raw good, its exportation to the factories of Marseilles and Lyons enabled by a web of finance that held if not the promise of material and literary progress, then certainly that of capital flight.

In the early 1800s, Beirut, eclipsed by Tripoli to the north and Acre to the south, was not yet a center of Mediterranean trade.[1] It was not until the 1830s, as Jens Hanssen notes in his study of late Ottoman Beirut, that "European commercial expansion—especially the silk trade with Mount Lebanon—propelled Beirut into the orbit of the Europe-centered world-economy."[2] In 1838 and 1840, Ottoman-European free trade agreements codified the region's increasing connectedness to a world economic system, and in 1856, the first branch of the Imperial Ottoman Bank opened for business in Beirut.[3] Following the Druze-Maronite War of 1860, foreign and especially French intervention in the economic affairs of Beirut and Mount Lebanon increased tremendously, centering on the light and valuable commodity silk as they ushered in an age of finance capital. As the historian Boutros Labaki points out, the French troops sent to Mount Lebanon in June 1860 "were charged with the reconstruction of houses and with putting the silk industry [*séricicultur*e] back on its feet."[4] In the wake of this intervention, the silk industry was restructured and industrialized to the benefit of French businessmen and bankers, as well as, in the short term, the growing local bourgeoisie. It was a new economic order, apprehended by the Sublime Porte as a growing threat to an earlier age of merchant capital and taxation, culminating in the early 1870s in the speculative nightmare of *papillonnage*, so many silk moths, detained by their Ottoman taxers, imagined to have rent their chrysalises, Beirut's fortunes in flight.

Over the course of the 1860s, capital was amassing in Beirut: it was silk money but also a growing web of finance, marking the city's incorporation into a changing world economy. The telegraph, the opening of the Suez Canal in 1869, and the ever-increasing rate of steam-powered industrialization all contributed to the accelerating pace of this first age of finance capital. Over the course of the 1860s, the booming silk industry cultivated a vastly changed geography and economy for Beirut and its markets. With the exception of the summer of 1865, when a cholera epidemic killed thousands and forced many to evacuate Beirut, the city witnessed growing prosperity. If some of the capital was finding its way to French banks and French factory owners, the 1860s seemed to promise a future of local material prosperity enabled by the workings of global finance. Beirut, the nightmare of 1860 receding, could again be imagined as an Eden of, as Khalīl al-Khūrī put it in 1859, "literary and material progress [*al-taqaddum al-adabī wa-l-māddī*],"[5] that would culminate in the gardens and novels of the Arabic press in 1870.

Coming on the heels of the profits of the 1860s, the early 1870s were marked, however, by unstable, falling returns on silk. As Akram Fouad Khater notes in his book *Inventing Home: Emigration, Gender, and the Middle Class in Lebanon, 1870–1920*, a sense of "growing uncertainty" emerged in the 1870s,[6] one that resonates with the serialized form of long fictional narratives such as *al-Shābb al-maghrūr* and *al-Huyām fī jinān al-Shām*. As discussed in chapter 1, the repetition of the coda "the remainder is to come" at the end of each installment of a serialized story could be read as a homology of notions of steady progress so central to nineteenth-century utopias of the future, taking form in 1870 Beirut as a garden dream of *Nahḍah*. Yet, serialization also cultivates in its readers the habit of speculation, with the understanding that the future may not turn out as one might have hoped or expected. As investment in silk built precarious fortunes in the city of Beirut, the suspense generated in these serialized narratives limned the tension between an audience's investment in material progress and gardens of literature and knowledge, and their uncertainty and even fear in the face of the future. At least one contemporary of this period, reflecting back in 1908, likened the entire silk industry to "gambling," for one "does not know when he will win or when he will lose, for his winnings are great and his losses greater such that the majority of the people of our country who occupied themselves with it lost their fortunes [*amwālahum*] and their status [*aḥwālahum*]."[7]

While the 1870s would disappoint many of Beirut's investors and sericulturalists, 1860s Beirut teemed with merchants, brokers, and entrepreneurs profiting from the raw materials being exported and the manufactured goods being imported, and the new standards of living this activity afforded. Villas were built, gardens cultivated, and silk fabrics and European fashion clad the aspiring bourgeoisie. Not only finance, but the logistics of industrial manufacture connected Beirut to a global market at a moment of changing fortunes in the

Mediterranean silk industry. Khater observes that "increased weaving of silk textiles in France in the nineteenth century required more silk thread than could be supplied by European sericulture. This was especially the case after 1865, when a blight decimated French and Italian sericulture; industrialists of Lyons and Marseilles needed to find alternative supplies for their factories."[8] Coupled with rising French demand for silk, a series of strikes by French silk factory workers in the 1860s made the importation of silk thread a pressing concern for French industrialists.[9] European- and especially French-owned silk spinning factories transformed the landscape of Mount Lebanon and Beirut. By the 1860s, local entrepreneurs, too, had capitalized on the production of steamed raw cocoons and silk thread, opening their own filatures. While the number of foreign-owned filatures dropped considerably over the course of the 1860s, Lyons-based finance continued to fuel the silk industry via the banks of Beirut.

This moment is the rise of Arabic's first age of finance capital, that realm of capital that Arrighi reminds us is "hard to see because of the actual invisibility or the complexity of the activities that constitute it."[10] While it was born of cotton money in Egypt, in Beirut it took form around the growing silk industry through French credit and the pressures of Ottoman taxation, as Labaki points out in his study of the economic history of Syria, producing a sense of palpable risk motivating a sophisticated securities and futures market among local merchants and brokers. In 1856, the Ottoman government, under pressure from European powers, issued a proclamation as part of the modernization project known as the Tanzimat. It stated, as Labaki writes, "that the creation of credit would be encouraged, [and] that the monetary and financial system as well as public finances would be reformed."[11] The institutions extending credit to those in and around Beirut were in large part local banks backed by Lyon-based financiers, though wealthy locals also extended credit. Labaki points out that the concomitant rise of the silk industry and credit-based finance "is explained by the necessity for the silk trader to have at his disposal a rather large amount of monetary capital in order to set in movement the circulation of this light and valuable merchandise."[12] He notes: "almost no local filature had at its disposal such sums."[13]

Industrialization through the spread of French banks and the shift from a cottage silk industry to a new geography of filatures connected to factories in the South of France exposed Syria's silk industry to risk on a new scale. If it leaves a trace in French consular records, as discussed in the introduction, in the form of the fear of *papillonnage*, of Ottoman taxation overwhelming French and local industrial efforts; in Beirut's markets, it created an opportunity to gamble through the trade in silk futures, and the buying and selling of debts of considerable magnitude. These merchants and brokers of Beirut, the local weavers of the web of finance underpinning Syria's silk industry, are the subject of Fawaz's *Merchants and Migrants in Nineteenth-Century Beirut*:

> Much of the investment in silk came from import-export houses of Marseilles and Lyon. These houses advanced capital to the silk manufacturers either directly or through brokers in Beirut. . . . A number of brokers also maintained their own business on the side, buying cocoons from the silk cultivators and selling them to the silk-reeling manufacturers or to commercial houses. They borrowed capital to buy the silk crop, sometimes gambling on futures at usurious rates that guaranteed the brokers a low price for the future crop. . . . A whole range of successful silk entrepreneurs soon rose to the top of the economic ladder, which traditionally had been occupied by older, more established merchants, landowners, and notables. . . . This initiated a social revolution not only in the urban milieu where the entrepreneurs flourished, but also in the nearby countryside.[14]

The price of silk peaked in the 1860s and early 1870. With the new kind of volatility that finance capital introduced,[15] as Khater argues, "silk helped change th[e local] state of affairs by clearly establishing money as a signifier of social status," with this newfound wealth manifesting as a "new and more expensive standard of living."[16] Among the changes taking place in and around Beirut during this period was the emergence, traced in chapter 1, of a bourgeois reading class looking from the gardens of Beirut, Aleppo, and Damascus toward Europe as a model for their dreams of "literary and material progress," symbolically congealing in new reading habits and a particular penchant for French textiles, especially silks.

Salīm al-Bustānī's and Yūsuf al-Shalfūn's novels were serialized in Beirut's journals, which also published updates on harvests, new production techniques, shipping schedules, lists and prices of exported and imported commodities, advertisements placed by local and foreign merchants, financial information, announcements of bankruptcy, and currency values. Newspapers of Beirut also regularly featured telegrams sent from European cities, translated articles from the European press, and long and short pieces on the state of affairs in Europe, but most particularly in France. Jürgen Habermas in a

European context observes that "the traffic in news that developed alongside the traffic in commodities" accompanied "the expansion of trade," for "merchants' market-oriented calculations required more frequent and exact information about distant events,"[17] something On Barak's *On Time* corroborates in the case of Egypt.[18] The spate of journals that began publication in 1870 and 1871 in Beirut provided their readers with a range of trade-related information, while also serializing, as we have already seen, several novels.

Despite Edenic hopes, 1870 proved an inauspicious year in the region's silk trade. Silk cocoons harvested around Beirut and Mount Lebanon (though not in the Bekaa) reached their highest value in the months before *Al-Jinān* and *Al-Zahrah* began publication in January 1870, and Beirut merchants and bankers would never see the price of silk recover following the poor harvest of that year.[19] Though the production of silk would increase throughout the 1870s and into the next century, the price per *bālah* continued to fall.[20] In its early May 1870 issue, *Al-Jinān* captured the sense of anxiety and fear surrounding the impending silk harvest: "Although some of the crops that were eaten by locusts [*jarād*] have been replanted a second time thanks to the plentiful rains, despite this the speed with which the [silk] worms fell and the recent cold and its damage to the mulberry leaves and the new armies of locusts [*jarād*] make us fear the occurrence of a decrease in the silk harvest."[21] Fear of locusts, like that of *papillonnage*, was a fear of impending capital flight, haunting the unseasonably cold gardens of progress in 1870 Beirut, and for years to come.

Serialized novels, like Salīm al-Bustānī's 1870 *al-Huyām fī jinān al-Shām* and Yūsuf al-Shalfūn's *al-Shābb al-maghrūr*, gave literary form to the speculative hopes being undone in the mulberry orchards of Mount Lebanon. The installment of *al-Huyām* published in *Al-Jinān* early that May cathects the fears (and, for some of the gambling brokers, perhaps the hope) roused by armies of locusts among the many readers whose fortunes rested on the increasingly threatened silk harvest of 1870. A general air of anxious suspense persists throughout the late spring and early summer, when the fortunes of that year's silk crop hung most pressingly in the balance. In these installments of al-Bustānī's first novel, his protagonist, Sulaymān, and the group of foreigners with whom he is traveling face the armies of Bedouin about whose warring ways they have been repeatedly warned. The early May installment sees a pause in the battle that erupts, though "dangers threaten,"[22] and the installment ends with Sulaymān's cohort left preparing to meet the far larger Bedouin army darkening the horizon. By mid-May, the group has been captured, and the issue ends with Sulaymān preparing for his imminent execution. A fearful current runs through these installments of *al-Huyām fī jinān al-Shām*, articulating the sense of suspense flooding Beirut and its environs, as May anxieties surrounding the year's silk harvest gave way to a tenor of despair come June.

When *Al-Jinān* reported on the locusts that had been ravaging the mulberry groves in its tenth issue, printed in mid-May 1870, the update was no doubt met with some hope by those whose assets were tied up with the year's silk harvest. It read: "The high degree of determination that was demonstrated and continues to be demonstrated by the government of [Mount] Lebanon and its inhabitants in annihilating the locusts [*jarād*] calls for the thanks and gratitude of all. Because were it not for this determination then the locusts [*jarād*] would have destroyed the Mountain and the rest of the country."[23] The installment of *al-Huyām fī jinān al-Shām* that appeared in this issue of *Al-Jinān* recounted the fate of Sulaymān and his entourage of foreigners after their first battle with Bedouin forces following their sightseeing visit to the ancient city of Tadmur, or Palmyra. While they thought that they had perhaps escaped, in fact an enormous army returns and captures them, placing the group in confinement "after they had stripped us [*jaradūnā*] of most of our clothes [*baʿd an jaradūnā min akthar malābisinā*]."[24] Thirteen pages earlier in the same issue, readers of *Al-Jinān* may have been comforted by the efforts expended in fighting the armies of locusts (*jarād*). Yet the army that returns in great numbers to capture the protagonist of al-Bustānī's novel along with the rest of his group metaphorizes the feared fate of the silk harvest, laying it bare, as it were. The reader recognizes the multiple layers of this metaphoric operation, not only at the level of unfolding events but also at the linguistic level, through the repetition of the root *j-r-d*, to strip or lay bare: the army of Bedouin "stripped" (*jaradū*) the protagonist Sulaymān along with his foreign friends of their fine clothes, just as the "locusts" (*jarād*) laid bare the mulberry trees. The next issue of *Al-Jinān* makes plain this defeat, directing its readers to the economic downturn that is expected: "It is thought that the price of silk this year will not exceed the middle point, for it is heard that the harvests in Europe and especially in France were very good. It is the nature of these losses to stop the gears of trade [*tijārah*] which turn when the steam of the harvest's quality moves them."[25]

Al-Jinān, as it pivots around derivations of the root *j-r-d*—locusts, stripping or laying bare—underscores, too, that newspapers—*jarā'id*, also from the root *j-r-d*—played a role in the literary and financial speculations threatening Beirut's gardens of progress with ruin in the early summer of 1870. At the same time as Beirut's press enabled many a speculative venture, profiting off the new kinds of information and stories on which they relied, the press also held out to its readers, a bourgeoisie seduced by dreams of gardens, novel material for closer reading, an account of the workings of finance capital just beginning to come into view in early 1870s Beirut.

The brokers who gambled on silk futures and the financiers who backed them built their fortunes through speculation, riding currents of suspense, of hope and fear at the harvest's outcome. The very source of the narrative in *al-Huyām fī jinān al-Shām*, namely the well-heeled protagonist Sulaymān, the hero of the love story who hides in an early eponymous garden scene in a shady grove of trees, the one who was "hard to see," is revealed in the pages of issues 15 and 16 of *Al-Jinān* to himself be caught up in speculating in silk futures. He explains his finances to the novel's enframing narrator:

> My hands did not hold at that time a single dirham because my money was in the hands of the brokers. I am not saying that I practiced usury, far from it, for I hated the usurers or those who give the poor what would cover their needs and take from them much. Rather I had placed my money in the hands of those whose presence has been made necessary by the present organization of the world which has bound all that you have in the world together with commercial [*tijāriyyah*] relations. For they take the money from those in ease in order to widen the operations of those that, despite their being of easy circumstances, need an extension of money in order to fulfill their commercial [*tijāriyyah*] operations at a specific time, such as during the days of the harvest, in order to increase the amount they buy so as to increase their gain and facilitate trade [*tijārah*] by taking papers acknowledging the given amount in a given place in order that they collect their value at a later time than in the time in which they paid their amount and in a place other than the place in which they arranged them before. Exposing themselves to the calamities that might be produced by a lack of these pieces of paper standing in for the money that they paid for them.[26]

Sulaymān speaks of "calamities," referencing the considerable risk involved in speculating in the silk harvest for not only the brokers but also for their financiers, such as Sulaymān himself. While lenders attempted to secure their future returns through the guarantee of "pieces of paper standing in for money," it is understood that in the event of a disastrous silk harvest, all might be lost. As Gaston Ducousso, a Frenchman working in Beirut as part of the French Consulat Général, observed in his 1918 study of the silk industry in the region: "The [financial] backers in these sorts of operations were extremely prudent; yet, despite all the guarantees that they could surround themselves with—mortgages, signatures of notables of the borrower's village guaranteeing his solvency, arguments were not rare and these sorts of differences provided the indigenous courts with a good part of their affairs."[27] Ever looking to the future, speculating as to the "remainder to come," the rise of a complex financial system in the region resonated with the tenor of hope and fear punctuating the new serialized Arabic novels being published in Beirut's journals, enabled by and themselves participating in the textualization of a new mode of capitalist speculation.

Prior to that May, *Al-Zahrah*'s serialized novel *al-Shābb al-maghrūr* [The conceited or tempted youth] had been a love story, even an allegorical love story, perhaps, of silk. Throughout the spring, the suspense in *al-Shābb al-maghrūr* hinged on Khalīl's relationship with his young, engaged neighbor Anīsah, linked as it was to the mysterious reappearance of a lost letter. The possibility that this relationship might grow into a love affair, drawn out in the pages of *Al-Zahrah* for over a month, finally evaporates when Khalīl decides to leave the city of Damascus. Even with Anīsah out of the way, though, *al-Shābb al-maghrūr* still promised a love story: in Khalīl's ensuing travels around Syria, he falls for a young and beautiful woman named Ghirrah, her name the stuff of illusion, seduction, and risk, derivations of the glinting edge of the blade of a sword. Upon their return to Damascus, that plot of romance is decisively interrupted when the narrator loses track of Khalīl. He begins to search for him, as he senses that Khalīl has been hiding something, and he wishes to hear the rest of his story. He, like those whose futures were bound up in the region's silk harvest, is in a state of suspense, chasing after illusion, left to wonder what was to come.

Late nineteenth-century Arabic novels, like the Victorian novels Caroline Levine studies, "flaunt their secrets."[28] Indeed, Beirut's novels are as ostentatious in flaunting their secrets as the local bourgeoisie was in commodifying its wealth. Those secrets will in the end govern the plot of this and other nineteenth-century serialized Arabic novels, and the story they tell will neither be one of *nahḍah*, nor will it end in a garden. When *al-Shābb al-maghrūr*'s narrator finally finds Khalīl at Ghirrah's house in Damascus in the twenty-first installment of this serialized novel, appearing in late May 1870, the novel suddenly ceases to be the tale of love it had just promised to be. The narrator discovers an ornately appointed home in the first June 1870 installment, though, as he notes, it contained "strange furniture, useless for anything but decoration."[29] Two weeks earlier, in the installment of *al-Huyām fī jinān al-Shām* in which Sulaymān and his friends are, like the mulberry trees, stripped nearly bare, Sulaymān warns against the widespread and ostentatious consumption of commodities, as fear of ruin hovers at the horizon. The bourgeoisie, like Khalīl, "purchases jewelry or furniture or food or drink or real estate or carriages or horses or donkeys and whatever else that make the ignorant imagine that in his action is pride or greatness or honor."[30] The extravagant uselessness of Ghirrah's "strange furniture" for anything but ostentation underscores what the bourgeoisie is hiding behind the many material commodities that suddenly overwhelm these novels' plotlines, as the dream of the gardens cultivated that spring begins to erode.

It is a game of risk. With a poor silk harvest immanent, the knock at the door in a June installment of *al-Shābb al-maghrūr* reverberated with the fortunes of many involved in sericulture, trade, and finance in the region. The fictions subtending their fortunes were, like Khalīl's own secrets, born of illusion and about to be suddenly exposed, no longer "hard to see." Speaking softly lest someone hear, in the next episode, Khalīl takes the narrator at the door on a tour of Ghirrah's house. It is a palace of debt: all of the furniture costs 15,000 *ghirsh*, or piasters, none of which he has yet paid. He furthermore owes his servant Isṭifān 4,000 *ghirsh*, while at present he has only 20 *ghirsh* to his name. The tally accumulates over the course of the issue, running to more than 30,000 *ghirsh* of debt, and the next knock is one of Khalīl's creditors.

Spiraling debt was a plotline that Sulaymān, the protagonist of *al-Huyām fī jinān al-Shām* had warned against in the pages of *Al-Jinān* a month prior, as if speaking from the pages of one 1870 Beirut novel to the protagonist of another. Complaining of the many who prioritize luxury goods over daily necessities, Sulaymān laments: "How many of the young borrow the money of another and throw themselves into the arena of poverty."[31] The narrator of *al-Shābb al-maghrūr* intercedes to manage Khalīl's accounts, working out an agreement for the payment of Khalīl's debt in eight days time. When Khalīl tells the narrator that he will just borrow some money to get by for a few days, the narrator replies: "And what will you do after that? Will you die of hunger?"[32] This installment of *al-Shābb al-maghrūr* was published in early June, when *Al-Jinān* announced that the poor silk harvest had "stop[ped] the gears of trade." The questions that the narrator puts to Khalīl in *al-Shābb al-maghrūr* vocalize the internal dialogue of Sulaymān in *al-Huyām*: "He imagines that he would be satisfied with the attainment of what he does not hold in his hand but when he attains that he seeks something else, and so on until what God wills."[33]

Come the summer, hope is to be found in neither Beirut's novels nor its silk industry. The list of Khalīl's debts grows yet longer in *al-Shābb al-maghrūr*, adding to those of which we have already read another 500 *ghirsh* to his boy servant, 400 *ghirsh* to the owner of his second house (rented at 60 *ghirsh* per month), 200 *ghirsh* per month for his house with Ghirrah (on which he owes three months, and which he has rented for a year). As each of the narrator's suggestions for balancing Khalīl's accounts meets with a list of yet more debts, the narrator jokes, "Has it occurred to you to throw yourself into one of the rivers?"[34] Sulaymān, the protagonist of *al-Huyām fī jinān al-Shām*, for his part weighed the hope of success, of material progress, against the uncertainty plaguing *Al-Jinān*'s readership:

> It is among the most difficult of affairs for a person to be unsettled of mind, not knowing if good or bad fortune will come upon him in a matter whose occurrence he awaits. Especially when he sees the soldiers of bad fortune preparing for battle against him . . . for a person finds comfort in the hope of future success. And without that, despair throws him in a hole of distress and degradation. And so he walks, paralyzed of hand and bound of leg, not knowing how to free himself from the fetters of confusion that the soldiers of worry have led him to.[35]

A new credit economy was ensnaring Beirut's reading public in the seductions of finance, leaving Mount Lebanon and the greater region of Syria in a precariously risky position, "paralyzed of hand and bound of leg, not knowing how to free [it]self from the fetters of confusion." It was not an accident of global finance that a mounting sense of economic "distress and degradation" generated by the disappointing silk harvest of 1870 was overwhelming the region, that its serialized Arabic novels had given way to a future of mounting debts as the knock of the creditor ever threatened at the door, and the "soldiers of bad fortune" hovered on the horizon. Rather, this was finance capital's ruse, the risk and uncertainty off which it fed: to hold out a garden of progress, that "comfort [of] the hope of future success," and to meet those hopes that had made gamblers of the region's brokers and silk cultivators not with the dreamy alchemy that seduced them, but with a ledger of debt and the persistent fear of impending capital flight.

The historical juncture was eclipsing the hopeful alchemy of a garden set apart, of a press that would serialize novels where suspense would be the stuff of botanical romance. This garden phantasmagoria was briefly revived in 1870 by Salīm al-Bustānī's sister Adelaide, in her short story entitled "Henry and Amelia," published that summer in two installments in *Al-Jinān*. Set not in the gardens of Damascus, like the early installments of the novels Salīm and Yūsuf al-Shalfūn published that spring, but now in an idyllic nameless geography of seashores, beautiful views, a forest, and a spring, the garden was already transformed: a cultivated space that defied geography, nestled in a setting where the landscapes of Europe and Syria converge, the garden is now enframed not only within the pages of *Al-Jinān*, delimited by a break between installments, but it has been moved indoors. It is a hall "decorated with green vines and beautiful flowers such that if you entered it you would think that you were in the most beautiful little garden."[36] Through a scene staging its own artifice, the seductions of a fiction of a global bourgeoisie living the alchemy of progress dreamed in the gardens of chapter 1 are broadly legible.

Debt, bankruptcy, and a narrowing horizon of "hope of future success" continued to punctuate the journals of Beirut throughout the 1870s, persistently running counter to the hopes stoked in the Edenic scenes of romance figured in Beirut's *riwāyāt*. Though 1871 witnessed a far better silk harvest than the previous year, the pages of the journal *Al-Najāḥ* nevertheless regularly featured announcements by the Mercantile Court or *Maḥkamat al-Tijārah* regarding the settling of debts. On May 29, 1871, the Mercantile Court published an announcement in *Al-Najāḥ*, "in accordance with the fourth paragraph of article twenty" of the court legislature, stating that such announcements had to be published in *jurnālāt*, legislating the role of the press in the web of finance, debt, and bankruptcy securing as it upended the Beirut economy. The announcement told of a creditor named Jirjis Ilyās Ṭāsū who had lost track of a man named Sarūfīm Kasūnīfūn who used to live in Beirut and was overdue in paying back the 1,845 *ghirsh* that he had borrowed from him.[37] The letters of Daniel Bliss, founder of the Syrian Protestant College, too told a familiar tale of debt overwhelming romance. A young woman named Layla's engagement was likely to be cut off, for her fiancé "has nothing to live on, is in debt, and continues to run in debt more and more."[38] A few days later, Bliss relates that "Layla's intended" has managed to broker a deal whereby she will marry for "a piece of land worth eighty dollars and . . . dresses to the amount of seven hundred piasters [*ghirsh*]," though Layla's father suspects that "the young man's creditors will not allow him to give her the land until they are paid."[39] Financial woes, the product of a credit economy and the speculative practices of an international bourgeoisie, were ransoming the dreams of 1870s Beirut.

Credit, extended through French banks and local Beirut brokers, was indebting the newly emerging bourgeoisie, a story Salīm's *al-Huyām fī jinān al-Shām* intimated already in the late spring of 1870. Finance capital, even as it enabled the trade in silk, caught Syria in a web of speculation and impending capital flight. The entourage of travelers setting out to visit Tadmur with Sulaymān find themselves captured in the Syrian countryside, forced to "either surrender or pay 5,000 *ghirsh* in ransom for each person."[40] The group had not taken such a threat into account, and as a result can amass between them only 20,000 *ghirsh*. As they number twenty-two men and two women, this leaves them 100,000 *ghirsh* short, in debt to forces with whom they cannot negotiate. They send a messenger to try and bargain the ransom down, telling the Bedouins "that we will not pay anything other than half that amount, and that only after our arrival in Damascus."[41] Their counteroffer is refused, and so they increase it, proposing that they have someone sent to Damascus, where they will pay 3,000 *ghirsh* for each of them. This too is refused, the entire group is taken hostage; they are about to be stripped bare, like the mulberry orchards, and though Sulaymān and his beloved rose Wardah enjoy a moment of that dream in the garden, it is but a brief reprieve. Next Wardah is captured by a band of robbers, the novel's readers asked to speculate as to what could possibly free this would-be love story from its shackles, from the robbers who would ruin it; *al-Huyām fī jinān al-Shām*, a tale that would seem to have eponymously promised Love in the Gardens of

Damascus from its first installment, can in the end only imagine romance through a flight to the southern shores of Italy.

Meanwhile, though Khalīl has managed by *al-Shābb al-maghrūr*'s penultimate installment to pay off many of his debts with the help of the narrator, finance continues to beget fiction. It never was a love story, at least not with Ghirrah; it was only ever a dream of one. Khalīl's entire downward spiral of debt is revealed as a ploy on the part of Ghirrah and her mother, Fitnah, who are rumored to be prostitutes who have since set their designs on another wealthy man. Though he has paid his debts, Khalīl remains unable to redeem his reputation: finance begets durable fictions of ruin. He explains:

> When I paid her mother the *dirhams* that I owed her, it did not occur to me at the time to take the records she had regarding the matter, and now I see her showing them to everyone she sees, saying that I am in debt to her, and that when I bought something for Ghirrah, I took a promissory note from the vendor in her name. Now she shows people these pieces of paper saying that I am not owed anything by her, for everything that she has at her place she bought herself and not I, and all that based on these papers.[42]

As *al-Shābb al-maghrūr* writes itself into being as a novel of debt, usurping the fantasy of a would-be love story and replacing it with a plot of conspicuous consumption and falsified promissory notes, it is the very artifice of finance—the fictitiousness of its capital, what made its practices "hard to see"—that shows through. These novels, Sulaymān's fears, Khalīl's spiraling debt, the speculations of the reading public of 1870s Beirut—they are all "based on these papers," on the textualization of finance capital and its fictions.

Al-Huyām fī jinān al-Shām too is a fiction premised upon the tools of textualization enabling and enabled by a credit economy founded in promissory notes and a network of bills of exchange holding so many in late nineteenth-century Arabic in suspense, grabbing at scraps of paper in the face of a game of risk dissimulating a dream of *nahḍah*. Sulaymān asks the narrator, Salīm, "Would you permit me to ask you to take this check [*ḥawālah*] to my broker in Beirut and collect its value from him and send it to me in Tripoli with the first mail?"[43] Salīm, the enframed narrator of the novel, recounts that Sulaymān "gave me a check [*ḥawālah*] drawn for his money changer in the amount of 50,000 *ghirsh* and told me please send me half and buy for me with the other half a bill of exchange [*suftajah*] from the Ottoman Bank so that I can cash it when necessary. . . . But he did not ask me for a receipt [*waṣl*]. For he said there was no need as he relied on me."[44] Salīm then "took a piece of paper and wrote for him a receipt."[45] It reads like a routine financial act and some good advice, but the very surfeit of such narrative figures in novels of not just late nineteenth-century Beirut but soon Cairo insists on the duplicitous foundations of finance, perhaps especially in Arabic as France and Britain's own imperial designs were reshaping the textiles trade in silk and cotton. Written ledgers, receipts, checks, promissory notes, mortgages, at the moment that they posed as securing the economy, through their very immateriality and the fictions of exchange they enabled, introduced a new form of risk and uncertainty off which the serialized novel form like the journals in which they appeared capitalized. Fiction loomed within finance: speculating in Arabic became the province of novelists and financiers alike.

Advertisements placed by insurance companies in the pages of a journal like *Al-Najāḥ* further bring into focus the intimacy of fiction and finance in what Ian Baucom identifies in the context of the Black Atlantic as a "system-wide determination to credit the existence of imaginary values."[46] The fictions of a capitalist world economy grounded in a global web of finance both encoded and profited off fears of loss and capital flight, making their fictitiousness both harder to see and easier to trade. Threatened by ravenous locusts and the specter of a cloud of silk moths hovering above the stalled steam chambers of local filatures, there was ever the worry that silk would be exposed, like Wardah and Sulaymān in *al-Huyām fī jinān al-Shām*, to "maritime dangers." A fear, a risk when seen by most from the port of Beirut, when viewed from the other side of the Mediterranean, offered but one more opportunity for gamble and profit: in May 1871, an advertisement appeared on the back cover of *Al-Najāḥ* publicizing that a French insurance company, with "six million francs in capital" and its "headquarters in Lyons" now had a representative in Beirut. Called the Kūmbāniyyah Sīkūrtāh Baḥriyyah, or Maritime Insurance Company, their advertisement would continue to run for months.

As Beirut was incorporated into a global age of finance capital enabled by the telegraph, steamships, and the opening of the Suez Canal, ever seeking to profit off fear and hope for the future, there was a sense that the speed of change was intensifying. In Arabic, it reconfigured an early age of merchant capital, a narrative time of not just Sindbad and *A Thousand and One Nights* but also the anecdote,[47] now appearing not in the *adab* anthology but in journals like *Al-Jinān* and *Al-Zahrah.* In its second issue, *Al-Jinān* ran an anecdote entitled "al-Irtiqāʾ al-sarīʿ" or "The Quick Ascent," whose young protagonist, dreaming of joining the "others among the sons of my nation [*waṭanī*] acquiring fortunes . . . and wearing silk,"[48] begs his father to lend him "some capital [*rās māl*] with which to do business and be finished with this miserable way of life."[49] In the end he makes a tragic miscalculation that sunders him both from a narrative of rise born of dreams of silk and "some capital with which to do business," and perhaps too the very reading public of Arabic.

Jurjī Zaydān, too, dreamed of a "quick ascent," of leaving behind the "miserable way of life" he had been born into, but his father feared a ruse. One day in 1877, Zaydān bought Nāṣīf al-Yāzijī's book *Majmaʿ al-baḥrayn* at half price from a young boy who came by his father's restaurant with a copy for sale. Zaydān recounts that his father "did not know its value because he did not know how to read. So he thought someone had cheated me and became angry. He hit the book with his hand and said, 'Did you pay nine piasters for this book, trading *dirhams* for paper?'"[50] Later that evening their neighbor came by to visit and asked Zaydān's father why he was so upset, as he explained that his son "spends *dirhams* buying useless paper." To which the neighbor responded, "I thank God, Abā Jurjī, that your son uses up his *dirhams* buying books and not getting drunk or the like."[51] Jurjī Zaydān would go on, as I show in chapters 4 and 5, to be one of the most successful entrepreneurs of the literary *Nahḍah* apace in Arabic. He remembers that his father, however, who was illiterate, sensed a ruse in the "trading [of] *dirhams* for paper," even if his neighbor found it preferable to outright intoxication. The new class of readers of which Jurjī Zaydān was becoming a part were invited by the newly publishing Arabic journals of Beirut to dream of a "quick ascent," of futures clad in fine silk textiles, exalting in Edenic dreams of material and literary progress, even as their access to the journals, newspapers, and printed books of the *Nahḍah* was a matter of material privilege and considerable capital investment.

Journal subscriptions were expensive: the bimonthly *Al-Jinān* (thirty-two pages per issue) cost roughly 140 *ghirsh* in Beirut and Mount Lebanon, with another 13 *ghirsh* or so added for postage for those living outside the region. Come year-end, for 150 *ghirsh,* one could order a bound copy of the year's issues or backorder an issue at a rate of 6 *ghirsh* per issue; while the weekly *Al-Zahrah* (eight pages per issue) was something of a bargain at 40 *ghirsh* for a yearly subscription in Beirut and Mount Lebanon, adding 10 *ghirsh* for postage outside the region.[52] Books and journals during this period were very much a bourgeois pleasure, and workers laboring in the mulberry orchards and silk factories around Beirut could hardly afford such a luxury. In 1870, the male overseer in a French filature made 10 *ghirsh* per day; male workers made from 3.25 *ghirsh* to 6 *ghirsh* per day depending upon the season and the grade of silk they produced, while a male apprentice would make as little as 1 *ghirsh* for a day's labor. Women made between 2 and 3 *ghirsh* per day, though they would also receive "monetary bonuses and dresses as gifts."[53] It would thus cost more than two weeks' wages for a silk factory overseer to purchase a subscription to *Al-Jinān*, while the far more affordable *Al-Zahrah* would cost the average worker in the off-season (when yearly subscriptions were often announced) two weeks wages for a yearly subscription. Indeed, it appears that few workers or peasants were among the growing readership for periodicals in the region; while five merchants and twenty-three industrialists responded to the biblical trivia contest in *Al-Nashrah al-Usbūʿiyyah* in 1871, only one person from the worker and peasant category responded.[54]

Looking to the novels themselves underscores how very many stood well outside the gates of the gardens of the Arabic press. For the price of a year's subscription to *Al-Zahrah* through the mail (50 *ghirsh*), a resident of Damascus in 1870 could have paid a month's rent on a room for Ghirrah in the journal's serialized novel *al-Shābb al-maghrūr*; while a subscription to *Al-Bashīr* at a cost of 60 *ghirsh* would have paid one month's rent on Khalīl's second home. A resident of Beirut could have sold one *uqqah* (or 1.28 kg) of *baladī* silk in 1871 for 268 *ghirsh*,[55] purchasing a bound copy of the previous year's *Al-Jinān*, along with a year's subscription to *Al-Najāḥ* or *Al-Zahrah*, and a full-price copy of Nāṣīf al-Yāzijī's *Majmaʿ al-baḥrayn*. With a little industry, the readers of the American Protestant *Al-Nashrah al-Usbūʿiyyah* learned, an *uqqah* of *baladī* silk could be sold for the materials to make 158,013 *ghirsh* worth of buttons,[56] nearly enough to pay off Khalīl's army of creditors as well as the Bedouins holding Sulaymān and his friends hostage. Yet as the reader of 1870s Beirut journals knew well, local factories for finished goods were rare; Beirut exported its raw materials, importing the finished goods so coveted by a global bourgeoisie looking to Europe.

In 1871, *Al-Najāḥ* listed the imports coming into Beirut's port following that year's silk harvest:

> 13 cases of various fabrics; 96 cases of cotton fabric; 6 cases of silk fabric; 415 bundles of English manufactured goods; 50 cases of various English fabrics; 26 bundles of broadcloth; 7 cases of ṭarbūshes; 11 cases of various *objets d'art*; 17 bundles of leather; 12 cases of shoes [made of red or yellow leather]; 122 bundles of paper; 12 bundles of cardboard; 49 cases of candles; 10 cases of cosmetic creams and spirits; 6 cases of perfumes and soaps; . . . 185 cases of matches; 117 sacks of coffee; 50 barrels of sugar; 53 barrels of salty prepared foods; 12 barrels of oil; 6 sacks of dried foreign peas; 49 barrels of wine; 16 cases of various beverages; . . . 152 barrels of beer; 2 cases of *ʿaraq*; 5000 cases of petrol; 35 barrels of gas; 35 barrels of salt; 3 cases of [silk]worms; 614 sacks of English rice; 7200 sacks of Italian rice; 5 bundles of cork; 69 cases of glass and china; 33 cases of vegetables; 73 cases of different metals; 76 barrels of nails; 19 barrels of lead [*raṣāṣ*]; . . . 6 pieces of furniture; 100 sacks of flour.[57]

Al-Najāḥ also listed Syrian exports to Europe for the same period:

> 572 bundles of wool; . . . 110 bundles of factory silk thread; 45 bundles of perforated [silk] cocoons; 29 bundles of cotton; 32 bundles floss/flax; 2 bundles of hemp; 201 bundles of leather; 3 bundles of carpets; 15 bundles of sponge; 1055 sacks of spices; 93 cases of citrus; 600 barrels of tar; 1 case of candles; . . . 4 cases of roots for red dye [madder]; 53 bundles of tobacco; 14 sacks of aniseed.[58]

Syrian exports to Europe and especially France overwhelmingly took the form of raw materials, with silk representing an extremely light and valuable commodity, while they in turn imported a wide array of manufactured goods and textiles. The disadvantages in this balance of trade were a matter of considerable concern and debate in late 1860s and early 1870s Beirut.

In 1869 in a lecture before the Syrian Scientific Society of Beirut that was later published in its distributed proceedings, a member named Salīm Kassab critiqued this balance of trade, troubled by the conspicuous lack of local industry:

> If we went down to the markets we would see them laden with different commodities . . . but made in foreign countries. If we considered our homes we would see that they are furnished with the nicest of various fabrics and utensils and abundant containers but where are they from? From abroad. If we considered the clothes that are upon our bodies, men and women alike, we would see that they are covered in good fabrics, but made by foreigners. . . . Why, then do . . .

> we send silk and cotton and wool and leather and madder and rags and other products [to Europe] and some of them return to us having multiplied in value?[59]

The local bourgeoisie was not positioned in the world economy to extract the surplus value created by workers in European factories as they transformed the raw materials exported from Beirut's ports into finished manufactured goods. Rather, they themselves imported and consumed the very finished goods whose raw materials they furnished to those European factories, leading Kassab to rhetorically ask: "What is it that increased their value and multiplied their price? Is it not industry?"[60] Silk fabric and clothing in particular were increasingly imported from Europe as the number of local weavers dwindled and no local silk fabric factories replaced them.[61] The year after Kassab addressed the Syrian Scientific Society, one of its members, Yūsuf al-Shalfūn, founded *Al-Zahrah*, printing in June of that year a similar critique. Calling attention to the number of locally owned silk filatures in the region, *Al-Zahrah* complains that as soon as someone "builds a silk [filature] . . . you see a bunch [of people] undertake the same project without thinking at all about finding another project such as a factory for silk goods, or for cotton or other factories such as iron or brass or glass."[62]

The circulation of commodities—enabled by a credit economy that usurped garden dreams of romance in 1870 serialized Arabic novels—was a subject reported on, debated about, and decried in the pages of Beirut's journals. At the end of an issue of a journal, though, there would sometimes appear advertisements for these very same goods, wooing readers to become consumers while also helping to keep the publications printing these ads economically viable. Not only did journals circulate alongside commodities such as French silks, but their circulation among the reading public of Arabic in Beirut and far beyond both enabled and was enabled by the circulation of not only material commodities (coveted even as they were maligned as the region's undoing), but by a hard-to-see global web of finance.

A short article entitled "On Fashion [*al-mūḍah*] (or Changing Styles)" ran in *Al-Zahrah* in 1870, drawing attention to the role of the changing textiles trade in the uneven incorporation of Arabic into a global web of finance capital, at the moment that *al-Shābb al-maghrūr*'s Khalīl found himself caught in a spiral of debt dissimulated as romance until the poor silk harvest of 1870. The author deems Beirut, "this city of ours, the Arab Paris," going on to say that "we have done a good and beautiful service to the women of our neighboring cities such as Damascus, for example, or Tripoli or Latakia for I have been informed that their clothes there are still as they were in Beirut previously."[63] Though living in an Arab Paris, Beirut's "women are not content with what is found in [the] city in the way of goods and fabrics but rather compete in demanding new styles from European countries and from Alexandria."[64] The next page dramatizes Alexandria's position as an Arab hub in the European finished textiles trade, that much closer to the workings and ravages of a new age of finance capital making fortunes off Egypt's cotton. Alexandria's department stores, some of which were founded by emigrants from Beirut and its environs, are figured as teeming with European luxury goods and clothing.[65] A conversation takes place between a man and his wife, who is upset:

Woman: "The reason [that I am upset] is that you always disrespect me and do not treat me as other women [are treated]."

Man: "How do I disrespect you? . . . [M]y love for you is great and the witness to that is that I got you a diamond the day before yesterday."

Woman: "Yes yes but if you loved me as you say, you would have gotten me an outfit of silk velvet from Alexandria like the one that Abū Yaʿqūb got for his wife, and others besides him. For I will not accept being treated other than my peers and the cost of this outfit is no more than three or four thousand *ghirsh* and it is payable in installments."[66]

A bourgeois financial order, negotiated through textiles, connected the Eastern Mediterranean to the factories, banks, and imperial capitals of Europe through debt. "Payable in installments," like the next episode in a never-ending serialized Arabic novel, "the remainder was to come," and its name was empire.

Silk in the region was underpinned by a web of finance radiating out from Lyon and Marseille, the center of the global silk industry at the time. The local bourgeoisie of Beirut was in debt, paying European silk factories and manufacturers quite considerable sums as they imported their transformed exports on credit, cladding themselves in a garden dream of Arab Paris. A growing critique called for local industry, while finance capitalism's role in it all remained encrypted in clouds of locusts, an eavesdropping narrator hidden in a shady garden grove, dreams of silk, and the suspense subtending the serialized novel form. In 1869, Kassab asked fellow members of the Syrian Scientific Society: "Where has the money of this country been buried? . . . Is it not in Europe?"[67] The next year *Al-Zahrah*'s editor, former Syrian Scientific Society member Yūsuf al-Shalfūn, bemoaned this situation, telling its readers that if they considered "our country's profits from trade, we see that most of them are in the hands of Europeans."[68] Salīm al-Bustānī placed a similar critique in the mouth of *al-Huyām fī jinān al-Shām*'s protagonist, Sulaymān, as he complains that foreigners "go to their country with much money when the sun of their lives is about to set," after making it in the silk industry in Syria.[69] Though Sulaymān asks to be taught the workings of this industry so that he can prevent this money from being taken outside the country, this never takes place in the novel's pages, and his role in the trade is limited to that of a local silk financier. Kassab, like others, urges a diversification of local industry, calling for local silk factories to be established and for them to produce "new and pleasing types of [silk fabric] that are appropriate for the needs of our people,"[70] and for the circulation of "printed notices urging people to refrain from buying [imported] velvet for example for vests . . . and to replace it with silk fabric" made in local silk fabric factories.[71] Local industry poses as the answer to the riddle of Syria's buried treasure, to why it is "hard to see": a bulwark against capital flight at sunset in an age of empire.

In 1871, al-Bustānī serialized a novel entitled *Zanūbiyyā*, set at the end of the third century when Tadmur "was the axis of the East's industry and a center of its trade," to which "merchants came from all regions,"[72] asking his Beirut readers to stand before its ruins like the pre-Islamic poet and learn the lessons it has to offer their times.[73] The novel begins well into the reign of Zanūbiyyā, queen of the ancient city of Tadmur, whose ruins the characters of his 1870 novel *al-Huyām fī jinān al-Shām* visited; and yet the novel is explicitly marked as not only a comment upon but also a product of the historical conjuncture punctuating its serialization. Al-Bustānī "implore[s] . . . each reader" of this novel to

> overlook what he sees in the way of mistakes and errors . . . [for] I was unable to correct the proofs but rather presented them to the printer piece by piece without reviewing them thoroughly because of a lack of time and the piling up of work . . . [in the case of] this [novel] and all writings and translations in *Al-Jinān* . . . from the

> first sentence it is printed in all haste from the first draft and many of my friends and those serving in the circles of work here [at *Al-Jinān*] know that and have seen it and for that we deserve to be forgiven for the errors that there is no doubt we have committed through our haste and the piling up of work.[74]

Like the regular installments of *al-Huyām fī jinān al-Shām* and *al-Shābb al-maghrūr*, as well as later serialized novels, the publication of each installment of *Zaynūbiyyā* was deeply interwoven with the rush of everyday life in late nineteenth-century Beirut, a time of "haste and the piling up of work." Salīm al-Bustānī insists on the contingency of the novel he is serializing and, as Raymond Williams argues, in turn "develop[s a] mode of analysis which instead of reducing works to finished products, and activities in fixed positions," can "discern . . . the finite but significant openness of many actual initiatives and contributions."[75]

In the novel, Zanūbiyyā's Tadmur has been taken hostage by imperial Roman forces, and both Zanūbiyyā and her daughter Jūliyā are held captive. At her moment of defeat, Jūliyā's clothing choices are shown to be emblematic of her love of country and her resistance to a European empire. Intervening in Beirut's ongoing debate on foreign textiles in the markets of Beirut, al-Bustānī breaks the novel's frame to directly address his contemporary readers:

> He who looks at the affairs of our country in this age and the affairs of Jūliyā in her time sees an enormous difference for she liked to have something from the products of the foreigners but she did not wear foreign things if they meant that there was no hope for her country in them. . . . [A]s for us we see foreigners wearing our fabrics but we look down on wearing them, for our silk fabrics do not circulate except for in foreign countries for our women do not wear them but rather prefer to buy foreign fabrics . . . however if they wore them . . . the industrialists [of our country] could improve their production and advance in it bit by bit.[76]

Despite Jūliyā's loyalty to local fabrics, Zanūbiyyā and her daughter end their days living comfortably in Rome, the former glory of Tadmur forever lost. In the final installment of the novel, readers in 1871 Beirut stand, like the characters of the previous year's *al-Huyām fī jinān al-Shām*, before the ruins of the ancient city of Tadmur: "From that time Tadmur began to decline until now it has become a village of about thirty huts built along the edge of its great temple and its residents are fewer than one hundred and are poor and ignorant to a great extent. . . . This is what remains[77] of that great city."[78]

The trope of standing before the ruins runs throughout the course of Arabic literature, inherited from pre-Islamic poets as they cried at the site of the beloved's former encampment. In *Conflicted Antiquities*, Elliott Colla surveys discourses surrounding Egypt's ancient Pharaonic past, placing the focus of his analysis on the colonial period. He observes how the traditional Arabic textual legacy that precedes this period, with its focus on reading ruins as lessons about the passage of time, converges with nationalist visions projected in the works of writers such as Rifāʿah Rāfiʿ al-Ṭahṭāwī and ʿAlī Mubārak.[79] Journals published in 1870s Beirut, too, navigated a range of ways of reading the ancient ruins of the region. While the Protestant *Al-Nashrah al-Usbūʿiyyah* featured a regular column describing the remains of ancient cities in Syria with a focus on narrating the region through a biblical lens (the landscape that had so captured the imaginations of American missionaries, and soon the Zionist colonists), a novel such as *Zanūbiyyā* fell more in line with the works of al-Ṭahṭāwī and Mubārak, seeing in past glories a hope for future progress, a hedge against a fear of its demise.

Zanūbiyyā figures ancient Tadmur at the height of comfort and yet on the brink of decline, a country riddled by contradictions. Jūliyā's loyalty to the local textile industry and her attempts to serve as a model for the women of Tadmur are juxtaposed with "the lack of regard" among some Tadmuris "for the common good and their preoccupation with their own pleasures and gathering money for themselves," which leads to the "ruin (*khirāb*) of politics."[80] The novel warns from its first page that "for every [time of] prosperity there is the ruin of that prosperity,"[81] rendering ominous later scenes of luxury and wealth. In the February installment of *Zanūbiyyā*, Jūliyā denounced the Tadmuri "women of the middle class [who] spend nearly all their husbands' money in order to adorn themselves with useless pieces of jewelry." Salīm al-Bustānī again breaks the narrative frame:

> There is no doubt that what Jūliyā said was correct and how correct it was. For the Tadmuris liked to imitate, thus if Zayd's wife saw ʿAmrū's wife wearing beautiful clothes and expensive jewelry she would ask her husband to get her similar [goods] even if they had less money than ʿAmrū. And if he did not meet her request she would bring upon him the armies of enmity and complaint and dissatisfaction and make his life that of a tired and anxious mind. The furnishings of the middle class and their jewelry and their clothes and their food almost became better and more expensive than the furnishings

> and jewelry and clothes of the rich and the commodities of the poor are better and more expensive still than the commodities of the middle [class]. And nothing gets in the way of this situation except ruin (*khirāb*).[82]

Though returns on the silk crop would be better in 1871 than 1870, a fear of risk tilting toward ruin becomes increasingly palpable in the Beirut press. This current of nervous apprehension— threatening both the alchemy of the gardens of material and literary progress and the industry apace in the mulberry orchards with clouds of locusts and a spiral of unpayable debt on the installment plan—stood as the narrative conditions of 1870s Beirut and the rise there, as elsewhere, of finance capital.

CHAPTER 3

Fictions of Capital in 1870s and 1880s Beirut

Over the course of the 1870s and early 1880s, the Beirut press confronted the contradictions that finance capital wrought in the region. Bankruptcies were announced to readers who comprised a new class of rising financiers, merchants, factory owners, and perhaps a factory worker or two; Beirut was imagined as an "Arab Paris" even as Paris and its Commune were burning; and though early serialized Arabic novels would begin in the gardens of Aleppo and Damacus, their plots seem to only find resolution in a flight to Europe.[1] As the decade continues, new journals joined *Al-Jinān* and *Al-Jannah*, notably Fāris Nimr and Yaʿqūb Ṣarrūf's *Al-Muqtaṭaf* (Choice clippings) in 1876 in Beirut (later to move to Cairo in 1884), which offered a vision of the local economy, grounded for a moment in commodity production and industry. In its Beirut years, *Al-Muqtaṭaf* critiqued the novel, apprehensive that the genre was an entertaining distraction that was corrupting the younger generation, the household economy, and in turn the region's future, as both Samah Selim and Elisabeth Kendall discuss in the context of the late nineteenth-century Arabic novel in Egypt.[2] While *Al-Muqtaṭaf* and other journals of the Arabic press called for increased local agriculture and industry, Salīm al-Bustānī's serialized novels instead brought into view something that was and remains difficult to see, namely the fictions subtending the financial markets, built as they were on a bourgeois idyll of future palaces of industry and agriculture. His 1872 *Budūr* (Budur), 1875 *Bint al-ʿaṣr* (Girl of the age), and 1882–84 *Sāmiyyah* (Samia) take up Beirut's uncertain future and finds there, again and again, not *nahḍah*, but a time of risk and deception.

Come 1875, not only was the future of the silk industry in and around Beirut in question, but so, too, was that of the Ottoman Empire. As Jens Hanssen notes, with the 1875 bankruptcy of the Ottoman Empire, "the subsequent financial control by the European-controlled Public Debt Administration (PDA) neither turned the Ottoman empire into a formal colony, nor integrated it into the 'informal empire' of one particular imperial power."[3] Some of the same commodities that *Al-Muqtaṭaf* would encourage its readers to produce and that featured as the stuff of speculation for Beirut's novelists and brokers in the 1870s were identified as a source of revenue for the PDA: "In order to service the Ottoman debt, the PDA farmed out tax monopolies to European public/private companies that siphoned taxes off spirits, salt, hunting and fishing licenses, silk, and tobacco."[4] As Beirut was increasingly knit into a global capitalist market with structural disadvantages for those in cities beyond the metropoles of France, England, and the United States, commodity production was strained by a combination of diminishing returns, the contradictions of both industry and speculation, as well as taxation.

These uncertain conditions are the setting of the 1875 serialized novel *Bint al-ʿaṣr*, in which al-Bustānī narrates the web of forgery, debt, and credit subtending the markets of Beirut. Pointing to the shuttering of many stores soon after their doors open, Salīm breaks the frame of the narrative to address the fate of Beirut as it witnessed "an increase in the hands of merchants and decrease in the causes for retail."[5] While raw materials such as silk comprised the bulk of the city's exports, the limited local production of commodities and the high price of finished European luxury goods caused its own problems in the markets themselves. The number of merchants proliferated without enough commodities available for local sale, with increasingly complex financial markets providing a means for a wealthy group of brokers and traders to dominate the local financial scene and drive prospective competition out of business. Salīm al-Bustānī's serialized *Al-Jinān* novels persistently critique these speculative financial practices.

In 1876, the year after al-Bustānī serialized *Bint al-ʿaṣr*, Nimr and Ṣarrūf, two local residents of Beirut who both taught at the Syrian Protestant College after graduating from its medical school, began to publish a different kind of journal with the college's support. *Al-Muqtaṭaf* targeted the class of industrialists and agriculturists whose ranks were growing in 1870s Beirut, and it was to become one of the most influential Arabic periodicals of the *Nahḍah*, relocating from Beirut to Egypt in 1884. Fīlīp dī Ṭarrāzī notes in the second volume of his seminal *Tarīkh al-ṣiḥāfah al-ʿarabiyyah* (History of the Arabic press) that as *Al-Muqtaṭaf* grew in esteem, "readers bestowed upon it the nickname 'the shaykh of Arabic journals.'"[6] Offering lessons each month in chemistry, geology, biology, and other natural sciences as well as practical, do-it-yourself advice, the journal addressed itself to the production of material commodities through local industry and agriculture.

Al-Bustānī's novels tracked the ruses of the marketplace through allegory and plots of deception. *Al-Muqtaṭaf* imagined reading practices of a different sort, especially for those members of its audience who found themselves among "those with little experience of reading and especially those among the industrialists." To read *Al-Muqtaṭaf* was not like being entertained by the stories on which the aspiring industrialists had been raised; if the reader "wanted to understand it [the contents of *Al-Muqtaṭaf*] as he understands stories without taxing his brain he will not understand anything."[7] The audience of *Al-Muqtaṭaf* is encouraged to instead read each sentence carefully, to use a dictionary, to try out the journal's suggestions (more than once), to measure exactly, to explain to friends (which is, the journal details, useful to these acquaintances, while the reader will discover in the process much that remained unclear), to write ideas down, to use a picture, and finally to write in with questions if they needed clarification.[8] By 1877, questions came from all over Greater Syria, including Mount Lebanon and especially Beirut, as well as Baghdad, Tunis, and various cities in Egypt, tracing the contours of a growing reading public of Arabic, whose attention was being turned to material commodities and the surface of the text.

As discussed in chapter 2, in 1870 in the pages of his satirical journal *Al-Zahrah*, al-Shalfūn bemoaned the lack of diversification in the local economy, observing that the moment an aspiring industrialist "builds a silk factory . . . you see a bunch [of people] undertake the same project without thinking at all about finding another project such as a factory for silk goods, or for cotton or other factories such as iron or brass or glass."[9] *Al-Muqtaṭaf* aimed at remediating this state of affairs. Its early issues contained information for the entire production cycle of finished silk goods, from how to handle silk eggs and harvest silk cocoons in the mulberry orchards, to finishing silk fabrics for sale in local markets. *Al-Muqtaṭaf*'s first issue ran an article on how to drape silk and muslin,[10] while the next issue published a long feature on silkworms and mulberry trees,[11] with instructions on how to refine silk coming at the end of the issue.[12] Later issues in *Al-Muqtaṭaf*'s first year ran responses to a number of questions regarding the best methods for dying silks.[13] The journal also featured advice and practical knowledge for readers interested in blowing glass,[14] making matches,[15] dipping candles,[16] shining and tanning leather,[17] and working with silver, copper, and brass.[18] *Al-Muqtaṭaf* taught its readers how to shine leather, silver, cotton, and brass; to produce fine silks, to drape their weave, so the cultivated fibers caught the light; to render the appearances of luxury and productivity in shop windows and on the diversifying factory floors.

Late nineteenth-century Beirut was bent on keeping up appearances. Consider the well-dressed visitor to Saydah's salon appearing in al-Bustānī's 1882–84 novel *Sāmiyyah* (Samia), that "youth wearing fine clothes . . . his hair treated with scented oil and on his fingers diamond rings and on his chest expensive pins and in his hand a beautiful walking stick."[19] The reader of *Al-Muqtaṭaf* could help manage the hairstyle, with a recently printed recipe for hair pomade [*pūmādū*] made from pig fat and rose water.[20] That reader could even discern if the many diamonds studding such rings were real,[21] or if looks were deceiving; and learn how to make mirrors,[22] the better for the youth to assess their fine clothes. Goods produced through a careful, applied reading of *Al-Muqtaṭaf* are transposed in the pages of *Al-Jinān* as novel material, which in form and plot give shape to the fictions underwriting late nineteenth-century Beirut.

At the end of the seventh installment of his 1872 novel *Budūr*, al-Bustānī breaks the narrative frame, leaving behind the collapse of the Umayyad Empire and with it another garden of Damascus. Al-Bustānī laments that among the contemporary audience of the novel, "many . . . deceive themselves and think that knowledge of reading and writing and the principles of grammar (*al-naḥw*) and inflection (*al-ṣarf*) and prosody (*al-ʿurūḍ*) and a foreign language make industry and agriculture beneath them [*dūna maqāmihim*]."[23] Many look down upon

> trade and political and scientific [*ʿilmiyyah*] positions despite the fact that if a person joined knowledge with industry or the agricultural sciences [*al-ʿulūm al-zirāʿiyyah*] he would be able to progress and gather of wealth and knowledge what would make him like the merchant if not more respected than him if he became famous for

> invention or the like for it is not concealed that trade and politics and science [*al-ʿilm*] are not able to employ all those who stand before the doors of knowledge [*al-maʿārif*] and count [*yaḥsubūn*] themselves in its palaces.

It is the dream of progress and industry now confronting the gardens of knowledge, but already "it is not concealed" that neither is enough: "So they must replace the truth with appearance so you see them borrowing money and spending it on clothes and delicacies and jewelry and the like."[24]

Things are not as they seem: something lurks beneath the shining surfaces and well-draped silks in the pages of *Al-Muqtaṭaf*. Real like real estate, credit provides the material means to "replace . . . truth with appearances," to give the illusion of a utopia in which trade, politics, and science deck all those in the garden standing before the doors of knowledge in clothes and jewels. "Industry and the agricultural sciences" deemed "beneath them," readers of Arabic in the late nineteenth century, paying subscribers to *Al-Jinān* and maybe even *Al-Muqtaṭaf* at a moment so often figured as a *Nahḍah*, built palaces not, as it might have seemed, of knowledge and trade, or industry or agriculture, but often of debt and surface appearances.

The volatility of the 1870s pitted a financialized credit economy against the materiality of the many villas being built and sometimes (like the village homes) lost in the region: palaces of debt, the uncertainty of the markets threatening at the horizon of the future. It was a persistent object of critique in Beirut's early serialized fiction, one that al-Khūrī intimated in *Way, idhan lastu bi-ifranjī* and that al-Shalfūn began in *al-Shābb al-maghrūr* (1870), and that found its complement in a number of al-Bustānī's novels, including not only *al-Huyām fī jinān al-Shām* (1870) and *Zanūbiyyā* (1871) but also later works like *Budūr* (1872), *Bint al-ʿaṣr* (1875), and *Sāmiyyah* (1882–84). Serialized novels, interrupted stories of financial suspense and the trials of the lower classes, were meted out in fortnightly installments, testifying to the haste and piling up of work in Beirut and its printing presses, ratcheted to a new sense of time, of hoping and fearing the remainder that was to come, as the Ottoman Empire was increasingly eclipsed by the British and French.

Salīm's 1872 novel *Budūr* was set, like the previous year's *Zanūbiyyā*, at a moment of historical transition between empires in the region's past. As in al-Bustānī's contemporary Beirut, wealth was changing hands, and appearances were not what they seemed.

As the Umayyads fell and were replaced by the ʿAbbasids in the east, and al-Andalus emerged as a center of Arab rule and culture in the west, the future of the eponymous heroine Budūr was in a state of flux. A daughter of the former Umayyad ruling class, Budūr must flee Damascus. Her cousin ʿAbd al-Raḥmān manages to escape the massacre, and Budūr has just enough time to fall in love with him before the historical juncture necessitates that they both leave the city. *Budūr* charts their trials and travails before a happy reunion in the novel's final pages. Over the course of 1872, the novel details how Budūr, with the help of her servants, hides in a small Syrian village until she is captured and imprisoned by the new ruler, Sifāḥ, escaping to navigate a course past pirates in the waters of the Mediterranean and through the Pyrenees. Finally Budūr makes it to al-Andalus, where ʿAbd al-Raḥmān is now ruler, fighting at the head of the Arab armies conquering Spain. Secrets and disguises repeatedly appear in the novel, and if its readership is to make out its plotline, they must be skilled in decoding what the surface of the narrative would at times keep hidden.

While Sabry Hafez bemoans how al-Bustānī's novels "suffer from authorial intrusion and interruption of the narrative," something Hafez identifies as a "complete reliance on telling with very little showing,"[25] an eye to the generic porousness and general novelty of the novel form in this period underscores instead how imperative it was at that moment to break (the better to attend to) the novel's frame. Throughout *Budūr*, as in Salīm al-Bustānī's contemporary Beirut, things were often not as they seemed. Readers are let in on the secret identities of Budūr, ʿAbd al-Raḥmān, and other characters in authorial asides, all of whom otherwise spend large portions of the novel in disguise or in hiding. Letters are written that conceal their true messages as well as the identities of the correspondents from other characters. The reader of each installment, quite new still to the novel form, must know who is who and what they are really saying in order to enable the inner workings of the plot. Readers are further warned that Budūr at times speaks ambiguously, demanding that her statements be read on multiple levels;[26] and in the sixteenth installment Budūr boasts, "deception [*al-khidāʿ*] is my weapon."[27] To follow *Budūr*, then, a reader must be in on the ruse of deception, to read past the surface, alert to the tendency to "replace the truth with appearance[s]."

Reading *Budūr* allegorically, taking Budūr at her word that "deception [*al-khidāʿ*] is [her] weapon" and reading for the meaning that is concealed, yields a trail of wealth that leads the reader from the opulence of the palace she must now flee, to the village home. Published in *Al-Jinān*, in its third year, the garden dream of alchemical knowledge comes into focus as a site of dissimulation, of moonlit disguises and hidden jewels, emerging as a sustained critique of surface appearances, implicating the novel form as the genre that allowed for narrative, time, hope, fear, and romance to be leveraged, reconfigured, traded, bought, and sold. In this period, the Arabic novel cannot be read as the sort of novel later imagined by Bourdieu's sense of semi-autonomous spheres; still less in keeping with the New Critics or later the "New Formalist view of the artwork's sovereignty over itself, its autonomy from ideology," as characterized by Stephen Best and Sharon Marcus. Rather, the serialized Arabic novel itself staged its own "materialist criticism . . . as an expression of struggles with its historical conditions and limits."[28] Fictions, technologies of suspense at the heart of both industrialization's dreams of progress and finance's games of risk, take shape in *Budūr* as a call to read what lurks beneath appearances and the surface of the text.

The protagonists and the novel's very plot often move in *Budūr* only with the labor of the lower classes. As *Budūr*'s seventh installment opens, the servant Saʿd brings ʿAbd al-Raḥmān (who is unable to leave the Golan Heights due to a lack of money) a letter from Budūr containing money, and ʿAbd al-Raḥmān is finally able to set off to Egypt, where he will hide among the Bedouin and tend sheep. Before leaving, ʿAbd al-Raḥmān sends Budūr a letter in response, signing it "in the name of the eunuch without mentioning his own name."[29] The letter will be delivered by the servant Saʿd to Budūr's eunuch and then on to Budūr, held captive in an ʿAbbasid prison. While the readers of *Al-Muqtaṭaf*, *Al-Jinān*, or *Al-Zahrah* read words inspiring them to become industrialists, factory owners, or agriculturists of repute—residents of palaces that might rival those of the merchants—in *Budūr*, servants are the very narrative means by which the plot continues, by which the remaining installments appear. These palace abodes of capital will forever be stalled, debt-ridden fictions without the labor of the lower classes.

As Bruce Robbins observes in the case of the Victorian novel in *The Servant's Hand: English Literature from Below*, "the discourse of labor, which joins rulers and ruled in a hegemonic bond, by the same token lays out common ground where ruptures, recognitions, and renegotiations can take place between them."[30] The social upheaval accompanying the fall of the Umayyads and rise of the ʿAbbasids produces a moment of "rupture" and "renegotiation," a moment not unlike the historical juncture being lived by al-Bustānī's contemporary audience. Robbins points out that "rather than grapple with the new and exotic industrial worker, no longer ruled by custom and deference but by the cash nexus, novelists turned to those vestigial, unrepresentative members of the same class who lived in their homes, whose hands opened their doors, cooked and served their meals."[31] In *Budūr*, the plot cannot go on, no progress can be made, without the dutiful labor of servants. They are as indispensable to *Budūr* as the "new and exotic industrial worker" is to the industry the Arabic press called for, and the palaces of which it dreamt. The *Nahḍah*, as the characters and very form of al-Bustānī and al-Shalfūn's novels tell us, is not a moment of material prolificacy, but a phantasmagoria of commodities subtended by unpaid debts, a haunted garden of spectral value, the hope of alienating the labor of others, enunciated in Arabic.

As Budūr plans her escape from the Umayyad palace as the ʿAbassids come to power, she obscures her wealth and identity, and again, we are in the gardens of Damascus. She hides money and jewelry in a box, placing it in the branches of a tree growing in the palace's gardens. While Budūr is busy hiding her jewels, the servant Saʿd flits across the local geography, visiting the markets of the city to purchase clothing and face paint, and the neighboring countryside to rent a small house. The clothes, face paint, and small house are all the makings of a disguise to help Budūr escape to their modest refuge in a Syrian village, where she will play the part of an exiled Umayyad prince bestowing gifts and edification upon the village residents. In order to escape the confines of her quarters in the palace undetected, Budūr paints her face the dark color of her servant's, and Budūr's servant lends her her *burquʿ* to complete the ensemble. Cloaked, in shadows, her identify obfuscated, Budūr borrows her servant's invisibility in order to circulate freely, molting. The princess flees the Damascus palace through its gardens, an analogue of restive capital's own impending flight.

Budūr's jewelry like her disguises demand that readers look beneath the surface. Before leaving the palace grounds for her exile in a Syrian village, Budūr takes some of this jewelry from a box hidden in a garden tree and has her eunuch carry it to the small house Saʿd rented. Fleeing in her servant's *burquʿ*, when Budūr reaches the house, she and the eunuch change into the clothes that the servant

Saʿd purchased at her request. Now disguised as a young man traveling with his servant, "Budūr took out the jewelry that had been in the box [hidden in the tree] and hid some in her clothing and the rest in the eunuch's clothing."[32] Quite a bit is happening in this scene, as Salīm's novel flaunts that something is being hidden, and something revealed. Wealth is first hard to see because it is hidden unseen until the appointed hour in the branches of a tree in a garden of Damascus, a scene that can be read as allegorically pointing to the web of finance cultivating the mulberry orchards surrounding Beirut. Plucked, like so many silk cocoons destined for filatures and export, from among the branches of a garden tree, the jewels are immediately concealed and redistributed, some in Budūr and some in her eunuch's clothing.

Budūr is now able to travel through the countryside dressed as a young man, in whose garments are hidden untold riches. The ruse works for a short period, and Budūr lives a prince's happy life of exile in a small village house in Syria. Soon, believing they have stumbled upon ʿAbd al-Raḥmān, the ʿAbassids send their forces to bring him in. Budūr is forced to reveal her identity, but not before she "had buried jewelry and cash in the small house,"[33] informing the servant Saʿd of its location. The wealth that had been hidden in a tree, and then in clothing, is now hidden in a small village home. The jewels are capital in a covert spiral of alienation, staging a midnight return to the source. While a reader in 1870s Beirut might have found decrypting an Umayyad princess's jewels through a lens of industrialization something of a leap of faith, the villagers of Mount Lebanon in the late nineteenth century knew all too well the changes apace, as Akram Fouad Khater documents in the early chapters of *Inventing Home: Emigration, Gender, and the Middle Class in Lebanon, 1870–1920*. Villagers were being transformed into industrial agriculture workers, a cottage silk industry disarticulated into mulberry orchards, distant filatures, and ships leaving Beirut's port for the factories of France, as industrialists and large-scale commercial farmers were building villas alongside those of merchants and other members of the wealthy bourgeoisie on the outskirts of the growing city of Beirut.[34]

Budūr is an anxious novel, unable to keep up with the deceptions of its own plot. When Budūr goes into hiding as a benevolent Umayyad prince, she takes a new name and hires a servant to help her maintain the small house. In these installments of the novel, Salīm al-Bustānī repeatedly alternates between the names Ṣādiq and Ṭālib when referring to the exiled Budūr-in-disguise.[35] Whenever Budūr goes as Ṣādiq, her servant is Ṭālib, and vice versa. At no point in the novel does al-Bustānī acknowledge these slippages, which create a perpetual carnival of class and gender, the spectacle of an older social order being upended at any and every moment. Later in the same installment of *Budūr*, al-Bustānī warns his 1872 readers of threats to "our name or our position."[36]

A decade after *Budūr* and on the eve of his death, Salīm al-Bustānī began publishing *Sāmiyyah*, a long, serialized novel that would run in the pages of *Al-Jinān* from mid-June 1882 through the early spring of 1884. The diffuse class concerns encoded in *Budūr* metamorphose in *Sāmiyyah*; the poor, working class exerts pressure on the texture of the narrative with a specificity and a degree of organization not in evidence in al-Bustānī's early novels. While in 1870, al-Bustānī's *al-Huyām fī jinān al-Shām* pivoted around the romance of a silk financier and a spectral fear that might strip the bourgeoisie of its trappings; and in 1872's *Budūr*, readers were incited to read for deception and ambiguity, laborers were allegorized as servants, and the silk industry flickered through Umayyad palace gardens and a trail of jewels, by the early 1880s with *Sāmiyyah*, al-Bustānī's audience met with a novel staging the Beirut economy's dependence on speculation and the labor of others in considerably more direct terms. The shrouded allegory and geographical specificity of al-Bustānī's *Budūr*, and the fears lurking in *al-Huyām*'s repetition of the root *j-r-d*, to strip or lay bare, gives way in *Sāmiyyah* to sharp critiques of the status quo placed in the mouths of sometimes villainized characters, occurring now in an unrooted landscape, one untethered from an alchemical dream of the gardens of Damascus. *Sāmiyyah* instead directly engages pressing questions stirred by the global rise of finance and falling returns on silk, debating socialism, capitalism, and the future of local industry and agriculture.

Sāmiyyah is the story of the gambling socialist Fāʾiz, in love with the beautiful, edified, and charitable Sāmiyyah, who in the end falls for another man. Despite the title, the narrative takes as its center of gravity not the perspective of the eponymous Sāmiyyah (as *Budūr* had Budūr) but rather that of Fāʾiz. Readers are privy to Fāʾiz's internal monologues, and while many of his socialist tactics and ideals are portrayed in an unflattering light, the novel equivocates. If his gambling socialist ways seem to threaten a capitalism grounded in industry and the material production of commodities as championed by *Al-Muqtaṭaf*, and Jūliyyā in *Zanūbiyyā*, Fāʾiz at the same time curbs the winnings of a rampant finance capitalist as he trumps him in a game of risk and justice.

From the 1870s, writers in the Beirut press mused over the socialist and communist movements in Europe. As Matti Moosa points out in his chapter dedicated to the work of Salīm al-Bustānī in *The Origins of Modern Arabic Fiction*, al-Bustānī followed the news of socialist and communist movements in Europe from the early 1870s, "mention[ing] the Second Communist International" in an article in *Al-Jinān*'s early March 1873 issue.[37] Even before this issue of *Al-Jinān*, however, the journals of Beirut were discussing communism. In September 1871, *Al-Bashīr* printed an article on "*sharikat al-intīrnāsyūnāl*," in which it quotes from the International's official newspaper and meetings. Translating from an article run on March 25, 1869, in the International's newspaper, *Al-Bashīr* reprints for readers of Arabic in 1871 the International's principles: "We want the administration of the people [*idārat al-shaᶜb*] to be headed by the people and [we want] an end to the right to the personal inheritance of property [*amwāl*] and tools of labor and for all land [*arāḍī*] to become public property."[38] *Al-Bashīr* quotes this and other declarations by the International, the Paris Commune, and international socialist groups in order to warn against what it sees as a growing threat to European civilization, or at least its bourgeois, capitalist underpinnings. Critiquing communism for an audience only beginning to hear about such movements in Europe, however, by reprinting the International's words in the first-person plural "we," *Al-Bashīr* at the same time broadcast their message to sympathetic readers of the Arabic press.

In her recent study *The Eastern Mediterranean and the Making of Global Radicalism, 1860–1914*, the social historian Ilham Khuri-Makdisi devotes a chapter to the discourse on socialism and communism printed in the pages of *Al-Hilāl* and *Al-Muqtaṭaf* after their editors Jurjī Zaydān, Fāris Nimr, and Yaᶜqūb Ṣarrūf had already quit Beirut and established themselves in Cairo. She opens the chapter entitled "The *Nahḍa*, the Press and the Construction and Dissemination of a Radical Worldview": "In the early 1890s Arabic reading audiences in Beirut, Cairo and Alexandria began regularly (if not too frequently) encountering articles on socialism (*al-ishtirākiyya*) and anarchism (*al-fawḍawiyya*) in the pages of two formative and influential opinion-making periodicals: *al-Muqtaṭaf* . . . and *al-Hilāl*."[39] While Khuri-Makdisi traces the lineaments of this debate through the beginning of World War I in the pages of *Al-Hilāl* and *Al-Muqtaṭaf*, these journals were in fact inheriting a debate about the progress and perils inherent in socialism and communism that had animated journals such as *Al-Bashīr*, *Al-Jinān*, *Al-Jannah*, *Al-Najāḥ*, and *Thamarāt al-Funūn* since the 1870s.

More than a decade before Salīm al-Bustānī serialized *Sāmiyyah* in *Al-Jinān*, the Beirut press was discussing communism through the lens of the 1871 Paris Commune and the ensuing destruction in the streets of Paris. If the appearances being kept up by so many in the region donning French-finished silk garments was a debt-funded materialization of an "Arab Paris" in the streets of Beirut, the fires and destruction in the streets of Paris in the fall of 1871 were difficult to square. The twice-weekly *Al-Najāḥ* serialized interrogations of members of the Commune and, along with *Al-Bashīr*, ran updates on the cost of reconstruction,[40] as *Al-Bashīr* lamented the "barbaric actions" of the Paris Commune and the "destruction of the finest buildings and most beautiful traces of the civilizing of the backward" in the city of Paris that spring.[41] *Al-Jinān*, on the other hand, offered "praise" to the Communards in Paris.[42] Matti Moosa identifies in al-Bustānī's writing "an inherent, deep-seated distrust of the masses," even as he "seems to advocate a moderate form of socialism."[43] A conflicted narrator of novels whose surfaces themselves would sometimes equivocate, Salīm al-Bustānī's fictions struggle as they confront "the present organization of the world which has bound all that you have in the world together with commercial [*tijāriyyah*] relations," as his first protagonist, the silk financier Sulaymān, observed.

Al-Bustānī's last and longest serialized novel, *Sāmiyyah*, worked through these contradictions—of an Arab dream of a Paris of silk velvet, when Paris itself was on fire—in the figure of Fāʾiz, an eloquent, well-educated, but misguided figure, plagued by "the corruption of his socialist thoughts."[44] Fāʾiz equates socialism with being a "peer [*sharīk*] in wealth,"[45] and in the early pages of the novel, it is the finance capitalist Wāṣif, Fāʾiz's wealthier rival for the hand of Sāmiyyah, whose peer he wants to be. Wāṣif, the reader learns, grew rich through "financial means that placed [wealth] in the palm of his hand through happenstance and the labor of others."[46] Fāʾiz is the "cleverest gambler in the city,"[47] and as Fāʾiz's winnings increase, "he distanced himself from his socialist principles,"[48] becoming more and more like the capitalist financier Wāṣif, whom he was bent on beating, we realize, at his own game.

While the card table proves to be Wāṣif's undoing, it is speculation in the socially sanctioned commodities market that threatens Fuʾād/Nadīm, the moderate capitalist whose love Sāmiyyah reciprocates. "One morning," in the novel's sixth installment, "a telegram came to Fāʾiz from which he learned that the prices of some international paper had dropped a great deal and that was in the winter so he met with Fuʾād and showed him a telegraph whose date was previous to the mentioned telegram by one day."[49] Fāʾiz urges Fuʾād/Nadīm to buy paper at the high price shown in the previous day's telegraph, and Fuʾād/Nadīm ultimately follows Fāʾiz's deceitful advice, losing a good portion of his wealth in the process. Deception in trading commodities and deceit at the gambling table cast Fāʾiz and the socialism he touts in a poor light. Simultaneously, however, these scenes of ruin, like the socialist discourse in the pages of the novel, offer a trenchant critique of the financial practices animating the markets of Beirut in an age of finance capitalism, a new experience of simultaneity enabled by the telegraph and a global market facilitating profits off not only material good but their futures, too.

Tactics borrowed from the card table, with the potential to ruin the bourgeoisie in the span of an evening of gambling or a morning of business as usual, al-Bustānī's last *riwāyah* critiqued, too, the role of the Arabic press in all of this. For if *Al-Jinān* might warn readers against duplicitous socialists twisting the markets to their own ends, of financiers profiting off "happenstance" and the "labors of others," two of the journals published by the extended al-Bustānī family—*Al-Jannah,* and Salīm al-Bustānī's cousin and brother-in-law Khalīl Sarkīs's *Lisān al-Ḥāl*, available for a discounted subscription rate when purchased along with *Al-Jinān*—were the source of this very novel's plot material, namely telegraphed international commodity prices. As readers paid the price of the rather expensive journal subscriptions considered in chapter 2, they became members of the reading public, subscribers—in Arabic, *mustashrikūn*, a word whose root *sh-r-k* kept intimate company with not only the capitalist specter of socialism, *ishtirākiyyah*, but also the institution of the corporation or company, *sharikah*, that was playing such a decisive role in knitting the markets, banks, filatures, and mulberry orchards surrounding Beirut into a global silk economy.

The men who vie for Sāmiyyah's affection represent the spectrum of characters trading in the markets of Beirut, and Sāmiyyah herself is a daughter of the commodity-coveting, finance-minded bourgeoisie.

In the novel's first installment, we read that "nothing but material things influence Sāmiyyah's mother,"[50] while Sāmiyyah's father spends so much time overseeing his commercial affairs that it is "as though he sleeps between his account books and papers."[51] The palaces of *Budūr* and the encrypted futures of its villagers give way to a direct critique of sharp material inequality in *Sāmiyyah*. While Sāmiyyah is surrounded by material comforts, Fāʾiz's comrade observes that "you do not see in the cities and the villages more than five percent of souls attaining what they have a right to attain in terms of living and clothing and education."[52] In the next installment, Fāʾiz's comrade goes on to denounce wealthy capitalists for making money by using people as "tools [*alāt*] for their greediness and luxury and corruption,"[53] much as Wāṣif, and no doubt some of *Al-Jinān*'s own readers, had.

Though "the social structure was changing," the novel describes Sāmiyyah's father as being "fixed in his ways and while the social position of wealth devoid of manners was in decline he deluded himself with his/its rise. He was extremely fearful for his money and did not pay attention to anything except the uprisings on the part of the people [*al-ʿāmmah*] in some countries against the owners of wealth until one day Fāʾiz said to him that socialist [*ishtirākiyyah*] principles are on the rise to the point that I have come to fear for those who have a great deal of money such as yourself."[54] A merchant in 1880s Beirut, "extremely fearful for his money" and his future, threatened by socialism at home and abroad, would likely have also been a reader of the Arabic press, where he could have learned of "the uprisings on the part of the people in some countries against the owners of wealth" in newspapers and journals such as *Ḥadīqat al-Akhbār, Al-Jannah, Lisān al-Hāl*, and *Thamarāt al-Funūn*.[55]

Social and economic volatility vex 1880s Beirut. While Sāmiyyah's mother urges her to marry Wāṣif and his great fortune, Sāmiyyah's response underscores the financial instability that came to structure Beirut life by the early 1880s. She asks, "Do you know that of those who held financial fame thirty years ago three-quarters of them have been ruined and lost their wealth?"[56] Sāmiyyah's servant herself is a daughter of ruin and lost fortune; she tells Fāʾiz: "My upbringing was not to become a servant for I learned to read and write and embroider and I was prepared to be served like my mistress except that time took its course with my father and when I was 14 years of age he died and I had to descend from the rank for which I had been created."[57] The servant's fate embodies a fear felt in Beirut and its environs in the early

1880s at card tables, in the silk markets, and in the attendant trade in debt and commodity futures. Changing fortunes, the decreasing silk revenues of the turbulent 1870s, a lack of diverse local industry, the growing ranks of factory laborers, and mulberry orchards ever haunted by the nightmare of 1860 now taunted a future that appeared increasingly uncertain.

Offering an apprenticeship in fiction in an age of finance capital, it is al-Bustānī's 1875 *Bint al-ʿaṣr* that made broadly legible the lineaments of finance—the rules of the game that Wāṣif the finance capitalist, Sāmiyyah's father, Sulaymān the silk financier, along with the novelists Khalīl al-Khūrī, Yūsuf al-Shalfūn, and Salīm al-Bustānī, were all playing by. A reader could not parse this novel's plot, could not wait in suspense for the next installment in *Al-Jinān* in 1875, without a sophisticated understanding of how the trade of securities, currencies, debt, and commodities futures, too, were nothing but the stuff of appearances. Gamblers' ruses, confidence games, tales of suspense, deception, and dissimulation, and dreams of romance governed novels and markets alike.

In *Bint al-ʿaṣr*, the wealthy securities broker Anīs vies against the moderate capitalist Mājid for Rīmah's love; it is a serialized romance, and another lesson in how to read. In the parlor with Anīs and Mājid, sisters Rīmah and Jamīlah read a novel together: a pedagogical scene. Jamīlah, interested only in the love story, bemoans the author's inclusion of other material. Rīmah invites her sister to continue "to read the novel with her for she [Rīmah] saw in it shortcomings in comportment similar to the shortcomings" of her sister.[58] While Rīmah pushes Jamīlah to read beyond the frame of the love story, she likewise critiques Anīs's reading practices, limited to the sections of newspapers listing commodity prices and updates on finance; the other sections of newspapers, he insists, have nothing to do with the economy.[59]

What *Bint al-ʿaṣr* teaches readers new to the private Arabic press is that neither the novels serialized at the end of each issue of a journal like *Al-Jinān* nor the financial updates printed in newspapers such as *Al-Jannah* and *Al-Najāḥ*, and later *Lisān al-Ḥāl, Thamarāt al-Funūn*, and *Al-Muqtaṭaf*, are to be read in isolation; they each tell the story of the other. Initiating a discussion of the securities (*al-awrāq al-māliyyah*) market, Anīs immediately turns to Rīmah to apologize for discussing such matters in her presence. Rīmah—an eponymic "girl of the age" and model of idealized reading comportment in 1870s Beirut—insists, however, that in fact she "like[s] to find out all news related to the prices of securities for they are generally an indication of political affairs that our comfort and financial positions rest upon."[60] *Bint al-ʿaṣr* critiques the myopia that would obscure the contingency of the markets and novels of a city such as Beirut, that would see one as the stuff of securities, the other as the province of romance, never the twain to meet.

Finance capital's gambling ways in *Bint al-ʿaṣr* index how risk, debt, and sudden changes in fortune chart the futures of its protagonists. In his efforts to secure Mājid's downfall, Anīs teams up with Ṣāliḥ, the son of a miserly landowner who made part of his fortune gambling. While Anīs's considerable holdings were, he tells us, "bought . . . all with my money and not through credit unlike Yūsuf and Ṣāliḥ and Khalīl and the other merchants of this city and their brokers,"[61] Ṣāliḥ, on the other hand, is depicted as an indebted merchant who

> makes appearances of his high social standing and large amount of money while in fact he is always in need given that he is on his father's limited account and his father was in the beginning a broker [*simsār*] famous for lying until he ruined a third of the merchants and joined a group gambling with the price of a watch that he sold and it was his wife's watch and he won, and in a year he had gathered a not small amount of money and built a beautiful villa [*dār*] and the wealthy started to respect him and visit him as though he were one of them[,] overlooking his original position.[62]

Ṣāliḥ is the son of a landowning gambler, raised in a villa built on the ruins of a third of Beirut's merchants and the winnings made on borrowed time at the card table. This palace of debt and bankruptcy is the admiration of the city's bourgeoisie, who themselves, as al-Bustānī critiqued a few years prior, would go into debt, perhaps to the very likes of Ṣāliḥ, in order to keep up appearances and live in their own beautiful villas. The seductions of wealth are here characterized as being both volatile and destructive, and readers are invited to imagine a third of the city's merchants going bankrupt in the time it took to read a novel such as *Budūr*, *Zanūbiyyā*, *al-Huyām fī jinān al-Shām*, or *al-Shābb al-maghrūr* in serialization.

"One of the rich who live off the income from their land" held a banquet that Ṣāliḥ attended.[63] Briefly an aspiring journalist, he records the passing conversations and idle gossip of partygoers, replete with the poor Arabic pronunciation of foreigners, complaints about the local wine, shock at card-playing gamblers, and declarations that foreign manners should not be emulated because "we are not," after all, and despite the fantasies espoused earlier in the decade, "in Paris,"[64] a scene no doubt familiar to readers of the Arabic press in Beirut, Cairo, Alexandria, and beyond in the late nineteenth century. Showing his efforts to a friend, Ṣāliḥ is counseled not to publish this too-telling portrait of bourgeois life. The intimation is that it is unfit for the press, and yet it is as novel material for *Bint al-ʿaṣr* that we encounter it, giving the sense that we are on the inside, seeing beneath the surface of the appearances being kept up in Beirut and its journals.

Much of the plot of *Bint al-ʿasr* centers on decoding deceitful appearances, in a prolonged ruse orchestrated by Anīs and Ṣāliḥ with the aim of using falsified promissory notes to ruin Mājid. The novel lets the reader in on many details of how this plot will unfold. In its fourth issue, Ṣāliḥ explains to Anīs: "We will write [Mājid] a check . . . [backed] by promissory notes with your signature to be changed by one of your agents . . . and we will not tell the agent about the promissory notes so he will not accept them and when they are returned we will deny your signature or more precisely will show that it is not your signature and I will make the sale from my hand and deny that too."[65] This scheme is predicated on the reliability of Anīs's signature, which in a later issue is said to be "among the best in the city."[66] The novel announces from the beginning that appearances will deceive, while at the same time giving readers the sense that they are in on the plot, being instructed as to how to spot the sorts of underhanded dealings by which a third of the merchants were ruined at the hands of Ṣāliḥ's father. In order to pull off the ruse, Anīs and Ṣāliḥ work with Fāris, a man unconcerned with his reputation who is "willing to make known [his] bankruptcy in order to make some money."[67] The reader learns another detail of the plan: Ṣāliḥ will approach Mājid about going into business together.

Once the plot is put into action, however, while the reader anticipates a financial scheme based in forgery, the novel does not disclose which aspects of the trades and exchanges are false. Fāris establishes himself as a successful new merchant, and Ṣāliḥ and Mājid interact in the markets on a regular basis. One day, Ṣāliḥ visits Fāris in his shop while Mājid is there. Ṣāliḥ announces that he read a telegraph stating that "the price of bond[s] for such-and-such a country have risen and you have in your box more than 15,000 lira of them and it is best that you sell some of them."[68] Fāris asks Ṣāliḥ if he knows someone who will buy them, to which Ṣāliḥ replies that he does, "on condition that you hand over the papers [bonds] at the time" of the trade. Ṣāliḥ then returns "with a sheet with Anīs's signature on it stating that we have bought in the amount of 5,000 lira bonds issued by such-and-such a country from Fāris and we will pay him the price after five days."[69] A fairly straightforward financial interaction is depicted in this scene, with telegrams, printed bonds, and signatures posing as securing this act of financial speculation. Throughout this exchange, Mājid, like the novel's readers, are witnesses, observing what appears to be a regular afternoon in the market. Though the reader has been asked to be on watch for forgery and sleight of hand, none reveals itself in this scene.

Later on the same page, Fāris approaches Mājid about doing business together. The reader, reading for forgeries and ruses, is once again on guard. Fāris offers to buy some of Mājid's cotton, and Mājid, a cautious, small-scale merchant unsure of Fāris's reputation in the markets, checks with Anīs, one of the wealthiest and most successful traders in the city. The reader is predisposed to doubt Anīs's word. When Anīs tells Mājid, however, that though he does not like Fāris, he has a good deal of money and commodities and so does not represent a risk financially, it reads like business as usual. Indeed, Mājid and the reader saw earlier on the same page that in fact Fāris has in his box a considerable sum in foreign bonds. Mājid decides to go ahead with the transaction, "the contract of sale occurred and the merchant received the cotton and Mājid received the debenture notes and the job ended."[70] The reader is asked to be suspicious of any trade deals into which Mājid enters, and though a reader would be hard-pressed to see where Mājid may have gone wrong, the debenture notes that he holds from the cotton merchant Fāris appear to be the most threatening.

Another trade occurs immediately. This time, Ṣāliḥ comes to Mājid with "promissory notes in a large amount with Anīs's signature on behalf of Fāris," announcing that "Fāris wants to sell these bonds so do you want to buy them?"[71] The appearance in the narrative of Anīs's signature creates an immediate air of doubt and concern, given the novel's warning of an impending forgery. When Mājid is told that Fāris holds these bonds due to a cotton deal that he had brokered which fell through, the novel takes on an ominous tone. Nevertheless, Mājid is compelled to buy the bonds as he "need[s] to send money to another country."[72] He "bought them and gave Ṣāliḥ a contract stating that he would pay the money three days later and so Mājid sent the bonds to Europe . . . and paid the price of the promissory notes with them and found that he had earned in this commercial job nearly 500 lira."[73] While Mājid celebrates his windfall, a lingering feeling that things are not as they seem hovers over the pages of this installment.

Indeed, Mājid's moment of financial success is brief. In the final page of this issue of the novel, Fāris's business collapses, and at the beginning of the next installment of the novel, we discover that Fāris no longer has "the many international bonds that he had."[74] The narrative explains that following a large fall in the value of securities, Fāris, who had purchased securities with credit, could not pay Anīs the money he owed. Both Mājid and Anīs are left holding Fāris's debt, and Mājid thus loses the cotton he sold to Fāris, as well as the value of the bad debt. In an effort to stem his losses, Mājid goes to Anīs with debenture notes in hand from Fāris (backed by Anīs's signature). When Anīs tells Mājid that "there is no note of them in my registers and no mention of them in my letters,"[75] Mājid recognizes the extent of his bankruptcy at the hands of dishonest brokers. In the next issue of *Al-Jinān*, Mājid attempts to maintain appearances so as to prevent a run on his business by creditors who might become anxious about the debts he owes them. Fāris for his part confesses to forging Anīs's signature, ruining his already damaged reputation in the market and further threatening Mājid's. Mājid now worries about his prospects with Rīmah: "How will he clothe her in expensive silk clothes and . . . buy her gold jewelry and hold banquets and dinner parties?"[76]

Bint al-ʿaṣr is a tale of serial debt and forgery. With Fāris and Mājid in apparent bankruptcy, the novel lets the reader in on the inner workings of the ruse that the reader could not work out alone. In fact, Fāris's commodities and wealth, and all the trades and transactions carried out by him—narrative elements the reader witnessed—were an exercise in duplicity engineered by Ṣāliḥ and Anīs to secure Mājid's trust and ultimate downfall. For the plot to work, al-Bustānī played their accomplice. Behind the reader's back, Anīs had placed the bonds in Fāris's box to lend him the appearances of a wealthy trader. Anīs had also recorded fake transactions between himself and Fāris in his registers, making sure that Fāris's registers agreed with the false accounting. Even Fāris's confessions of forging Anīs's signature were planned by Anīs. *Bint al-ʿaṣr* called upon readers to be on the watch for just this sort of fraud. Though the plot was disclosed from early on, and though the reader is told that Mājid will be outwitted by Ṣāliḥ and Anīs, the novel obscured the inner workings, keeping readers in suspense, hoping and fearing, their perspective aligned with the character being deceived. Duplicity becomes inherent to the very workings of the plot, investing readers in a narrative economy that would entrap them, too, through the ruses of speculation.

Mājid pursues legal action against Fāris and his dishonest dealings in the market, yet the courts, rife themselves with corruption, found Fāris's ledgers to "be exact and correct from all angles."[77] An honest judge becomes involved in the case, just as Anīs enters Ṣāliḥ's home to discuss the financial fictions that just netted the two 7,000 lira. As in *Budūr* and later *Sāmiyyah*, and throughout the eighteenth- and nineteenth-century English fiction studied by Robbins, so too in *Bint al-ʿasr*, a domestic servant, that unrepresentative member of the working class, appears in a novel's pages: "Ṣāliḥ had an unfaithful servant and so when Anīs entered his master's house and met with him in his private room that servant entered the adjoining room without their knowledge and listened to their conversation by means of a locked door between the rooms and knew all of what was intended and was determined to put it to use for himself."[78] Anīs is revealed to be a "rich man [who] stole thousands of liras through forgery and trickery and covered the matter up with clothes and money even though despite his riches he is the great thief."[79] In the process, *Bint al-ʿasr* trains its audience to read past the appearances concealing the corruption undergirding the lifestyles of the bourgeoisie and the financial deals brokered in the city's markets, but not without revealing the imbrication of the serialized novel and its reliance on suspense in the culture of speculation upending Beirut.

In the penultimate installment of *Bint al-ʿaṣr*, Fāris goes to prison and Anīs pays fines in restitution. Mājid is recompensed for his losses by the judge, who, if honest, also happens to extort money from the novel's offenders in order to pass it along to their victim. In the final installment, Mājid tells Rīmah what Ṣāliḥ's servant overheard, and this time it is Jamīlah, enamored of the novel's villain, Anīs, who is eavesdropping. Anīs has a change of heart and falls for Jamīlah, and the novel ends happily ever after as two sisters prepare their weddings, with one caveat. Mājid has Anīs write him a letter stating the truth of everything that happened, which Mājid can then publish if Anīs mistreats Jamīlah. The novel's final installment holds out the possibility that the narrative that is coming to a close *is* that letter written by the fictional Anīs: the residue of a failed romance, erupting onto the pages of *Al-Jinān*, the novel becomes a vehicle for social critique, reform, even revenge. Serialized fortnight after fortnight, Salīm al-Bustānī's novels held readers in suspense, as a deep sense of doubt accumulated around the appearances being kept up in the markets, streets, and homes of Beirut, and the remainder that was to come. To read *Bint al-ʿaṣr* as a tale penned by Anīs is to read of a Mājid twice deceived in a novel whose narrator sometimes acts like a dishonest finance capitalist, cautioning vigilance in reading both the surface of the text, and the fictions of capital it conceals.

was able to sleep for a few hours. When he awoke he was feeling much better, and by the afternoon, "he was at ease and the pain of the sickness diminished and he received those present speaking to them with the eloquence and kindness for which he was well known and frankly discussed with us the joy he had attained and resolved to return to Beirut the next day."[5] The reader, with the heavy black outline of an obituary page staring back, feels no relief. This is not fiction; there is no space here for hope, and there will not be another installment but only impending tragedy. The doctor continues, "As he spoke to us a sudden painful [heart] attack struck him half an hour after noon and it took his life in less than two minutes leaving in our souls the most painful of blows and the most calamitous of misfortunes."[6]

Salīm al-Bustānī did indeed return to Beirut the next day, to be the silent witness to a public outpouring of sorrow and elegy. When the funeral procession reached the grave, the sounds of the sobbing mourners filled the air as his body was lowered into the earth: "Then the voice of the eulogist rose up from a height beside the grave and the gazes of the crowd turned to it and it was . . . our colleague Fāris Nimr one of the editors of *Al-Muqtaṭaf* and he eulogized the dead with fine speech exceeding in eloquence."[7] Several times in the course of this heartrending obituary, the plea for patience repeats in the wake of Salīm al-Bustānī's death. The *Nahḍah*, a dream of rise and renaissance, confronted elegy; still others would soon be leaving behind the gardens of Beirut.

Fāris Nimr was himself preparing to quit Beirut, no longer a viable location from which to cultivate the gardens of knowledge that had provided the city with a dream of Eden in 1870. The cofounder and editor of *Al-Muqtaṭaf*, a journal devoted to "choice clippings" from the fruits of the sciences, like his fellow editor, Yaʿqūb Ṣarrūf, Nimr had until quite recently also been an instructor at the Syrian Protestant College. There is growing scholarly interest around what many refer to as the "Lewis affair" at the college in 1882, when Professor Edwin Lewis referenced Charles Darwin's theory of evolution at commencement, arguing for the need to "pair knowledge with science."[8] The lecture provoked a censorious response from a powerful conservative contingent of evangelical professors at the college, among them Daniel Bliss, then president of the college. In December of that year, Lewis lost his job teaching at the college, and students responded with a strike that protested Lewis's removal as well as a range of educational concerns. Some students were expelled or left the college, among them Jurjī Zaydān, who recounts in his unfinished memoirs the role he played in organizing and leading protests against the administration. In the aftermath of Lewis's speech and the student protest, most of the more liberal professors, including Lewis, Cornelius Van Dyck, and Van Dyck's son William, left the college.[9] The Syrian Protestant College administration and faculty became increasingly strident, as Jeha recounts, "resolv[ing] to deprive natives from holding professorial ranks, to exclude them from decision-making positions, and to entrust such responsibilities to Americans or, in certain cases, to other foreigners."[10] Editors of the already renowned scientific journal *Al-Muqtaṭaf*, Nimr and Ṣarrūf were both gravely affected by this policy and its fallout.

While the administration briefly equivocated on their position, in July 1884, two months before Nimr would eulogize Salīm al-Bustānī at his public funeral, Nimr and Ṣarrūf received written notice announcing the college's decision to terminate them. The press historian Nadia Farag argues in a pivotal early study of the fortunes of the scientific and industrial journal *Al-Muqtaṭaf* that Nimr and Ṣarrūf moved to Cairo as a direct result of the policies of Bliss and others at the Syrian Protestant College, taking *Al-Muqtaṭaf* with them. The persistence of articles on the Lewis affair over the course of 1884 in the pages of *Al-Muqtaṭaf* would certainly support this argument, as would a mournful letter from Dr. Cornelius Van Dyck printed in *Al-Muqtaṭaf*'s first Cairo issue. Nimr and Ṣarrūf continued to publish updates on Beirut's intellectual scene and their former college, only now from Cairo, and *Al-Muqtaṭaf* persisted well into the twentieth century as the *shaykh* of Arabic journals and a central institution of the *Nahḍah* being dreamed in Arabic.[11]

Upon the departure of *Al-Muqtaṭaf* and its editors, Van Dyck was left to wonder "if it was the fate of Syria to lose all her young men famed for their earnestness and erudition who had striven to better [Syria's] situation and raise her affairs, and if she has fallen through great sin [*jannat dhanban ʿaẓīman*] such that her noble sons would abandon her?"[12] To Nimr and Ṣarruf, former colleagues at the Syrian Protestant College and pillars of the scientific and cultural community it nurtured in Beirut, Van Dyck writes that "Egypt has won you and attained your journal but Syria lost in losing you, oh what a loss," ending the letter, "hoping that Syria has only been forbidden from its riches until a time when God will once again grace them upon her and we will say, 'These are our goods returned to us.'"[13] Van Dyck's reference is to *al-ʿIqd al-farīd*, to the rise of al-Andalus as it cribbed from Baghdad's annals of Arabic literature, serving in 1885 as a vector through which to hope for the future return of Syria's "riches," and to recognize the serialized novel form's indebtedness to Arabic's long legacy of popular storytelling.

In his influential and oft-cited *Tarīkh al-ṣiḥāfah al-ʿarabiyyah* (History of the Arabic press), Fīlīp dī Ṭarrāzī narrates the changing fortunes and collapsing hopes of Beirut's press with an eye only to censorship. Ṭarrāzī writes that *Al-Muqtaṭaf* moved to Egypt in 1884 because, "when censorship on publications intensified in the Ottoman Empire [Ṣarrūf and Nimr] saw no other option in continuing this great service save to move their journal to the capital of the Egyptian nation. So they emigrated to it in 1884,[14] and the first issue that they published there was the sixth of the ninth year."[15] The fate of *Al-Muqtaṭaf*, the only journal that physically relocated to Egypt, an Egypt occupied since 1882 by the British, is taken as symbolic of the general shift of gravity in Arabic press activity from Beirut to Egypt, away from the collapsing Ottoman Empire, and to the future of European imperial control. This narrative of migration and flight, influentially charted by Ṭarrāzī, overlooks the many intersecting paths—personal, social, and economic—changing the shape of Beirut's press in the early 1880s. Indeed, Donald Cioeta argues in a compelling article on censorship during this period that the reasons for this shift from Beirut to the Nile Valley were overdetermined and much more rooted in economic and social factors such as the Lewis affair than in censorship per se; "journalists in Egypt," Cioeta explains, "did not enjoy greater freedom than those in Beirut when *al-Ahram* was founded [in 1875], or indeed until 1885."[16] And it was not, Cioeta argues, until 1889 that Ottoman censorship of the Beirut Arabic press became particularly acute.[17]

Rather than a matter of censorship (as Ṭarrazī would have it), the fall of the Edenic gardens of the Beirut press reads as a story motivated by pressing material concerns in Cioeta's work: "By 1878, Beirut was already a highly competitive journalistic center, while Egypt was largely untapped territory. Moreover, a prosperous, literate Syrian business community in Egypt was willing to finance and read newspapers and magazines. Such publications were not at the mercy of subscription revenues as were their counterparts in Beirut, and provided opportunities for educated men to express their views while earning a living."[18] Ami Ayalon, in his *The Press in the Arab Middle East: A*

History, like Cioeta saw the opportunities available in Egypt as a primary motivation for this press migration, though Ayalon figures the question in terms more of capitalist competition than patronage, noting that "the press, like other commercial areas, involved competing for a limited market."[19] This material question of the market for Arabic journals, their means of support, and of the livelihoods this market afforded, predated the British occupation in 1882. Ayalon points out Khedive Ismāʿīl's "pull . . . for the Syrian intellectuals' skills, alluring them with options that their country could not offer."[20] Sarkīs remarks in Salīm al-Bustānī's obituary in *Lisān al-Ḥāl* that Salīm "received praises from every noble and in the Nile valley he met with abundant luck from the khedival government. . . . [H]e went to Egypt twice and returned with suitcases that spoke of the magnanimities of his eminence the Khedive."[21] The 1870s saw Syrian émigrés establish new periodicals in Egypt, most notably the still-publishing newspaper *Al-Ahrām* begun by the Taqlā brothers in 1875 with French support. Come the 1880s, Beirut's press and markets were torn asunder, leaving behind mostly religiously minded journals, with the exception of the Ottoman-supported *Ḥadīqat al-Akhbār*, and the still thriving *Thamārāt al-Funūn* and *Lisān al-Ḥāl*.

By the 1880s, the silk industry was faltering. In August 1882, Salīm Ibrāhīm Naṣr published a detailed article in the pages of *Al-Jinān* entitled "Silk Cocoon and Silk Production in the World."[22] He opened the article: "The decrease in prices for silk cocoons these past years has made a few think that this species has reached the point of collapse [*suqūṭ*] and . . . that it is most appropriate to replace the growing of mulberry trees with planting another useful crop such as tobacco or coffee."[23] The growing doubt in the silk industry surrounds too the future of agriculture and real estate around early 1880s Beirut: perhaps it is a time not of mulberry trees but of tobacco or coffee. Naṣr attempts to allay his readers' fears by pointing out historical fluctuations in silk prices, arguing that though "the decrease in prices has been steady since 1874,"[24] the price of silk has historically over the course of the nineteenth century "changed[,] going up and down in such a way that we cannot say that this species has collapsed and that its drop [in price] is perpetual and increasing."[25] Naṣr captures the tenor of early 1880s Beirut on the eve of the deaths of Buṭrus and Salīm al-Bustānī and just before a wave of student protests and intellectual upheaval that would significantly alter the city's most important institution of higher learning, the Syrian Protestant College. Even before the city was to lose both *Al-Jinān* and *Al-Muqtaṭaf*, the fortunes of the silk that had underwritten Beirut's bourgeois reading public were in the balance. Silk—"an important crop from which a large portion of the world lives from the results of its returns"—was becoming in the pages of *Al-Jinān* a commodity "whose reputation it appears has collapsed among the people."[26] The Beirut hope in progress, spun of 1860s and 1870s silk and its returns, both financial and cultural, in 1882, on the eve of protest and funerals that would devastate the city's literary scene, yielded a new sort of speculation in what was to come.

Many members of the Beirut bourgeoisie, among them a few who were to play a pivotal role in the future of the Arabic press, relocated to Egypt in the late 1870s through the 1880s.[27] Capital was in flight.[28] They were, as Cioeta suggests, greeted by an established group of Syrian entrepreneurs poised to patronize new journals. Kendall points to how "running a journal presented a business opportunity for smaller entrepreneurs—it required little investment and could be run by a couple of people. The Syrian emigres were instrumental in this early development of Egyptian journalism."[29] Syrian émigrés in Egypt by the late 1870s owned large and profitable businesses, such as the Sidnawi department store in Cairo, run by brothers from the Syrian village of Sidnayah. Some of the most popular items sold in Egypt's department stores were *dentille* lace, silks, and *articles de Paris,* the very goods so coveted by Beirut's bourgeoisie, tapped into the markets of an increasingly global European fashion industry.[30] Syrian émigrés already in Egypt, merchants and entrepreneurs in search of opportunity and new markets, witnessed the flight from Beirut of individuals who would play a decisive role in the future of the Arabic press and most particularly the novel form. As Nimr, Ṣarrūf, and Zaydān and others arrived in Egypt, they left behind a Beirut rent by protest, economic doubt, and elegy.

Al-Jinān republished many of the elegies composed for Salīm al-Bustānī in the journal's first two issues following his death in early and mid-November 1884, revealing a changed terrain for the Arabic press. Alongside eulogies appearing in Beirut journals and newspapers such as *Ḥadīqat al-Akhbār*, *Thamarāt al-Funūn*, and *Al-Nashrah al-Usbūʿiyyah* were a number published in Egypt, in *Al-Ahrām*, *Al-Maḥrūsah*, and *Rawḍat al-Iskandriyyah.* There was also the piece printed in *Al-Muqtaṭaf*, as the voice of its editor, Fāris Nimr, "rose up from a height beside" Salīm al-Bustānī's grave, "eulogizing the dead with fine speech exceeding in eloquence," in a public act of mourning that deeply resonated in a changed Beirut, the city he would soon leave for Cairo.

Cairo inherited Beirut's literary and intellectual legacies. The year 1892 serves as a watershed, marking the first issue of Zaydān's *Al-Hilāl*, which was to significantly inform the history of the Arabic press and the Arabic novel form. While the first Cairo issue of *Al-Muqtaṭaf* looked back to Beirut, the first issue of *Al-Hilāl* contained an elegy of sorts for the newspapers that had come before, with a section devoted to the Beirut press of the 1870s and early 1880s. The article was entitled "Arabic Newspapers in the World" ("Al-Jarāʾid al-ʿarabiyyah fi-l-ʿālam"); published in September 1892, it represents one of the first attempts to historicize the development of the early Arabic press. The metaphors of culture and cultivation of the early 1870s stage a return, as Mehmet ʿAlī—*manbit ghirs al-tamaddun al-ḥadīth fī al-bilād al-sharqiyyah*, or the "cultivator of the seedling of modern civilization in the Eastern countries"[31]—is credited with planting the first seed with the official khedival newspaper *Al-Waqāʾiʿ al-Miṣriyyah*, followed by another (often) official Ottoman paper, Beirut's *Ḥadīqat al-Akhbār*. Official government newspapers (including *Al-Rāʾid al-Tūnisī*) then give way to the private press; the "seedlings of the sciences and knowledge [*maghāris al-ʿulūm wa-l-maʿārif*] had begun to grow [*tanmū*] in Egypt and Syria,"[32] and Buṭrus al-Bustānī founded first *Al-Jinān* and then *Al-Jannah*.[33]

Al-Jinān and then *Al-Jannah*—their titles like their editors' family name harkening to an Edenic early moment in the Arabic press—appeared in the pages of Jurjī Zaydān's first issue of *Al-Hilāl* under the heading "Newspapers That Appeared and Then Disappeared from Sight, Either Suspended Indefinitely or Closed Forever."[34] These two titles joined the list that included *Al-Junaynah, Al-Zahrah,* and *Al-Naḥlah,* as well *Al-Taqaddum* and *Al-Najāḥ*. But *Al-Muqtaṭaf* was plucked from a future of indefinite suspense, of being closed forever, by a footnote informing readers that the journal "was not suspended but rather moved to Cairo and will be mentioned in [the section of] Living [*ḥayyah*] Newspapers of Cairo."[35]

By 1890s Cairo, when Zaydān—having grown up on the margins of al-Bustānī's Beirut, hearing both the old storytellers' tales from the threshold of the kitchen he worked in and reading the new narratives inking the pages of the Beirut press—began serializing and publishing his own fiction, Cairo itself was caught up in a wave of cotton and real estate speculation taking form through the press, the stock market, and the institutions they enabled. Zaydān inherited Beirut's legacy of the serialized Arabic novel, a novel that bore its saturation in the economic in both form and content. But as chapter 5 argues, he dreamed another iteration of finance for the Arabic novel, one whose plotlines staged a distance from the markets copiously woven through the works of al-Khūrī, al-Shalfūn, al-Bustānī, and later Ṣarrūf. He dreamed a novel that would even part ways with the suspense-driven imbrications of the serialized form, turning its back on a nineteenth-century global web of finance in the fictions of Beirut, including not only Salīm's oeuvre (1870–1884) but also Khalīl al-Khūrī's 1859–60 serialized novel *Way—idhan lastu bi-ifranjī* (Alas, I am not a foreigner), and Yūsuf al-Shalfun's 1870 *Al-Shābb al-maghrūr.* At the hands of Zaydān, the novel emerged all the more heavily capitalized: it was a commodity, one that in its very form and circulation betrayed the Edenic, impossible dream of an Arabic novel untroubled by speculation. Fictions of capital were accumulating again in the garden, this time Ezbekiyyah, and would soon culminate in the 1907 Cairo stock market crash.

Zaydān arrived in Cairo following the 1882 Syrian Protestant College student protests in which he played a prominent role, as he records in his memoirs.[36] Those memoirs went unpublished until shortly after his death, appearing in *Al-Hilāl* in installments, an act of spectral self-eulogy from beyond the grave. The memoirs chart Zaydān's rise, from a waiter and bookkeeper in his father's small Beirut restaurant to a medical student at the Syrian Protestant College before the ensuing protests.

Zaydān's father worked at a *lūkandah* that served as the initial site of Zaydān's introduction to Beirut's literary scene, both high and low; as a young boy he used to listen to the storytellers at the edges of Beirut's markets from the back kitchen door of the *lūkandah,* while the restaurant's dining room would later introduce Zaydān to Beirut's flourishing intellectual, academic, and literary scene. Members of the Beirut bourgeoisie, students and teachers at the Syrian Protestant College, as well as some visitors to the city, would frequent the *lūkandah* for lunch, and Zaydān recalls in great detail the day that some teachers from the local schools first showed him an issue of *Al-Muqtaṭaf.* He was sixteen years old, "and during that time *Al-Muqtaṭaf* was publishing, and it was in its second year I believe. Some schoolteachers who would pass by showed me an issue of it in which was an article on eclipses. . . . I read in other issues an article on clouds and the reasons for rain, and my desire to study the laws of nature increased."[37] Looking back from Cairo to 1870s Beirut in memoirs made public only in death, Zaydān's tale of *nahḍah*, of his and the Arabic press's rise and renaissance, takes on a melancholic tone.

It is the melancholy of a portrait of a deeply ambitious, young Zaydān, looking to leave behind the life he was leading attending to the pots and pans, books and customers of his father's *lūkandah*. Zaydān did a brief stint as a bookkeeper for a silk merchant after a course in double-column bookkeeping.[38] But his true desire was to become one of the likes of his father's customers: Zaydān studied the affect and memorized the speech of frequenters of the *lūkandah*, such as the Shaykh Ibrāhīm al-Yāzijī and Salīm al-Bustānī's cousin ʿAbdallāh al-Bustānī;[39] and he bought himself a subscription to *Al-Muqtaṭaf*, recalling, "I had subscribed to *Al-Muqtaṭaf* in order to read it, and I took pride in being a subscriber [*mushtarik bihi*] and I liked for people to know that I read it." For Zaydān, the readers of *Al-Muqtaṭaf* represented a group to which he aspired to belong, yearning to see his own writing in its pages: "I wanted to embark on writing for it. So I wrote an article and strove to revise and embellish it to the extent of my abilities, though I did not know *iʿrāb* [here, Arabic grammar], but rather felt my way through writing it, for its topic was a critique of fathers who do not educate their children when they are young, for if they grow up the opportunity to educate them will be missed. That was my situation in those days."[40] After watching issue after issue of *Al-Muqtaṭaf* be published without his letter appearing in its pages, one of the journal's editors, Shahīn Makāriyūs, came to the *lūkandah* for lunch with some of his friends. Makāriyūs hoped that his next letter would be better, "setting [Zaydān's] self-confidence back by ten years."[41]

Finally securing himself a place as a student at the Syrian Protestant College medical school in Beirut, Zaydān took particular joy in his courses in dissection. He devotes a macabre section of his memoirs to the topic, first appearing in *Al-Hilāl* in 1924, ten years after his death.[42] In it, Zaydān relates that "dissection is very pleasurable [*ladhīdh jiddan*]," for it allowed one to "look upon what makes up the human body. And there was no way to study it but to procure the bones of a human skeleton." In early 1880s Beirut, "bones were scarce due to the difficulty of acquiring corpses, as people refused to allow the corpses of their dead to be dissected." The consequent high price of human corpses inspired the ever-resourceful Zaydān:

> I told myself that I would try to get a complete skeleton. And one day it reached me that a man from the people of Ras Beirut had died and been buried in a grave in the sand. So I arranged with one of my friends that we would go and steal it, and we took along a man and his trusted companion to unearth and carry the corpse. We went three or four days after the death and we figured that the corpse had been placed in a coffin so it would be easy to move as it was, so we went after midnight like frightened thieves, unearthing a number of graves as we had mistaken the location of the grave we sought, though we had gone by day to ascertain its location, and finally we found them though not buried in coffins. So we carried what we could of the bones for dawn had come upon us and returned frightened. No one at the college knew what we had done but my friend. The next morning people saw the open graves and accused the students of the college but did not find out who had done it.[43]

Well after midnight, interrupted by the break of dawn, the portrait of a frightened corpsesnatcher surrounded by open sandy graves, Zaydān's memoirs turned macabre,[44] later the stuff of a posthumous gothic chapter in the pages of *Al-Hilāl*, the journal he founded in 1892.

Zaydān's *Mudhakirrāt* ended after his departure from Beirut in October 1883, no longer a student at the Syrian Protestant College following his role in the protests. A new arrival in Cairo, he had planned to continue his medical studies at al-Qaṣr al-ʿAynī, having been awarded a diploma in pharmacy at the impromptu school Dr. Cornelius Van Dyck had established in his Beirut home following the departure of many professors, instructors, and students from the Syrian Protestant College medical school.[45] In Egypt, Zaydān began editing the small newspaper *Al-Zaman* (serializing novels of maritime suspense), but in 1884, as Matti Moosa recounts, "as war correspondent and interpreter, he joined the British expedition to the Sudan,"[46] spending ten months in their service.[47]

In his seminal four-volume study of the history of Arabic literature, *Tārīkh ādāb al-lughah al-ʿarabiyyah,* Zaydān makes a nod to the influence of Fransīs Marrāsh's polemical narrative and Salīm al-Bustānī's serialized novels as he writes his history of the Arabic novel.[48] Yet as Thomas Philipp was astute to point out in his dissertation,[49] Zaydān betrays some reluctance in attributing to Salīm al-Bustānī the pivotal and pioneering role his serialized novels played in the early history of the novel form in Arabic, a point also noted by Muḥammad ʿAbd al-Ghanī Ḥasan in his 1970 Arabic study *Jurjī*

Zaydān.[50] Narrating the Arabic novel's history in the third person in *Tārīkh adāb al-lughah al-ʿarabiyyah*, Zaydān records:

> Then writers set out to compose in this art [of novel writing] on their own in imitation of the foreigners, and among the earliest of those who worked in that [art] was Fransīs Marrāsh mentioned below, then Salīm Buṭrus al-Bustānī composed some historical novels that he published in *Al-Jinān*, and then the owner of *Al-Hilāl* [i.e., Zaydān himself] composed a series of novels on the history of Islam from its first appearance up to now, publishing 17 novels [as part] of it, in addition to his other novels.[51]

This introduction is then followed by a detailed review of the biographies of the "poets and prose writers [*udabāʾ*] of this *Nahḍah*," arranged (in keeping with a long tradition of Arabic biographical dictionaries) by date of death. The entry on Fransīs Marrāsh (d. 1873) comes as promised, under the section dedicated to those who died between 1867 and the "beginnings of the occupation" of Egypt by the British in 1882. We would expect the entry on Salīm al-Bustānī (d. 1884), then, in the following section, comprising those who died between the beginning of the British occupation of Egypt, and "now" (1914, on the eve of Zaydān's own death). Yet the first entry in that section, organized by date of death, is Shaykh Khalīl al-Yāzijī, who died in 1889. The entry for Salīm al-Bustānī, above whose grave the voice of Fāris Nimr had risen in eulogy in 1884 along with so many others, is nowhere to be found. His historical novels buried "in the pages of *Al-Jinān*," Salīm al-Bustānī makes only a spectral appearance, denied admission to Zaydān's sepulcher of "poets and prose writers of this *Nahḍah*."

Zaydān would return to Beirut, not only in his fictions and his posthumously published memoirs but throughout his life, underscoring the connectedness of Beirut to Alexandria and Cairo in this period. Though Zaydān worked as a translator for the British in 1884 as part of their Sudanese expedition, as *Al-Muqtaṭaf* related following his death in 1914, "the next year [1885] he returned to Beirut and studied Hebrew and Syriac and he and his friend the teacher Jabr Ḍūmiṭ wrote a book on linguistic philosophy building on the research of foreign linguists."[52] In 1885, Zaydān joined Al-Majmaʿ al-ʿIlmī al-Sharqī (The Eastern Scientific Academy), which "had recently been founded, in 1882 for research in sciences and industries, and how to benefit from them in order to return the country to wealth and prosperity." The fear that the progress of the 1860s and the hope of the

1870s might not be the remainder that was to come had given way to a different kind of Beirut: "Among the intellectuals who founded [Al-Majmaʿ al-ʿIlmī al-Sharqī]" we find familiar names: "Dr. Yaʿqūb Ṣarrūf, Dr. Fāris Nimr, Dr. Van Dyck, and Mawṣūlī Pasha, who were joined later by Dr. Wortabet, Dr. Iskandar Bārūdī, Salīm al-Bustānī, Shaykh Ibrāhīm al-Yāzijī and others."[53] Zaydān joined the academy in 1885, only a year after Salīm al-Bustānī's death, in a Beirut that was coming undone. Nimr and Ṣarrūf would soon leave Beirut, and Zaydān notes that "this academy did not long remain after the owners of *Al-Muqtaṭaf* moved to Cairo."[54] Zaydān himself would leave Beirut the next year, traveling with Ḍūmiṭ to London by ship via Port Said and Malta, departing in May 1886. In London, Zaydān was struck by the vibrancy of the press, the sometimes twice-daily newspapers, and the cheap prices at which they were sold.[55]

Zaydān left London at the height of the summer of 1886, having visited its museums, libraries, and parks, to arrive in British-occupied Cairo in July 1886, via Port Said and Alexandria. There he stayed in Bayt al-Zuhār, with a friend named Asʿad al-Ḥishmah. As he recalls:

> A moment after I arrived, al-Muʿallim Fāris [Nimr] came down as he was living on the floor above us, and met me and greeted me and invited me to dinner saying that the people of the house are awaiting your coming to dinner. So after washing and changing my clothes I went up with Asʿad to the *Muqtaṭaf* house and there we sat down to dinner with al-Muʿallim Yaʿqūb [Ṣarrūf] and Fāris [Nimr] and Shāhīn Makāriyūs and the Lady Yāqūt and Mariam. After dinner we spent the evening and the night talking of travels.[56]

Zaydān continued to pass by Bayt *Al-Muqtaṭaf* in the coming weeks, "discussing with them many matters and one day al-Muʿallim Fāris [Nimr] revealed their need for someone to take over managing the affairs of the journal and help them work the press and review the proofs. He confided that they could not rely on just anyone in this matter. And he hinted that they would be at ease if it were me."[57] Zaydān, who only a decade ago had been a waiter and cook at his father's *lūkandah*, unable to even get a letter that he "strove to revise and embellish" published in the pages of *Al-Muqtaṭaf*, was now managing the journal's production and receiving a valuable education in the technologies of periodicals publication.

The editors of *Al-Muqtaṭaf* later published a posthumous article on Jurjī Zaydān in their journal, an obituary of sorts after Zaydān, in 1914 on "the 22nd of July shortly before midnight after writing the last word of the twenty-second volume of *Al-Hilāl* and completing the final part of [the journal's yearly] supplement *Tārīkh adāb al-lughah al-ʿarabiyyah* died between his notebooks and inkwells."[58] The editors of *Al-Muqtaṭaf* looked back on that day in 1886 when Zaydān "returned to the country of Egypt and we handed over to him the management of our affairs for a year and some, then he quit and devoted himself to writing. He wrote *Tārīkh Miṣr al-ḥadīth* [The modern history of Egypt] and founded *Al-Hilāl* [in 1892] and took up writing novels and historical and literary books."[59] In 1892, Jurjī Zaydān announced for sale his early novel *Asīr al-Mutamahdī* (a title we might translate as "The captive of the self-made or so-called Mahdī"), several historical studies he had already completed, his geography of Egypt, and his linguistic treatise on Arabic, for purchase in book form.[60]

Inheriting Beirut's literary genealogies in a city with a rich cultural scene of its own, *Asīr al-Mutamahdī* stages a late nineteenth-century geography of literary and capital flight. *Asīr al-Mutamahdī* is the backstory of speculation in Arabic, both flaunting and concealing the shadow that the nightmare of 1860 continued to cast over Arabic and its novels, from the heights of Mount Lebanon and the hinterland surrounding Damascus, to the gardens overlooking Beirut, and sedimenting in Cairo's new public garden of Ezbekiyya. It is a novel that, fittingly, at times seems overwhelmed by the proliferation of the Arabic press and by the staggering preponderance of gardens in and around Beirut and Cairo.[61] If the Arabic press in 1870 could be imagined as a network of gardens, and if in 1892 in the first issue of *Al-Hilāl*, Zaydān could be found narrating a history of the Arabic press whose "seedlings of the sciences and knowledge [*maghāris al-ʿulūm wa-l-maʿārif*] had begun to grow [*tanmū*] in Egypt and Syria"[62] now for several decades, with *Asīr al-Mutamahdī*, Zaydān tells us something more. For these gardens, and most particularly Ezbekiyya, are from the start un-Edenic, ever troubled, even as they were figured as a space of refuge and retreat from the rampant speculation cultivating unruly cotton fields and real estate markets up and down the Nile.

Asīr al-Mutamahdī is prefaced by a brief "historical introduction" in which Jurjī Zaydān acquaints the reader with the tremendous changes that have occurred in Cairo as of 1878, the year in which the novel begins. Focalizing on Khedive Ismāʿīl and his desires to make Cairo "a piece of Europe," we are told of Ismāʿīl's efforts to "open [*fatḥ*] modern streets and establish new, organized quarters, following which were established thousands of homes and palaces and gardens [*ḥadāʿiq*] outside the original city, and wide, new streets were lined with trees on both sides, and the entire city was illuminated with gas, and its night became like its day and it grew in elegance and luxury, and public places in the city increased especially around the garden of Ezbekiyya."[63] A few lines later, Zaydān describes a diverse crowd, wrapt by the spectacle of military music being played each evening beneath the gaslights in Ezbekiyya. Zaydān addresses the reader in the second person—*wa-kunta idhā dakhalta al-ḥadīqah bi-l-masāʾ*—informing him (or perhaps her) what this gaslit evening garden in Cairo held for those who entered its gates.[64]

The first line of the novel reads: "On Shāriʿ al-ʿAbbāsiyyah in 1878 there was a house built in the modern style like the other modern homes there, but it was among the least grand and wide of them, and it had a simple small garden [*ḥadīqah*] that looked out upon the modern street shaded with ficus trees planted on both sides."[65] This is the home of our protagonist, Shafīq, to which his parents anxiously await his return. He has, for the first time, stayed out past dark. Just before his mother, Suʿdā, turns to her window overlooking this "simple small garden" and the "modern street shaded with ficus trees planted on both sides" to worriedly pass the time until her son's arrival, she announces to her husband her desire to share with Shafīq an article she had been reading in *Al-Muqtaṭaf*. Shafīq, it is widely thought, will soon be chosen by Khedive Ismāʿīl to study in England.

The Syrian émigré households that provide *Asīr al-Mutamahdī* with its protagonists are avid readers of the Arabic press, and fathers, mothers, sons, daughters, and servants share a particular predilection for reading periodicals published in the late 1870s by Syrian émigrés in Egypt or in the Beirut they left behind, including not only *Al-Muqtaṭaf* but also *Al-Ahrām*, *Al-Laṭāʾif*, and *Lisān al-Ḥāl*. Notably, *Al-Jinān* does not make the list. Mother and daughter are also prolific letter writers, and yet their letters frequently do not make it to their destination or are read by unintended audiences, obliquely registering a sense that women's writing was not making it to its audience, which would be partially remedied in 1892, when the first women's journal, *Al-Fatāt*, began publishing in Cairo.

This is not a novel of 1870s Beirut, though, but rather one that is haunted by the city's past, inheriting the legacy of failed silk speculations and the gardens since suspended in time. Shafīq's mother, Suʿdā, had been distracting herself from other worries as she read

Al-Muqtaṭaf that evening. Thinking that her son was already home and in his room "reading newspapers or something else,"[66] she herself had been anxious for the time to pass until midnight, the appointed hour when her husband would reveal the contents of a small box that he had kept closed and hidden since their marriage. Shafīq's mother now "forgetting or appearing to forget that matter of the box"—a box that will be revealed in the closing pages of the novel, in the mountains above Beirut, to contain a bloody secret of 1860: the family's Syrian genealogy and its flight to Cairo—Suʿdā "looks out the window not diverting her gaze from the street"[67] as the hour strikes ten, and then eleven. Her husband's efforts to comfort her, his telling her "there is no need to worry," that "the city is safe, and the streets are not empty of pedestrians until after midnight," and that "perhaps Shafīq went with his fellow students to Ezbekiyya garden to listen to the melodies of military music," fail to calm her heart.[68]

While the space of the garden in early 1870s Beirut temporarily elided debates that would persistently trouble the future of the Arabic press, in Zaydān's 1892 *Asīr al-Mutamahdī*, despite Shafīq's father's reassurances, the public garden of Ezbekiyya in 1870s Cairo reads at first as an entirely un-Edenic space, as everything that had threatened Beirut's gardens with a fall. In this novel, Ezbekiyya is the site of illicit midnight encounters of would-be lovers behind the backs of their fathers, aided by a well-dressed literate servant. And it is where our protagonist, Shafīq, is tricked into drinking his first cognac by his undeservedly dear friend ʿAzīz, in a coffeehouse in Ezbekiyya "set up for dancing and singing." When they arrive at this cabaret, Shafīq looks around him and sees:

> People in groups and alone drinking and singing and laughing, some of them swaying with delight at the sound of song, while another calls out at the top of his voice "*āh, kamān yā sitt*"—again my lady—while others toast and drink to one another.
>
> Shafīq looked at his friend in shock saying, "Where are we ʿAzīz?"[69]

It seems, in this evening Ezbekiyya, that we are somewhere far from Eden, that the novel has been reconfigured now not as dreamy encounters in Damascus gardens (though those, too, were troubled in their own way) but as a critique of disorienting Cairo gardens, which appear destined to persistently connote rapture, intoxication, and the promise of romantic encounters.

Before we dismiss this 1870s Ezbekiyya as entirely un-Edenic, we might skip ahead a few years to the first 1896 issue of *Al-Hilāl*, in which a curious Najīb Effendī Shāmī al-Ṣaydalī asks *Al-Hilāl*, "What was the tree from which our grandfather Adam ate in paradise [*al-firdaws*] and due to which he was sundered [from the Garden] and which the Bible calls the tree of good and evil but does not mention by name[?]"[70] It is presumably Zaydān who responds in the name of *Al-Hilāl* to offer two rather straightforward answers: that many believe it was an apple or another sweet, delicious fruit, while also suggesting that "the story [*ḥikāyah*] of this tree is symbolic." But then Zaydān offers a rather different account, one that harmonizes far more with Ezbekiyya after midnight than we might have expected. For Zaydān throws out the possibility that this "tree was among the elevating or intoxicating trees that now grow in some parts of India and Africa," reminding his readers in the closing line of this short exchange that "all that can be said about [the tree] is in the realm of guess and conjecture."[71]

Not that long before the events of the novel, in fact, Ezbekiyya as a European-styled public garden had itself been entirely "in the realm of guess and conjecture." Previously a pond fed by diverted Nile waters, by 1866 the area surrounding Ezbekiyya was drained and filled in, ready for a wave of city planning inaugurated by Ismāʿīl's 1867 trip to Paris, as he envisioned a new Cairo in which to host the Suez celebration. Returning to hire ʿAlī Mubārak as minister of public works, Ismāʿīl entrusted him with the task of making Cairo over as "a piece of Europe" in only two years, with a particular focus on the area surrounding Ezbekiyya, and the new area of Ismāʿīliyyah. New *maydān*s were planned throughout Cairo, with their formal plantings joining new streets newly lined with trees, in a vision of Cairo as a grand, modern city of boulevards and parks. Small private gardens and remaining agricultural land would slowly disappear as the area around Ezbekiyya was built up with the kinds of homes in which *Asīr al-Mutamahdī*'s protagonists and later Zaydān himself lived.[72] The area of al-Faggāllah, once a radish field irrigated by the Nile, was replaced with the new train station, streets, and modern-style buildings, one of which would later house Zaydān's Dār al-Hilāl's offices, printing press, and eventually bookstore and reading room.

As Janet Abu Lughod tells us, just prior to the opening of the Suez in 1869: "Ismāʿīl imported the French landscape architect—Barillet-Deschamps—whose work he had admired in the Bois de Boulogne and

Champs de Mars and commissioned him to redesign Ezbekiah as a Parc Monceau, complete with the free-form pool, grotto, bridges and belvederes which constituted the inevitable clichés of a nineteenth-century French garden. Thanks to the fast growing-season of Egypt, gardens were already flowering when the guests arrived in November."[73] It was a utopia of nineteenth-century French parks, and even more were imagined, such as a massive three-by-five-mile expanse of the West Bank of the Nile that was to be converted from farmland to an enormous park, a masterpiece only in its planning stages when Barillet-Deschamps died in 1874.[74]

Gardens abound in *Asīr al-Mutamahdī*.[75] This novel that would bury the gardens of Beirut charts a geography not unlike Zaydān's own from 1883 to 1887. Read sequentially, *Asīr al-Mutamahdī*'s gardens plot Zaydān's migration from Beirut to Cairo in reverse, save, of course, the gardens of Paradise (*al-jannah*) that are mentioned in one of the Mahdī's sermons to his army in Sudan. There are Ezbekiyya and the gardens lining the new streets of Cairo; the gardens of Qaṣr al-Nuzhah in Shubrah, where Khedive Ismāʿīl and later Tawfīq would go for weekly strolls (39); the gardens of Khartoum (89, 94); the green gardens of Beirut (109); the garden overlooking the Mediterranean at Dr. Nūn's Beirut home (who, we are told, was a former member of the Syrian Protestant College medical faculty) (119); the Ḥamīdiyyah public garden in Beirut by the police station (121); and the gardens of Mount Lebanon that are overlooked by the village of ʿĀlayh (145). In a later advertisement for *Asīr al-Mutamahdī* that appeared in June 1897 in *Al-Hilāl*, Zaydān is at pains to connect his own itinerary with the plot of *Asīr al-Mutamahdī*: "The author [Zaydān] witnessed most of the Sudanese events as an eyewitness and was present at the battles [*ḥurūbahā*] and saw the country [*wa-shāhada bilādahā*] and its people."[76] Zaydān, leaving behind Beirut's gardens of knowledge, charts an itinerary consonant with the rise of British empire in the region.

A chain of gardens reaches back from Ezbekiyya to the gardens of Beirut and Mount Lebanon, and a geography connected by the Nile, the Suez Canal, and the Mediterranean emerges. It not only traces Zaydān's life itinerary but also indexes the centrality of bodies of water to uncertain flow of commodities, literary strategies, finance, and empire for Cairo as for Beirut. Bodies of water are central to the events of *Asīr al-Mutamahdī*. Plans to attend the opening of the canal ultimately unravel with Shafīq finding himself in Ezbekiyya well past sunset, having gone for the first time to watch a French play at the new opera there. When they first arrive at the opera, ʿAzīz asks Shafīq: "Would you be amazed if I told you that Khedive Ismāʿīl built this and furnished it in five months?," going on to detail the debts Ismāʿīl incurred as he fêted the opening of the Suez Canal, which is used later in the novel to carry the British to the Red Sea as they embark on their Sudanese expedition. *Asīr al-Mutamahdī*'s many gardens and waterways evoke not only the "seedlings of the sciences and knowledge" that Zaydān left behind in Beirut but the *riwāyah*'s rootedness in water and irrigation (from *r-w-y*).

When Khedive Ismāʿīl came to power in 1863, Egypt had been at the height of a cotton boom, with prices high given the unavailability of the cotton of the American South during the Civil War. Turning the tools of irrigation to hydraulic city planning, Ismāʿīl set to work to build the Ismāʿīliyyah canal, in 1866 diverting water away from what had previously been the pond of Ezbekiyya. The next year, Ismāʿīl's trip to Paris left a deep imprint on him as he began to conceive of a new Cairo to host the opening of the Suez Canal, even as the price of Egyptian cotton collapsed, the war in America now over. The debts Ismāʿīl incurred in these years remain infamous and were an augury as to how French and British finance would shape Egypt's cotton industry, increasingly producing high-quality cotton fiber, now an industrial input calibrated to the needs of British textile factories and the speculations of an international bourgeoisie of cotton and real estate prospectors. These changes accrued in the garden of Ezbekiyya. Cultivated as a nonagricultural, nonindustrial utopia, Ezbekiyya was in fact an Eden of contradiction in an Egypt increasingly knitted into a capitalist world market governed by habits of speculation, hope, and anticipation with an eerie knack for disappointment.

A deep sense of anxiety and speculation hovers over the opening pages of Zaydān's early novel *Asīr al-Mutamahdī*. It is tethered first to a box not to be opened until midnight, one that in the novel's closing pages is revealed to contain the bloody secret of a hidden murder—the nightmare of 1860 all over again, divulged in the mountains above Beirut. Speculations abound, too, as to where Shafīq might be, out on his own in Cairo as midnight approaches, beyond the reach of his mother's gaze. She sits reading *Al-Muqtaṭaf*, perched in a window overlooking their garden and the street, "forgetting or appearing to forget that matter of the box."[77] Ezbekiyya is held out as a comforting hope, but as the novel and the garden's own history suggest, Ezbekiyya is but an Eden of contradiction. "Forgetting or appearing to forget" *Al-Jinān* and Salīm al-Bustānī's Beirut, Jurjī Zaydān leaves the city for Cairo, to publish novels that turn away from the fictions of capital reconfiguring the world economy, the better to make an industry out of the Arabic novel.

CHAPTER 5

Of Literary Supplements, Second Editions, and the Lottery

The Rise of Jurjī Zaydān

Migrating from Beirut to Cairo, *Al-Muqtaṭaf* and its editors, having eulogized the untimely loss of Salīm al-Bustānī in Beirut in 1884, now inherited the disappointed hopes of that city. Fāris Nimr, Yaʿqūb Ṣarrūf, Jurjī Zaydān, and many other Syrian émigrés arrived in British-occupied Egypt as finance capital was gambling on future fictions. If Khalīl al-Khūrī, Yūsuf al-Shalfūn, and Salīm al-Bustānī had serialized Beirut novels of the fictions of capital attending sericulture in the region, of deceiving appearances punctuated by hope and fear, the novels of Zaydān (in this chapter) and later Ṣarrūf (in chapter 6) would confront in Cairo a new terrain, grounded not in mulberry orchards but in Egypt's cotton fields, urban real estate, and for the moment, a booming stock market. As new newspapers and journals began to publish in great number, a diversified market for periodicals and fiction made the Arabic press and the novel itself a domain of speculation and potential profit.

In 1885, newly arrived in Cairo, the editors of *Al-Muqtaṭaf* speculated as to the future prospects of those tending "the seedlings of the sciences and knowledge" in Arabic. *Al-Muqtaṭaf* saw little hope for a return on the time invested in editing an Arabic journal. Like "all who manage the affairs of journals [*jarāʾid*] in general, and of scientific journals in particular," *Al-Muqtaṭaf*'s editors

> attest that their labors exceed their gains to a degree that cannot be measured and that those who found them [journals] in the East are making a tremendous mistake if they take them to be a means to earn money and distribute wealth. This is the cause of death for many

> scientific journals for they do not meet the needs of their owners in terms of attracting money and making great their standing and fame, and for that reason their life is not long. So let their likes be a lesson to those who would aim to found a scientific journal for if his first aim is not the service of the nation and knowledge his fortunes will be unlucky and his efforts ruined for sure, for knowledge [ʿ*ilm*] begets money but for other than its possessor.[1]

Al-Muqtaṭaf here calculates the return on a scientific journal in Arabic in 1885, a discourse animated by specters of Beirut. Having witnessed that their "labors exceed their gains to a degree that cannot be measured," the editors of one of the most important journals of the *Nahḍah* warn the aspiring press capitalist. The repeated invocation of money—that Arabic journals are not "a means to earn money," that they do not "beget money" for their owners, or "attract" to them "money and mak[e] great their standing and fame"—saturates the Arabic periodical in the language of the market.

Less than four years later, *Al-Muqtaṭaf* repeats the warning yet again, but this time "journals in the East" are compared with those of Egypt's British occupier, and they find themselves behind in salary, sales, and readers. The piece is entitled "The Salary of Newspaper Editors," and in it, *Al-Muqtaṭaf* warned readers that even Charles Dickens made only a modest yearly salary of two thousand pounds editing the *Daily News* from London. This, for a newspaper that every day published more than one hundred thousand copies, a number that *Al-Muqtaṭaf* claims is rather low for "a language that is spoken by more than a hundred million educated people." The sights of an editor of an Arabic journal should be set lower: "for the language that is spoken by not more than a few thousand educated [individuals], it is no wonder if only a few hundred of them subscribe to newspapers, their editors' pay having devolved [*inḥaṭṭat*] into what is less than a little."[2] Falling behind the British, this time of *nahḍah* is read in Arabic by *Al-Muqtaṭaf* as a time of *inḥiṭāṭ*, of decadence, devolution, and decline, indexed by the limited ranks of newspaper subscribers and the low salaries of their editors.

When *Al-Rāwī* [The narrator, from the same root as *riwāyah*, novel and *rayy*, irrigation] began publishing in Egypt just after the stock market crash of 1907, *Al-Muqtaṭaf* warned: "It will be difficult to attain his [the owner and editor of *Al-Rāwī*'s] hope and for the number of readers to be enough to prevent its failure and achieve a profit. For the English sell for two pence a novel containing five hundred large pages of fine print and only profit because of the number of readers it reaches. Only if *Al-Rāwī* earns a tenth of what the novels of Hall Caine or Conan Doyle do will there be sure profit for their author."[3] *Al-Muqtaṭaf* speculated as to *Al-Rāwī's* future in a Cairo chastened by the stock market crash but consumed with fiction: Samah Selim depicts the period "between 1880 and 1919 at least," as a time when "popular fiction in Egypt, translated and otherwise, constituted by far the lion's share of a burgeoning book and periodical market."[4]

Speculations abounded as to what kind of money could be made writing novels. While these sorts of stories never seemed to work out the same for Arabic, in the May 1905 issue of *Al-Muqtaṭaf*, under the title "The Profit of Writers [*Ribḥ al-muʾallifīn*]," its editors published a hopeful, even sensationalist tale of rich British novelists for readers of the Arabic press:

> Sir Walter Scott profited 80 thousand pounds from his pen and Miss Evans, known among writers by the name George Eliot, profited 7000 pounds from the novel *Romola* that she wrote. And Lord Roberts wrote his book *41 Years in the Life of a Soldier* [presumably his book *The Life-Story of a Great Soldier*, published in 1900] and was paid 10 thousand pounds for it. And the famous Mr. John Morley wrote the book *The Life of Gladstone* and received 10 thousand pounds for it. And Stanley received a like sum for his African travels and Marie Corelli received a thousand pounds for her novel *Ziska* and it is said that Mr. Hall Caine profited a hundred thousand pounds from his book by the name *The Christian*.[5]

Dickens's two thousand pounds for a year of editing the *Daily News* looked modest beside these staggering figures being reaped by British novelists. Ruses of imperial finance were indebting Egypt, prospecting in cotton land and real estate was rampant, and somehow British novelists were profiting handsomely.

Over the course of *Al-Hilāl*'s first year, Zaydān serialized installments of *Istibdād al-Mamālīk* (The oppression of the Mamluks), telling a tale of Ottoman despotism that would give way in Arab historiography to the *Nahḍah* (and European imperialism). In 1870s Beirut, serialization lent the Arabic novel its hopes and fears, apprehending through the merchant-capital-minded storyteller's frame tale a reconfigured mode of speculation in Arabic, pitched to the future: the simultaneous rise of finance capital and the serialized Arabic novel amid garden dreams of progress. And yet Zaydān's *Istibdād al-Mamālīk* is doing something else: still midstory when *Al-Hilāl* saw the end of its first year, Zaydān announced at the beginning of *Al-Hilāl*'s second year that the remainder of *Istibdād al-Mamālīk* would not be serialized in the pages of *Al-Hilāl* but rather would be sent to readers, and only at their behest, as a literary supplement. The sorts of frame tales that animated *A Thousand and One Nights* or Sindbad, those seas of stories told by the "trading seaman" returned from his journeys in Walter Benjamin's seminal essay "The Storyteller," had lent the early European novel and in turn the early Arabic novel their technology of serialized suspense. Yet 1890s Cairo is a moment in the history of the Arabic novel when Jurjī Zaydān begins to upend the ruses of storytellers past; it was becoming a time, as Benjamin had noted, when there is "no more weaving and spinning to go on while they are being listened to."[6]

Zaydān equivocated: for two years he did not serialize any novels in *Al-Hilāl*, and then in 1895, he returned to the serialized novel form with *Armānūsah al-Miṣriyyah*. The year 1895 witnessed a number of calamities caused by unruly caterpillars wreaking havoc on the Egyptian cotton and Syrian silk crops regularly appearing in scientific announcements and more politically minded editorials in *Al-Hilāl* and other Arabic journals concerned with science, agriculture, and industry, including *Al-Muqtaṭaf*. Economic misfortune hovered over the pages of the Arabic press, and yet the year Zaydān serialized *Armānūsah* in *Al-Hilāl* the journal witnessed a rapid increase in subscriptions that came as something of a shock to Zaydān.[7] Though cotton was in plight and silk in a state of blight, *Al-Hilāl*'s own affairs were on the rise. Zaydān's novels encoded the suspense of the ups and downs of the market as romance and history, turning away from both the material remainder that awaited his contemporary Cairo and the ruses and deceptions undoing its alchemical Edenic dreams.

If *Al-Muqtaṭaf* feared that the Arabic novel and press could not net future profit, the archive of first and second editions of *Al-Hilāl* reveals the novel's path to capitalization in Arabic, as it becomes untethered from the pages of the journal itself. First serialized midissue in 1892, in later years novels would appear at the end of an issue of *Al-Hilāl*; and still later in reprintings becoming a separate supplement appended at year-end. In an age of finance, Zaydān's novels turned away from the hope and fear attending the end of a monthly installment of a serialized novel to cultivate a new kind of posterity for the Arabic novel that could attend the dream of *Nahḍah* now casting Edenic fictions in the gardens of "the seedlings of the sciences and knowledge [*maghāris al-ʿulūm wa-l-maʿārif*] [that] had begun to grow [*tanmū*] in Egypt and Syria," and in its libraries.[8] As speculation hit a fever pitch in Cairo with the turn of the twentieth century, Zaydān imagined a novel in book form that could forget, that could seem to have never known how finance had reconfigured the silk and cotton markets of the region.

In *Given Time: I. Counterfeit Money*, Jacques Derrida reminds us that "the one who writes and his or her writing never give anything without calculating, consciously or unconsciously, its reappropriation, its exchange, or its circular return—and by definition this means reappropriation with surplus-value, a certain capitalization."[9] This kind of calculation in novel writing upset Egypt's "leading intellectuals," as the literary historian ʿAbd al-Muḥsin Ṭāhā Badr relates, filling them with scorn, anxiety and disapproval. The novel, Badr explains, had been seen as nothing more than "a means to promote the press [*wasīlah li-l-riwāj al-ṣuḥufī*]," making it "generally an object of disapproval [*istinkār*] among the leading intellectuals" of Egypt,[10] offering a history that both Samah Selim and Shaden Tageldin's recent research on Egyptian literature revisits.[11]

Badr identifies a category of Arabic novels at the turn of the twentieth century that he deems the *tiyār mā bayna al-taʿlīm wa-l-tasliyah wa-l-tarfīh*, or a trend that landed in an in-between, not entirely the stuff of pure edification (*tiyār al-taʿlīm al-khāliṣ*) but still falling under the overarching heading of "the edifying novel" (*al-riwāyah al-taʿlīmiyyah*). While edifying, Zaydān's novels had for Badr a taint of entertainment and diversion (*al-tasliyah wa-l-tarfīh*),[12] showing these categories to be something akin to poles at either end of a spectrum, terms of speculation on the long horizon of literary value, heralding rates of accumulation, capitalization, and amortization. Zaydān's fiction, beginning in 1892, "put entertainment in the service of knowledge,"[13] calibrating a space between edification and diversion, shuffling categories from older modalities of *adab* and the literary in Arabic, coming to mean differently in the late nineteenth century.

Attending to the archive of first and second printings of *Al-Hilāl*, we can see Jurjī Zaydān calculating the "reappropriation," the "exchange," and the "return" on his journal and the novels he published first serially, and later as literary supplements and stand-alone bound books. *Al-Muqtaṭaf* was not the only journal of the period doing the math. On a number of levels, the archival traces that the finances of publishing leave behind threaten the pure edification of the *Nahḍawī* dream, troubling the garden in which Zaydān's "seedlings of the sciences and knowledge" were growing. It was the "edifying novel"—*tiyār al-taʿlīm al-khāliṣ*—that for Badr would ward off this sense of uneasiness, narrate that ever-upward *telos* of rise, of the nation, of the *Nahḍah*'s persistent dream of renaissance and awakening, a dream that the novel's imbrications in the market interrupted with the promise of a fall. *Al-Muqtaṭaf* cautioned entrepreneurs against publishing Arabic scientific journals or novels for profit rather than pure edification; an empirical comparative literature, reading balance sheets along the axis of empire, the best Arabic's editors and novelists could hope for was 10 percent of the going rate in London, their pay in a state of perpetual *inḥiṭāṭ*. Zaydān looked at this same Arabic literary and periodical market and saw not *inḥiṭāṭ* but, like a revenant of 1870 Beirut, a chance for *Nahḍah*.

In 1870 Beirut, serialized novels briefly evoked the Edenic gardens of Damascus; its dreams of romance were upended by the early summer as tales of spiraling debt, ransom, and the shadow of locusts commanded the focus of Beirut's novel readers. The glittering gold invested in cultivating an edified reading public that had recently seemed to promise Arabic a future of progress instead found in the regular rejoinder "the remainder is to come" a current of anxious fear punctuating Arabic's new novels. *Al-Muqtaṭaf*'s editors critiqued the growing precarity of the Arabic press, the novel, and the region's lack of industry and commodity production; but Zaydān saw something else: a path in between, through the "seedlings of the sciences and knowledge," it leads Badr back to a garden—not those memorialized gardens of Beirut and Damascus but to Ezbekiyya, a garden of contradiction that in Zaydān's early novel *Asīr al-Mutamahdī* connoted the founding debts of British empire, and the intoxication of entertainment.

Searching for the immediate descendants of Jurjī Zaydān's fiction from the 1890s on, for authors whose work also fell between edification and diversion, Badr does not point to Yaʿqūb Ṣarrūf, or even Zaydān's Egyptian contemporary Muḥammad al-Muwayliḥī, or Faraḥ Anṭūn's *al-Dīn wa-l-adab wa-l-māl*, but instead turns up Al-Qāʾimqām Nasīb Bey's 1901 *Khafāyā Miṣr* (Secrets of Egypt), ʿAbd al-Ḥalīm al-ʿAskarī's really rather late (1927) novel *Suʿād,* and two novels—*al-Damʿ al-midrār fī al-maṣāʾib wa-l-maḍārr* (1898; Copious tears in calamities and losses) and *ʿIshq al-Marḥūm Muṣṭafā Kāmil wa-asmāʾ ʿashīqātihi* (1908; The passion of the departed Mustafa Kamel and the names of his lovers)—both signed only with initials: at the turn of the century, a novel of secrets and two hesitant signatories. It is, as Badr tells the reader, only "by chance" that these shy authors have made it into the literary register. The footnote for *al-Damʿ al-midrār fī al-maṣāʾib wa-l-maḍārr* tells us that while

> the author of the novel [*al-riwāyah*] did not want to divulge his name but rather designated it with two letters (R. G. in Egypt), the novel appeared in the year 1898 and was published by Jamʿiyat Mutanazzah al-Nufūs al-Adabiyyah [the Society of the Promenade of the Cultured Ones]. It appears that this novel's distribution was limited to a narrow circle of readers, and for that reason it is not indicated in the indexes of novels that I consulted rather I found it by chance in the stalls of Ezbekiyya [*muṣādafatan ʿalā sūr al-Azbakiyyah*].[14]

The author of *ʿIshq al-Marḥūm Muṣṭafā Kāmil wa-asmāʾ ʿashīqātihi*, too, "did not want to divulge his name but rather designated it with two letters"—this time "(A. F.)"—and "this novel, too, does not appear in indexes," but rather Badr "stumbled" upon it, too, "in the stalls of Ezbekiyya [*ʿathartu ʿalayhā ʿalā sūr al-Azbakiyyah*]."[15]

Badr stumbles upon these specters of Arabic novels that fall in between, *mā bayna* by chance in Ezbekiyya, book stalls now to be found along the paths to the bawdier entertainments of *Asīr al-Mutamahdī*'s late-1870s Cairo. Badr reads Zaydān's legacy through the ghostly traces of a genealogy of the Arabic novel, charting its course between edification and entertainment, the library and the bookstalls of Ezbekiyya, at the threshold of the *Nahḍah*'s gardens of knowledge and the un-Edenic speculations that haunted them. While Zaydān would leave Cairo Dār al-Hilāl, still publishing today, his name in gilt, in cheap newsprint, in so many Arabic libraries, and in every catalogue and bookstore, if also at every stall in Ezbekiyya, the authors of these novels, contemporary with Zaydān's growing series of historical novels, hesitate at the threshold: between edification and entertainment (*mā bayna al-taʿlīm wa-l-tasliyah*), making their way into the history of the Arabic novel only stumblingly, secretly, or by chance and initial. These novels, gathering the dust of years in Ezbekiyya as they await their chance encounter with Badr, betray, like Haykal signing as an Egyptian peasant, or *Al-Muqtaṭaf* publishing three novels on the heels of decades of disdain and critique, anxiety about the novel form. The dusty, spectral absence of the name of the author, its replacement by two letters here, two there, invite us to speculate as to what was at stake in being an editor and novelist in turn-of-the-century Cairo, a time when novel writing became "a thriving market, to which were attracted all who could hold a pen and tell the people a story."[16]

Journals and some novels were sold through subscription, and the process itself is the subject of a number of articles, letters, and announcements in Zaydān's *Al-Hilāl*. In 1900, in the section devoted to readers' letters, a curious Aḥmad ʿAbd al-Raḥmān expressed his "wonder at the reticence of some to pay for their subscriptions" to *Al-Hilāl* (a common refrain in other journals of the period, in both Cairo and Beirut). In his letter, ʿAbd al-Raḥmān—like the editors of *Al-Muqtaṭaf*, themselves fellow readers of *Al-Hilāl*—turned to British periodicals as a measure of successful business practices; their owners, ʿAbd al-Raḥmān pointed out, "do not send [their journals] except to those who have sent them payment for their subscription in advance."[17] Zaydān's response reveals a great deal about how he appraised the business prospects for an Arabic journal at the turn of the century; we see him "calculating" some of Derrida's "circular return" outside the colonial metropole:

> You are well aware that between our readers and English readers there is a considerable difference and that what befits one does not befit the other. We do not complain, however, of a small number of readers or from the stagnation of the commodity of literature [*kasād biḍāʿat al-adab*]. For the reception of knowledge and literature increases day by day and we have verified that through our practice of this industry [*ṣināʿah*] for almost ten years in this country. But we do complain of a habit among some of our readers. For among them is a group of people of wealth and culture [*al-tharwah wa-l-adab*] who you see with their desire to read *Al-Hilāl* and their praise of its design and their verbosity on its topics and their anxiety over its delay or interruption and their acknowledgment of its affordability and their desire to pay the cost of subscription and the availability of its price in their pockets—they, despite all of that, cannot bother themselves with the trouble of sending payment to the post office to wire to the administration of *Al-Hilāl* in Egypt or to exchange cash for postal stamps to send in a letter to the administration. . . . The way of the English and others among the nations of Europe of sending payment in advance is the best and simplest and most secure means, but we do not think that they arrived at it all at once, thus we hope that our esteemed readers will become accustomed to it gradually.[18]

Literature, then, is a "commodity," Arabic periodicals (for at least ten years) are "an industry," and the market for them is by no means, despite the concerns of the editors of *Al-Muqtaṭaf*, in a state of "stagnation." "Payment in advance" opens up a space time at the horizon of the future, which the British have "arrived at," though not "all at once," that, it is "hope[d]" the Arabic reader "will become accustomed to gradually."

Zaydān charts and calculates the capitalization of his journal in page after page of the archive of *Al-Hilāl*. An 1898 announcement to readers opens, "No two will differ on the wide extent of *Al-Hilāl*'s distribution and the magnitude of its readers for they number in the tens of thousands[19] and are spread across the kingdoms of the earth near and far, East and West, North and South." Zaydān is not only "calculating the return" on subscription payments from such an extensive readership but also staging another scene of capitalization, of "reappropriation with surplus-value"; Zaydān is selling *Al-Hilāl* to people who, presumably, have already bought it, and the effect is one of doubling, where not only Zaydān but also his readers in turn, are invited to capitalize on *Al-Hilāl*'s reputation and success. *Al-Hilāl*, just beginning its seventh year, is here being advertised as a journal so successful that "you scarcely know of a city or town or area in Egypt or Syria [*al-Shām*] to which *Al-Hilāl* has not been sent, to say nothing of its distribution in Europe and America." This, the reader comes to realize, is an advertisement for advertising. At the bottom of the page are listed rates by the page, half page, quarter page, and eighth of a page for advertisements appearing once, or repeatedly (six times, twelve times, eighteen times, twenty-four times). *Al-Hilāl*, Zaydān assures his readers, is the "best means for publishing advertisements among readers of Arabic"; it appears in "every city to which the Arabic language has spread," from the "Islands of the West Indies like Cuba, Puerto Rico, Santo Domingo" to "Mexico, Venezuela, Jamaica, all of Brazil, and in Argentina and Columbia" to "India, China, Japan, for it is widespread in Shanghai and Yokohama" and in "Calcutta, Hydrabad, Delhi, Burma, Bombay, and Lahore," not to mention "Singapore, the Philippines" and "Australia, Tasmania, New Zealand" and all over Persia, and of course in "Sudan," "Tunis, Algiers, Tripoli and Marrakesh," as well as "in Basra and Oman."[20] The reader and subscriber is invited to inhabit the role of would-be advertiser and join Zaydān in doing the math: how many cities, how often, in bold or fine print?

While in early issues of *Al-Hilāl* the journal published advertisements for books and local artisans in its pages, by the journal's fifth year, Zaydān had begun to issue a separate *bāb*, or section devoted to advertisements. In May 1897, Zaydān printed an advertisement for this section: "We direct the attention of doctors and pharmacists and inventors and merchants and all other types of businessmen to the advertisement section [*bāb al-iʿlānāt*] in *Al-Hilāl* for it has been proven in commerce and through experience that one *ghirsh* spent on it [advertising] returns to the owner of the advertisement thirty and sixty and a hundred [*ghirsh*] while it is known that *Al-Hilāl* is so widely distributed that it needs no proof."[21] The circular return, the reappropriation with surplus value, is here made plain: one *ghirsh* becomes thirty, sixty, one hundred. Businessmen, speculating on their own futures, should, Zaydān comforts them, find in *Al-Hilāl* a "proven" avenue for investment, so well established "it needs no proof."

The reader of *Al-Hilāl* in bound form—the only one generally available to researchers in the twenty-first century—is, however, unlikely to find this *bāb*, these traces of the commercial as it pressed against the literary journals of the period, for *bāb al-iʿlānāt* was published as a separate supplement. Contingent, of its moment, the commercial side of *Al-Hilāl* was not intended for the posterity of the bookshelf or the library. Rather, it was the stuff of *Al-Hilāl*'s own material present, Badr's "too commercial" showing through, alongside the novels Zaydān penned *mā bayna al-taʿlīm wa-l-tasliyah wa-l-tarfīh*.

A stray advertising supplement, however, slipped into *Al-Hilāl*'s archive, finding its way onto the shelves of Dār al-Hilāl's reading room library in Cairo, bound for posterity between the second and third issues of *Al-Hilāl*'s sixth year. Separately numbered, it contained advertisements for merchant cards;[22] an office in Paris;[23] the Al-Hilāl soap factory;[24] a French-Arabic dictionary of law and commerce terms;[25] a fabric shop with silks from India and Europe;[26] pills;[27] a journal to keep track of housekeeping;[28] a dentist;[29] the illustrator Salīm Ḥaddād;[30] another and less specialized French-Arabic dictionary;[31] a shop on Mūskī Street selling cigarettes and handkerchiefs of silk, toile, and cotton;[32] and an emulsion oil.[33] The commercial connections with Paris are unmistakable; the dominance of the pharmacy, the factory, and especially the international textiles market trace the contours of the advertisements punctuating issues of *Al-Hilāl*. Through this accident of the archive, this supplement separately printed and sent to subscribers of *Al-Hilāl*, "the commercial tendency" that Badr identified and decried in Syrian novels and journals from the turn of the century can be calibrated. Ephemeral and contingent, the supplement to a journal was supplemental not only to the periodical's contents but also because of ideas of what was fit for literary and cultural posterity.

Al-Hilāl was simultaneously a journal and a book publisher, maintaining an extensive inventory that was advertised in a separate, free book catalogue, a copy of which is announced in April 1897. Salīm Sarkīs, the editor of *Al-Mushīr*, having only two months previous heralded "The Migration of the Silkworm" from Beirut to Cairo (fleeing Ottoman *inḥiṭāṭ*),[34] received Zaydān's catalogue, announcing Zaydān's inventory of "most famous books" and "books for reading":[35] "The Al-Hilāl library in the capital [city of Cairo] has published a large list of about 80 pages of new books which will be sent for free to all who request it."[36] Zaydān announced that same year that *Al-Hilāl*'s Cairo offices also housed a newly opened bookstore and reading room,[37] and a "Special Announcement for Authors and Publishers" appeared in the pages of *Al-Hilāl:* "In encouragement of authors and to attract book printers and sellers we have made a special offer for book advertisements in the advertisements section of *Al-Hilāl* [*bāb iʿlānāt* Al-Hilāl]. We will not request the advertising fee for them in cash but rather will take its value in copies of the book being advertised such that those who wish to advertise a book or the like should contact the offices of *Al-Hilāl* in Egypt."[38] Jurjī Zaydān's capitalization on the return of his journal figured books themselves as a sort of currency. Zaydān's own writing, appearing in the pages of *Al-Hilāl,* had become so widely read and strategically capitalized that he was able to manipulate the "reappropriation with surplus-value" of his essays, novels, and editorials into not just advertising revenue and material for a reading room but also a press and bookstore through which he profited off the writing of others.

Subscribers to *Al-Hilāl* in later years were encouraged to purchase bound copies of previous years of the journal,[39] and as the rate of subscriptions to *Al-Hilāl* continued to rise over the 1890s, Zaydān had to reprint previous years for distribution as bound volumes destined for the growing private libraries of the *Nahḍah.* Something quite curious happened in the process, however, and again capitalization shows through in the pages of *Al-Hilāl,* leaving a palimpsestic trace that has confused a number of Zaydān critics over the years. In 1898, the second edition of the first year of *Al-Hilāl* appeared, carrying two dates: both 1892–93 and "the year 1898." The ephemeral materiality of 1892–93 competes in this new second edition with the literary capitalization afoot in *Al-Hilāl* by 1898. The picture of the khedive ʿAbbās in the seventh issue has been updated (his moustache is thicker and now turns up at the sides; he is considerably more decorated, as a sash intersects several medals; and he now looks at the reader straight on); a few novels published later in the 1890s are added to the list of books by Zaydān for purchase; some advertisements are replaced by others; but most striking at first is the shock at finding that the novel *Istibdād al-Mamālīk* has disappeared from the bound pages of *Al-Hilāl*'s first year. Previously meted out in installments in the middle of each issue, this 1898 bound volume and all subsequent reprints are short one incomplete serialized novel of oppressive Ottoman taxation.

Both original issues and later reprints of *Al-Hilāl*'s first year include an article entitled "Syrians in Egypt" ["al-Sūriyyūn fī Miṣr"], one that identifies a sense of envy among Arabic's readers as they apprehended an imperialist *Nahḍah* of industry and finance. The article reads as a caricature of Zaydān's fellow Syrian émigrés to Egypt. Coming from the "cradle of commerce [*al-tijārah*]" to Egypt in order to "promote their wares [*biḍāʾiʿihim*],"[40] Syrians are burdened with a terrible tendency toward "spending most of [their] time either at gambling establishments or reading novels or other things that do not greatly differ from those landing [them] in a state of confusion such that perhaps misery will lead [them] to emigrate to a place where no one knows" them, despite the Syrian being the "most skillful among them [the various peoples living in Egypt] in trade [*abwāb al-tijārah*] and the most capable among them in earning money [*iktisāb al-amwāl*]."[41] "Al-Sūriyyūn fī-Miṣr" reads like a critique of the turn-of-the-century Syrian that Badr could have written. Zaydān appears in later years determined to capitalize on this caricature, wooing his readers away from gambling establishments to spend their money instead on his journal, historical novels, books, or other edifying works available for perusal and sale through his reading room and bookstore, and worldwide by subscription.

In 1870s and 1880s Beirut, the gamblers were unproductive speculators and equivocating socialist protagonists; in 1890s Cairo, they are Syrian émigrés who would rather read novels than promote their wares. Beirut's hopeful gardens of knowledge sedimented in the Cairo garden of Ezbekiyya, where the many bad habits being debated in the Arabic press accrued, not least prostitution,[42] masturbation,[43] the imbibing of intoxicants, gambling,[44] and the funding of capitalist ventures with promissory notes and the promises of others. If reading, the press, and the literary in Arabic were offered in the late nineteenth century as an alternative to these dangerous tendencies, they likewise depended on the habituation of addiction and speculation—of readers, to borrow Zaydān's words, being "shackled by the chains of habit [*muqayyad bi-quyūd al-ʿādah*]"[45]—as they depended upon their readers in their other, thoroughly material role as subscribers.

Jurjī Zaydān was a literary capitalist at a moment when the Egyptian economy was the subject of extensive speculation—in the financial markets as in the pages of journals and novels—and his capitalization on his journal, books, and writing continued apace. Inspired perhaps by the great deal of gambling taking place in Beirut, Cairo, and other cities of the Arab world (not to mention the financial and real estate markets, the trading in cotton and silk futures (and their use as mortgage collateral), and other types of speculation under way), in 1898, *Al-Hilāl* announced its own lottery: Yā-Naṣīb *Al-Hilāl*.[46] Readers would find a number on the receipt they had received for full payment of their subscription, and this number entitled them to three opportunities each year to win a prize. This was both an incentive to readers to pay up and an invitation to speculate on and hope for a future literary windfall, and Zaydān points out in an announcement in early 1899 that the reader who wins once every ten years will have in effect been reimbursed "for everything he had paid for his subscriptions over that time period."[47] The first prize for the first drawing, held at 3:00 p.m. on December 31, 1898, and that went to Muḥammad Fuʾād of Port Said, was the value of ten years of subscription to *Al-Hilāl*—or 500 Egyptian *ghirsh* (Zaydān does the math for the reader)[48]—paid in francs (100 of them), along with "the entirety of the publications of the founder of *Al-Hilāl* well bound and gilded (as with all bindings of *Al-Hilāl*)."[49] In 1900, special offers were extended to paid subscribers, alongside the continuance of the *Al-Hilāl* lottery; subscribers received 20 percent off all of Jurjī Zaydān's works, as well as anything else published by the Al-Hilāl press, in addition to a discount of 5 percent on a suit at Zaydān's brother Yūsuf's shop in Egypt (only current receipts for *Al-Hilāl* subscriptions would be accepted).[50]

Heralding *Nahḍah*, finding profit in the "seedlings of the sciences and knowledge," Zaydān's novels would come to be offered, like the final installments of *Istibdād al-Mamālīk*, as a literary supplement to

Al-Hilāl. It might arrive in the mail with other supplements, like *Bāb al-Iʿlānāt*, featuring advertisements; or with the occasional book catalogue. Eventually stripped of the breaks that serialization would etch into the form, marking their historical contingency and the material needs of their author, Zaydān's novels became increasingly supplemental to *Al-Hilāl* as they approached the archive. Like advertisements for commodities that were simultaneously bought and sold in Zaydān's own historical moment and yet shielded from the posterity of the archive, a distance was staged through the literary supplement and Dār al-Hilāl's reprinting and binding practices through which serialized fiction was being distanced in the archive from the simultaneity of finance and fiction that appeared before the eyes of *Al-Hilāl*'s subscribers in the journal's first printing. At the insistence of its readers, in September 1896 *Al-Hilāl* created a separate section on commerce and trade—*bāb al-tijārah*—featuring detailed information on the stock and real estate markets as well as cotton prices. The following March, *Al-Hilāl* ran a story on political economy (*al-iqtiṣād al-siyāsī*). Zaydān reported that in England—the land of Cairo's occupiers, for whom Zaydān had served as translator during their Sudanese expedition—the study of political economy had "removed the veil from the border between the ruler and the ruled," leaving "the dominant class these days to see that the enlightenment of minds in this way was not in agreement with their interests." Zaydān identifies "a great need for books on this subject as what has been translated into our language is very little."[51] And yet as Cairo approached the crash of 1907, and even in its wake, Zaydān can be found repeatedly in the pages of *Al-Hilāl* not critiquing the financial markets for Egyptian cotton, real estate, and debt under British occupation but rather securing the capitalization of the Arabic novel by staging a turn away from the ruses of the market, the better to speculate in *Nahḍah*.

CHAPTER 6

It Was Cotton Money Now

Novel Material in Yaʿqūb Ṣarrūf's Turn-of-the-Twentieth-Century Cairo

Initially suspicious of the genre, by the early 1900s, *Al-Muqtaṭaf* editor Yaʿqūb Ṣarrūf began to translate and finally pen his own novels, published in monthly literary supplements to the journal. The speculative boom in stocks, cotton land, and Cairo real estate that would soon culminate in the crash of 1907 served as both the material for his first novel—*Fatāt Miṣr* (The girl of Egypt), serialized over the course of 1905—as well as the stuff of his own finances. It was something of a change of course for *Al-Muqtaṭaf*, founded in Beirut in 1876 as a beacon of science and home economics. Hailed in its time as the *shaykh* of Arabic journals,[1] previously *Al-Muqtaṭaf* could be found critiquing both the novel form and the concomitant habits of consumption and speculation restructuring the region's textiles industry in Arabic's first age of finance capital.[2]

In 1885 *Al-Muqtaṭaf* moved from a Beirut disappointed by returns on the silk industry and calling on locals to buy Syrian cloth, to a Cairo enamored of department stores and newly occupied by the British who would colonize it. The journal's editors, along with the many other Syrian émigrés who made that migration from Beirut to Cairo, were well poised to make out the signs of ruin stitched in the proliferation of stocks, mortgages, gambling, land development schemes, conspicuous consumption of European goods, and the stubborn flows of foreign capital. Ever threatened, the hope that this was *Nahḍah*, a time of resurgence and renaissance, was Cairo's as Beirut's, but as raw silk and cotton fibers continued to leave the Eastern Mediterranean for the factories of Europe, the balance of trade fell ever out of

Arabic's favor. The rise of finance capital in late nineteenth- and early twentieth-century Syria and Egypt was the rise, there as elsewhere, as Marx observed, of "fictitious capital,"[3] the stuff of hope and fear, and the novel, at least in Arabic, was its genre.

Fatāt Miṣr shares much in common with the earlier novels that Salīm al-Bustānī serialized in his family's Beirut journal *Al-Jinān* from 1870 to his untimely death in 1884, just before Ṣarrūf and coeditor Fāris Nimr themselves quit Beirut for Cairo. The reader uninitiated in the workings of the market—in how textiles futures, commodities trades, international lines of credit and insurance, and the private Arabic press itself were reshaping the region's economy through the industrialization and capitalization of silk and cotton—would have struggled to parse the plotline of serialized novels like al-Bustānī's *Bint al-ʿaṣr* (1875) or *Sāmiyyah (*1882–84), never mind Ṣarrūf's *Fatāt Miṣr.* But it was all eerily familiar. The many characters who speculate in cotton, stocks, and real estate in the early twentieth-century Cairo of *Fatāt Miṣr* are revenants of Beirut and its novels, of silk financiers, gambling socialists, tempted youth, and dishonest brokers, and of the disappointed dreams of material rise and progress they had cultivated. It was a fear of devolution, of *inḥiṭāṭ* that Jurjī Zaydān briefly revived in his early 1892 serialized novel *Istibdād al-Mamālīk* [The oppression of the Mamlūks], a tale of Ottoman taxation in the markets of Cairo, before staging a break between finance and the fictions of the novel as he persistently beheld instead an age of *Nahḍah.*

With scenes in Cairo, London, Tokyo, St. Petersburg, and the coast of India, the increasingly interwoven world of global finance articulates the rise and fall of Ṣarrūf's *Fatāt Miṣr.* Readers are left in suspense to wonder what might happen next as characters are shipwrecked in the Red Sea on their return from a business trip to Tokyo; as Cairo's markets rise and fall; as a London business deal presents an opportunity to speculate in cotton land; while Japanese securities are balanced against Russian as spies flit across the globe—and this is, of course, a love story, too. Engaged in the textiles trade, real estate speculation, and prospecting in cotton land, the characters of *Fatāt Miṣr* chart a financial web connecting Cairo to the world economy; and the happy-ending wedding culminates in yet another garden of the *Nahḍah*: a celebration of Egyptian-British cotton deals, a cosmopolitan, electrically lit Eden of empire.

If the speculative economy surrounding textiles—and particularly silk and cotton—repeatedly appears in the plotlines of Arabic novels from at least Khalīl al-Khūrī's 1859 Aleppo-based serialized novel *Way, idhān lastu bi-ifranjī* (Alas, I am not a foreigner), it is because the novel is a fiction of capital. Those "unconfessed but poorly disguised" dreams of progress observed by the French in Beirut,[4] the ever-impending threat of ruin, the surety that "no one is sure of his tomorrow"[5] noted in consular reports is also true of Cairo under the British, and it is the affective infrastructure of the serialized novel; the form's rise in Arabic cathects the rise of a new kind of speculation, eclipsing local markets and precipitating capital flight as it underwrites both fiction and finance.

This earlier history of the Arabic novel haunts ʿAbd al-Muḥsin Ṭāhā Badr's seminal *Taṭawwur al-riwāyah al-ʿarabiyyah al-ḥadīthah fī Miṣr* (The development of the modern Arabic novel in Egypt) discussed in chapter 5. For Badr, the literary efforts of Syrian émigrés to Egypt remained "too commercialist [*tijārī*]."[6] Bearing too much of the market, of the novel's debts there, Badr and many an Arabic literary critic favored the novel of the nation, something more like *Zaynab* or the literary production of later *nahḍawīs* like Ṭāhā Ḥusayn. That history of the Arabic novel eschews the market for the "rural imaginary" that so captivated later Egyptian novelists, a story that Samah Selim charts in her book *The Novel and the Rural Imaginary in Egypt: 1880–1985*.[7] It is the sort of novel that Benedict Anderson imagines for the nation, bounded by borders and tethered to the land, superseding an earlier geography of urban imperial centers. For Anderson, the newspaper is the novel's hyperform, a "one-day bestseller" that enacts his eponymous *Imagined Communities* of the nation.[8] The novel and the newspaper's rise in Arabic cathected a moment, though not yet of the nation-states that comprise our modern Middle East but rather of the rending of the Ottoman Empire's integrity by a new imperial order and its attendant finance capital.

Fatāt Miṣr, entrenched in the ups and downs of international finance, would be quickly forgotten and critically neglected for years to come. In 1921, Mayy Ziyādah, a prominent Syrian émigrée to Cairo, sent Ṣarrūf a letter, recounting a recent discussion of the novel at her weekly salon in Cairo,[9] which served as a key institution of the *Nahḍah*:

> I mentioned it [*Fatāt Miṣr*] before many of the literati and educated individuals who themselves were not endowed with the ability to write but had been following the literary movements of the *Mashriq* [Arab East], and I found that all of them were ignorant of its

> existence. Later one of them informed me that he had searched for it in bookstores and found no trace of it, and that the owners of some of the bookstores made it clear that they doubted your ability to write a novel or something like one [*riwāyah aw shibh riwāyah*]. He added that he had spoken to a group of fellow intellectuals [*akhwānihi bi-l-qalam*] concerning it and did not find them to be any more knowledgeable of it than he himself was. He concluded emphasizing that I was the only person who had told him that you had composed this novel and two or three others. . . . So I have come to you hoping that you will republish [it].[10]

At a time when new journals dedicated exclusively to the novel were beginning to appear,[11] when Zaydān's novels were entering their second and third editions, having taken flight from the pages of *Al-Hilāl*, Ṣarrūf's own forays in the genre were overlooked and forgotten by readers and booksellers alike. The very idea that such a prominent intellectual, renowned as a purveyor of edifying scientific knowledge in his capacity as editor of *Al-Muqtaṭaf*, would consider dabbling in the genre was cause to doubt that such a novel as *Fatāt Miṣr* even existed.

Indeed, *Fatāt Miṣr*'s serialization represented a change of course for *Al-Muqtaṭaf*, a journal that had persistently expressed concern at the material and moral dangers of investing in the novel form.[12] But by 1905, Yaʿqūb Ṣarrūf could himself be counted not just a translator (he had been doing that for some time), but also a novelist. Reminiscent of the departed Salīm al-Bustānī's novels published in *Al-Jinān* during *Al-Muqtaṭaf*'s Beirut years, and in format quite like the more recent successes of Jurjī Zaydān's historical fiction being offered in regular supplements to his journal, in January 1905 *Al-Muqtaṭaf* contained an announcement for Ṣarrūf's first novel, *Fatāt Miṣr*, that read: "We included as a supplement to this issue of *Al-Muqtaṭaf* four chapters of an entertaining literary novel [*riwāyah adabiyyah fukāhiyyah*] in which we aimed to include the most famous events that occurred in the past year and the most important social and philosophical subjects that scholars are presently researching."[13] Serialized as a supplement to *Al-Muqtaṭaf*, *Fatāt Miṣr* was advertised as a thoroughly edifying literary endeavor (if also an entertaining one). As readers awaited each month the remainder of the novel to come, the suspense that *Fatāt Miṣr* generated was a suspense born in tension with the hopes and fears of its own historical conjuncture.

Like Zaydān's 1895 *Armānūsah al-Misriyyah*, Ṣarrūf's 1905 serialized novel *Fatāt Miṣr* drew readers to *Al-Muqtaṭaf* in a way that its edifying scientific articles could not. The popularity of the novel form, its very ability to hold an audience who might otherwise be consumed with following an edifying history or serialized scientific study, was a cause of anxiety. One of Ṣarrūf's students from the Syrian Protestant College, Jabr Ḍūmiṭ, who had accompanied Zaydān on his sea voyage to London, wrote a critique of Ṣarrūf's novel, which ran the next year as a long article in *Al-Muqtaṭaf*, later to be reprinted as part of a critical introduction when the novel appeared in book form. Ḍūmiṭ's critique was thorough and very much in the first person, betraying a keen sense of fiction's entertaining and edifying potential. Of *Fatāt Miṣr*, Ḍūmiṭ wrote, "Truth be told I often would first read [the novel] before the remaining articles in *Al-Muqtaṭaf* not simply for the pleasure and entertainment intended in the writing of most novels but also for the architectural and political facts [it contained] and the manner in which it gestured toward reforming morals and habits and presenting some of what harms us."[14] Despite the novel's later fate among Cairo booksellers and their customers, in 1905, Ḍūmiṭ was not at all alone among *Al-Muqtaṭaf*'s readers in his impatience to read *Al-Muqtaṭaf*'s literary supplement: "As for the entertainment [*fukāhah*] in [the novel] I can attest that the author gave it its due in terms of the readers' yearning for the novel and their address within it and what I know of this matter I know from myself and my household and some of my friends who read *Al-Muqtaṭaf* for all of them, if *Al-Muqtaṭaf* was one day late imagined it to be a week and most of them from what I know turned first upon its arrival to *Fatāt Miṣr*."[15] At the moment of its serialization, *Fatāt Miṣr* captivated its audience, for whom the arrival of each installment of the novel marked the very passage of time.

Even for so educated a reader of *Al-Muqtaṭaf* as his own former student Jabr Ḍūmiṭ, Ṣarrūf's novel, issued in serialized literary supplements over the course of 1905, threatened to overwhelm the contents of the journal itself. Ḍūmiṭ's contemporary review focuses in particular on an excerpt from this edifying, entertaining novel fit for "the hands of our youth," that sheds light on what it was about this novel that felt so pressing to a 1905 audience, and yet so thoroughly forgettable less than two decades later. Ḍūmiṭ lingers over an excerpt from the novel depicting the figure of Lord Banshīld, a British newspaper mogul and venture capitalist, possessing

> more than thirty million pounds in wealth and a daily income of more than three thousand, while I heard that what he spends on

> himself in terms of food and drink and clothing is not more than three pounds per day. He eats in the morning an egg and drinks a cup of milk and coffee and eats in the afternoon a piece of fish and a piece of meat and some bread and vegetables and fruit and something like that in the evening . . . and he dresses like the simplest of people and he is nothing but an agent of his wealth concerned day and night with its investment and profits.[16]

He is one of those financiers who might have appeared in a novel by Salīm al-Bustānī, and yet in early twentieth-century Egypt, on the eve of a 1907 real estate and stock collapse brought on by high finance and capitalist speculation in the stock markets, he is not a well-dressed broker playing the markets of Beirut but rather one Lord Banshīld, an Englishman who is "nothing but an agent of his wealth concerned day and night with its investment and profits." *Fatāt Miṣr* offered to Ḍūmiṭ and his contemporaries a narrative of the international workings of finance, not at all the sort of novel that Zaydān, Badr, or Anderson imagined for the nation-to-come.

Serialized Arabic novels like *Fatāt Miṣr* would be read and reread, not only serially but later as a book. At the end of the year, readers would have individual issues of a journal bound together as a single volume, with the literary supplement affording the same possibilities for the novel. Subsequent editions of novels could be purchased as bound volumes as well, and novels would circulate between family members and friends, as well as through lending libraries. After having "read [*Fatāt Miṣr*] in sections at the time of its publication," Ḍūmiṭ then "returned to read it as a bound volume [*mujalladatan*] twice," which, as he recalls, "only increased my wonder at it and I remained of the opinion that it is among the best [of the novels] that have been written for edifying our youth and it is the most appropriate book up to now and we would do well to place it in the hands of our youth and ask that our schools read it."[17] Ḍūmiṭ sent his son a bound edition of *Fatāt Miṣr*; only twelve, he was just the sort of youth who could be edified by a novel like *Fatāt Miṣr*, a novel that Ḍūmiṭ was "not afraid of reading . . . to my student or to my son or daughter."[18]

Ḍūmiṭ's salutary review of *Fatāt Miṣr* extols the novel's ability to edify an audience given to speculating. His son, Ḍūmiṭ details, was moved by the character Amīn's "disgust at the stock market . . . the extent of his disdain for it and for those who ignorantly get swept up in its operations." Ḍūmiṭ continues: "He was entertained in his reading of it and benefited from it and the least of what he gained from it (and the greatest of its benefits) is that it gave birth within him to a strong disgust and displeasure with this hellish trap that has taken the wealth of many of our merchants and sons of the rich and powerful among us."[19] If the novel itself might be a commodity, it had the unique property in its most edifying and beneficial form—perhaps the likes penned by Ṣarrūf and read by the likes of Ḍūmiṭ's son—to be read and reread as a warning against the "hellish trap" of the imperial patterns of financial speculation that accompanied first the disappointments in Beirut's silk futures and soon the collapsing stock and real estate markets of Egypt. That novel, the one that Badr would disdain as being too commercial, could figure as an affective hedge against the loss of future wealth, against the fate of, as Ḍūmiṭ would have it, so "many of our merchants and sons of the rich and powerful among us," a fate that would only become more common come the 1907 crash. A warning against following an ill-fated path of speculation to ruin, the novel that absorbed the reading public in financial intrigue dreamed of a different sort of *nahḍah* to come.

The novel of finance that could both entertain and edify kept dangerous company. In 1905, the same year that *Al-Muqtaṭaf* published *Fatāt Miṣr* in monthly literary supplements to the journal, the journal also ran an article on the views of a range of British critics on the benefits and perils of novel reading. One Englishman saw something in the novel form that was not unlike what Ḍūmiṭ's son found: "The reason for the tendency of people to read [novels] is that the life of the industrialist and the worker and the merchant constricts the chest and restricts the soul. The preoccupations of modern civilization and its many worries lead people to seek deliverance [*khalāṣ*] from that condition either through physical exercise such as playing or through mental exercise like reading novels."[20] A space apart, figuring a geography not of nations but rather a place where "the industrialist" or "worker" or "merchant" might find some deliverance from capitalism's tendency to "constrict the chest and restrict the soul," that might save its readers from the "hellish trap of the stock market," novels were invested with the hope of a supracapitalist utopia of "deliverance" from "the preoccupations of modern civilization and its many worries."

It was a space not unlike that offered by the gardens of Beirut's early press—the likes of Salīm al-Bustānī's *al-Huyām fī jinān al-Sham* (Love in the gardens of Damascus) serialized in *Al-Jinān* (the journal title itself indexing so many gardens)—where speculative salvation from the perils of the financial market and the constricted lives lived under modern capitalism, with its unnerving tendencies toward crash and ruin, could be found. At the same time, however, the novel genre channeled a sense of attendant madness, of *junūn* that, in the minds of some, was not unlike addiction. One British novelist attested that "writing novels caused a nervous weakness in me from which I did not heal save from regularly playing ball," and a fellow countryman saw that "allowing the reading of novels to a degree resembling madness [*al-junūn*] led to weaknesses in the social structure."[21] Proffering both the promise of paradise—of *al-jannah*—and the threat of madness—of *al-junūn*—the addictive quality of serialized novels attracted subscribers of journals to their pages, as Ḍūmiṭ's personal experiences of reading and rereading *Fatāt Miṣr* in *Al-Muqtaṭaf* in 1905 and 1906 attest. Novels were commodities, indeed commodities to be consumed, that could promote the sale of journals, distract readers from matters scientific, make a day seem as long as a week; but they could also be bound, reread, offering sites of refuge from the uncertain future of finance capitalism in early twentieth-century Arabic.

For Badr and his study of the Arabic novel's development in Egypt, this is not what Arabic novels should have been doing. Badr somewhat disdainfully affiliates the legacy of the Syrian influence in Egypt with the novel as a "means for press promotion [*li-l-rawāj al-ṣuḥufī*],"[22] rather ambivalently noting the centrality of turn-of-the-century Syrian literary and press activity to the future of the novel form in Arabic. Badr laments that Arabic prose narrative through to the First World War (and perhaps not coincidentally therefore through the death of Jurjī Zaydān in 1914) "continued to turn in the same circle that the Syrian emigrants had delineated for it through imitation of the Western novel that pleased the popular taste of audiences of readers and that was dominated by a commercial [*tijāriyyaḥ*] tendency."[23] Syrian émigrés, Badr tells us,

> tried from the beginning of the Occupation to advance a *new* form in the literary arts which was the art of the novel [*al-fann al-riwāʾī*]. . . . Among the greatest factors that encouraged them in advancing this art was their control of journals like *Al-Muqtaṭaf* and *Al-Hilāl* and *Al-Jāmiʿah* and newspapers such as *Al-Ahrām* and *Al-Muqaṭṭam*. They were thus in need of attracting the greatest number of readers, and as the major intellectuals were not interested in novels [*riwāyāt*] during this period, the owners of journals and newspapers aimed to attract audiences of readers from the types of intellectuals

> who had grown in number since the age of Ismāʿīl and the [British] Occupation.[24]

The rise of the novel in Arabic was a product of *hijrah* from Beirut to Cairo, played out in the journals of Cairo that inherited Salīm al-Bustānī's Beirut and a new kind of reader under the British occupation, someone like *Asīr al-Mutamahdī*'s Shafīq, and his mother.

Intense debates in the Arabic press over the financial speculation in cotton, land, and stocks reshaping British Egypt in *Fatāt Miṣr* punctuated the Arabic press of the very early twentieth century. In the pages of *Al-Muʾayyad* in 1905, "airy speculations" and cotton worms were the twin plagues threatening Egypt's future.[25] The fertility of Egypt as a hopeful source of endlessly growing wealth was advertised widely in Cromer's reports as in the pages of the international press, earning it, "the reputation of an Eldorado of which the fabulous prosperity offered something truly supernatural. Capital imported from overseas doubled there in but a few months. Each [new] enterprise enriched its promoters before even being realized."[26] "Truly supernatural" fictions of the future became the stuff of material gain even as they were yet to be "realized," the better to be traded, and yet this Eldorado of finance capital was underwritten by financial tools that, even as they posed as securing investments—offering stocks as collateral against mortgages—whispered, too that the future was uncertain, and all might be lost.

For Yaʿqūb Ṣarrūf, a son of Beirut and coeditor of one of the most important journals of the *Nahḍah*, this "Eldorado . . . of fabulous prosperity" was a site of financial speculation in fictitious capital that saturates the plotline of *Fatāt Miṣr*. This 1905 novel that Ḍūmiṭ and his son read as a warning against the "hellish trap" of the stock market, could, however, at the same time be read not so much as a warning *against* but rather as an apprenticeship *in* practices of financial speculation. The novel manipulates both surface appearances and the deceptions that would produce real, material, widespread financial ruin come the 1907 crash, keeping readers in suspense. *Fatāt Miṣr* plots out how best to irrigate land to make it fertile for cotton; the likely sites of Cairo's apartments of the future; the dishonest dealings of Cairo's Jewish stockbrokers; British finance capital's insatiable and constant, imperially motivated wandering of the globe in search of high returns; and the global circuits connecting Cairo, Beirut, St. Petersburg, London, and hundreds of other cities, including

Tokyo, site of its own industrial, financial, and literary *nahḍah.* The romances animating the novel chart the distances finance was opening up between would-be lovers, their longings and affections serving as tenuous vectors of investment and speculation, imagining a future return.

Finance saturates the plot of *Fatāt Miṣr.* If Amīn's literal downfall (he trips on the tram tracks, too preoccupied by the stock market to see the oncoming car) is brought on by a trade of cotton shares driven by a compulsion that can only be likened to the addictive qualities of gambling; and if Amīn's first mistake was to trust ʿAzrah the stockbroker to be honest in both letter and word; in the end the audience is nonetheless left to celebrate the meting out of a British financier's cotton shares to fellow financiers in Cairo on the eve of an engagement. To understand this novel, one must understand how the stock and real estate markets work, must imaginatively inhabit the hopes and fears for material gain that undergird and set into circulation a financial system of bills of exchange, corporate shares, bonds, and debt that was reconfiguring both cotton land and urban spaces of the future.

Finance capital was, for Marx, "fictitious capital." All the capital in Ṣarrūf's *Fatāt Miṣr* or al-Bustānī's *Bint al-ʿaṣr* or any other novel is, of course, fictitious, enacting the fictitiousness of finance capital and its reliance on conventions of storytelling, suspense, and a dream of rise, of *nahḍah. Fatāt Miṣr* tells of a contemporary Cairo of familiar landmarks (the Splendid Bar, the Hotel Savoy, ʿAbdīn palace, and the railway station); and imaginary mortgages, bonds, bills of exchange, and cotton shares as they rise and fall in value, making money for some, leading others to despair, and in turn decisively changing both the urban and rural landscape of Egypt into real estate.[27] *Fatāt Miṣr,* its characters, and its readers all speculate in fictitious capital. Like Salīm al-Bustānī's *Bint al-ʿasr* thirty years prior in Beirut, *Fatāt Miṣr* neither encodes nor allegorizes the ups and downs of finance as seen from Cairo but rather lays them out before readers, revealing their fictions to be Arabic's very own, and the novel form to be saturated in finance capital.

Fatāt Miṣr, serialized in *Al-Muqtaṭaf* in the early twentieth century, is the story of the flight of commodity capital into the stuff of finance and fiction. As Jameson observes of finance capital's accumulation, the plot runs like this: "It was cotton money, or wheat money, textile money, railroad money, and the like. Now, like the butterfly stirring within the chrysalis, it separates itself from that concrete breeding ground and prepares to take flight."[28] All over Cairo, and in London, Tokyo, New York, and St. Petersburg—indeed, everywhere this novel's plot, like capital, would rove, seeking the next Eldorado—a sense of a butterfly stirring within a chrysalis, of the vertigo and potential volatility of a *nahḍah*, is palpable. Ṣarrūf, like al-Bustānī, al-Shalfūn, and al-Khūrī before him, writes fictions of capital.

One morning in *Fatāt Miṣr,* Lāvī, a wealthy Jewish Egyptian financier and landowner, awoke [*nahaḍa*] and began "thinking about matters of time,"[29] plotting out the rise and fall of markets. Turning first to the recent outbreak of the Russo-Japanese War and Japan's invasion of Manchuria, Lāvī thinks of how, with the fall of Russian bonds, "many financiers [*māliyīn*] went bankrupt." Next he ponders how "cotton rose and then fell and many of his friends lost [money] with its fall and especially Amīn ibn Wāṣif." The volatility of the cotton markets vexes Lāvī, who next considers the British bonds he holds, bonds he decides he should sell. Looking at a map, Lāvī decrees that for the moment, "I will limit my affairs to Egypt for the profits in it will increase with the increase in building and the rise in the population. We should focus on the suburbs of the capital [*ḍawāḥī al-ʿāṣamah*] and buy everything that we can in terms of soil and sand [*al-aṭyān wa-l-ramāl*] because all of it is destined to become land for building."[30] This is a scene of Lāvī's capital doing just what Jameson tells us it will, namely "jostling for more intense profitability." *Fatāt Miṣr* is a story in which finance capital appears repeatedly as a character in and of itself; it takes, again as Jameson tells us it will, "the form of speculation itself: specters of value, as Derrida might put it, vying against each other in a vast, worldwide, disembodied phantasmagoria." Lāvī's capital enters this phantasmagoria in the form of Russian bonds, rising and falling against British bonds, cotton shares, and plots of soil and sand in Cairo's future.

At the beginning of the twentieth century, the volatility of returns on Egyptian cotton meant that the price of land was unstable, though credit in various forms was available, good conditions for financial speculation, and, in Ṣarrūf's hands, for staging the fictions of finance capital. While there is no shortage of personages in this long novel, at moments the plot reads like an expanded version of Jameson's tale of the adventures of finance, as so many "specters of value . . . v[ie] against each other in a vast, worldwide, disembodied phantasmagoria." Take, for instance, a scene in which Lāvī encounters Shaykh Aḥmad who has just returned from Upper Egypt, and Lāvī's ensuing monologue:

> This rise [in the value of cotton land in the Ṣaʿīd] will not last long unless the price of cotton remains high, for if it falls a lot of people will be forced to sell what is dear cheap for last year the price of Egyptian cotton was approximately 18 million pounds and the entire country's exports [*ṣādirāt*] exceeded 20 million pounds, so if the price of a *qanṭār* of cotton fell one pound, and returned to two and a half pounds for instance, and this is not impossible, the value of exports would decrease six million pounds and the country would lose that and would not be able to otherwise compensate for it, as the value of its exports is more than 16 million pounds in addition to the servicing of its debt, and the debts of the government are approximately five million pounds, and if we added the price of exports and what tourists spend annually the total would not exceed what must be paid in terms of the price of imports and interest on the country's debts.[31]

When Shaykh Aḥmad then asks, "So do you expect then that the price of land will fall?," Lāvī informs him that "this depends on the price of cotton," mapping out the Egyptian economy's connectedness to the world economy not only through imports and exports but also through cotton fields in the United States and factories in Lancashire. The value of land is pegged to the price of cotton: "If the price of cotton stays as it is then [land] prices will rise as well and if it falls then prices would fall not long after that as many would need to sell their land. The catastrophe is for the one in debt[;] as for the one who is not in debt he is master of his time and has no fear as the product of his land satisfies its owners regardless of what happens."[32] In *Fatāt Miṣr*, specters of value hover over the cotton fields, and this fictitious capital often governs the plot. Fictitious capital visits its materiality upon those living in villas, as upon those addled by debt, whose land is mortgaged. Readers, protagonists, the narratability of the plot, and its apportioning out through suspense are all riveted to the price of cotton and the fictions of finance capital that threaten the Eldorado of Egypt and its gardens.

The novel opens "in one of the new quarters of the City of London where there is less traffic and more open space without buildings." There, the reader discovers "a large house or rather a magnificent palace built in the style of the old fortresses and surrounded by a vast, lush garden of intertwined branches in which the winds of autumn danced in the trees and verdant plants." Inside the London garden, "in a large room among the rooms of this house, heated by forced steam through pipes connecting the depths of the home where [the steam] is born and pushing it to all the rooms of the house . . . lit by electricity and in which are all sources of comfort and delight not to mention what it contains in the way of elegant furnishings and appointments," sit Henry and Dora, whose father, Sir Edward Brown, has just stood up from the table and headed to his office. Sir Edward is the owner of the *London News* and "earned from his newspaper a vast fortune for in one day during the days of the Boer War he would print more than one million, three hundred thousand copies. He turned the newspaper into a corporation with eight hundred thousand pounds in capital and founded other newspapers of different types with high circulations."[33] Like Lāvī, Sir Edward Brown—along with fellow members of the Press Club [*nādi al-ṣiḥāfah*] in London, such as Sir Henry Gray, owner of the *London Post*, and Sir Campbell Car, owner of the journal *Al-Mashriq* (*The East*), and other "owners of daily newspapers and weekly and monthly journals" including Lord Banshīld[34]—is concerned about American dominance in the cotton markets and what it means for those dreaming of Eldorado and prospecting in Egyptian land.[35] Sending Henry and Dora to Cairo, with the backing of the Press Club, Sir Brown entrusts his children to "discover the means by which the growing of cotton in Egypt can be increased,"[36] as capital from the British press, profiting off wars of empire, now (as Jameson said it would) "jostles for more intense profitability" in Cairo's cotton fields.

The novel's serialized format, meted out in monthly installments, generated a considerable degree of suspense among its readers as they wondered what was going to happen next, as Ḍūmiṭ's narrative attests. To be in suspense in this novel, though, is to impatiently await what capital will do next. Once in Cairo, Henry and Dora attend a ball at ʿAbdīn Palace, where they, along with the novel's readers, meet Wāṣif Bey, who explains to a Henry tasked with the project of speculating in Egyptian cotton, the centrality of irrigation to future land values:

> Widening the extent of summer agriculture depends on the presence of enough water in the summers and upon undertaking the engineering projects necessary for that. As for now, the waters of the Nile that recede throughout the summer and are stored in cisterns are not enough for most of what is planted in Egypt in terms of cotton, but if the reserves in cisterns were increased to double their hold of water and engineering projects were undertaken when the Nile is at its height such that much of its water was not lost the available water would be increased as well as the reserves and we could plant in

> terms of cotton double what we plant now, or put otherwise we could plant three million *faddan*s rather than one and a half million.[37]

Egyptian cotton would be so abundant, Wāṣif tells Henry, it could replace 5 million *bālah* of American cotton in the factories of England.[38] Industrial irrigation is central to this plot to invest in Egypt, and the need to materially intervene in managing agricultural cotton land in the Egyptian countryside is relayed by letter back to Sir Brown in London.

This novel, like others serialized in journals of Beirut and Cairo, revives a long tradition of the garden as site of knowledge and narrative:[39] the novel opens onto the garden of Sir Edward Brown's home on the outskirts of London, and it closes in the Cairo garden of Wāṣif Bey, whose daughter Bahiyyah has just been engaged to Sir Brown's son Henry. These fertile gardens enact a utopia of British financial intervention in the Egyptian economy, patterns of cultivation, and agriculture. The engagement party for Henry and Bahiyyah is attended by a cosmopolitan bourgeoisie whose members rejoice at the prospect of a future union of "East and West."[40]

These choice clippings, serialized as a supplement to *Al-Muqtaṭaf*, like al-Bustānī's narratives in the gardens of *Al-Jinān* and al-Shalfūn's flower of *Al-Zahrah* before it, are novels: *riwāyāt*. *Fatāt Miṣr*, as it identifies the centrality of irrigation to speculating in Egyptian cotton and land, once again annexes to the garden geography of *adab*, science, and knowledge an older etymology for the novel, one that, like speculating in cotton land, depends on irrigation (*al-rayy*). The Nile waters of the future are imagined in the pages of this *riwāyah* to flow at the behest, though, not of Arabic fictions of capital, but of those animating British capitalism in an age of empire. *Fatāt Miṣr* is a *riwāyah* in a garden of speculation, governed by the fictions of global capital.

Lāvī, Henry Brown and his father, Wāṣif and his son Amīn, and the stockbroker ʿAzrah and his agents all play a part in narrating the flow of capital in this novel, as profits accrue in the banks of London. The novel briefly breaks with its focalization around this international bourgeoisie comprised of agents of finance capital to attend to the voice of "the people" in chapter 25. While the novel is a cosmopolitan dream of literary, cultural, and economic *nahḍah*, that plotline is briefly suspended for a section narrated by "the people," an interlude that reminds readers of the fate of those being impoverished through debt and financial speculation. The chapter warns that this is happening all over the globe at the behest of "a group" that "is not satisfied with their lot . . . but rather you see them always in a state of avarice and greed that cannot be slaked or sated."[41] They are the contemporary "lords of wealth [*arbāb al-amwāl*] and those who resemble them among those who win from the loss of another."[42]

Fatāt Miṣr, despite the brief interjection by the voice of the people, is the story of this group that hopes to "win from the loss of another." In the closing pages of the novel, this includes not only the financiers and governing elite as might be expected, but among the "heads of trade," "directors of companies," and "property holders," we find too the "newspaper owners." Though as Ilham Khuri-Makdisi shows in her recent book *The Eastern Mediterranean and the Making of Global Radicalism, 1860–1914*, a discourse on socialism was now to be found with some regularity in an Arabic journal like *Al-Muqtaṭaf*,[43] the materiality of journal publishing cast newspaper owners such as Ṣarrūf and his coeditor Nimr, and al-Khūrī, al-Bustānī, al-Shalfūn, and Zaydān as well, in a role that paid "less than a little." Looking to the market, both Nimr and Ṣarrūf, as Thomas Philipp shows in his study *The Syrians in Egypt*, like Henry's father, Sir Edward Brown, and the financier Lāvī in *Fatāt Miṣr*, speculated in Egyptian land. In 1903, Ṣarrūf purchased 141 *faddān*s, and in 1906, Nimr and Ṣarrūf together, on the eve of the 1907 crash, purchased 781 *faddān*s.[44]

Fatāt Miṣr fictionalizes contemporary acts of speculation, exposes the serialized novel's imbrications in the kind of suspense tethering the financial markets of Egypt, its fictitious capital of futures, securities, and mortgages, already cross-collateralized by empire. The section devoted to the people is cut off by the voice of a narrator whom the reader, suddenly interpellated, has not yet encountered. The reader must leave "the people" behind to track these global flows of capital. The older kinds of stories that used to be narrated in Arabic at the edges of its markets here decisively give way; as Benjamin so tellingly observed, there is "no more weaving and spinning to go on while they are being listened to."[45] The narrator in *Fatāt Miṣr* almost rides the telegraph and telephone wires, announcing: "We will now travel with the reader to four capitals, and they are London, St. Petersburg, Tokyo and Cairo and hear what is being said in them that relates to the matters of our novel." In London, the reader encounters "three of the biggest financiers sitting in a room elegantly furnished and appointed, heated by steam pipes at times of cold and cooled by electric fans at times of heat and connected by the telegraph and telephone wires to most European and American capitals."[46] *Fatāt Miṣr* stages the global "meanwhile" of capital: Lord Banshīld and his financier friends are discussing profits in the tobacco and opium trades in an opulent London suite, while in St. Petersburg, Margiyūs and Fladimīr discuss the minister of war's recent telegram. In Tokyo, the minister of information, the minister of finance, and the minister of the navy, after reading the latest news via telegraph, discuss their war debts; and in Cairo, Esther and Bahiyyah "curse the stock market, for it kills the noble soul and weakens its determination."[47]

In Ṣarrūf's novel, it is this "curse" of fictitious capital that fells Bahiyyah's father following her brother Amīn's own fall. And it was a recent cotton deal he had commissioned, that was by the minute threatening severe losses in his holdings as he lay semiconscious, that so preoccupied him with what might happen that he did not see the oncoming tram. His losses are the stockbroker ʿAzrah's gain, who for his part does not fear prosecution, as any search by the courts of his registers will reveal his clients, at least half of whom "do not want it to be known of them that they play the stock market."[48] Finance begets the fictions that uphold it: the early serialized Arabic novel was the stuff of speculation and capital. It knew that the *Nahḍah*'s dream of rise and renaissance was in a state of suspense, haunted by the fear that all this speculation would end in ruin (and was already culminating in empire). It was a fear papered over by the novel of the nation, the archive at the heart of Samah Selim's *The Novel and the Rural Imaginary in Egypt.*

Fatāt Miṣr ends in a garden of the *Nahḍah*, one that has come full tilt from that Edenically envisioned in a Beirut just beginning to flourish from silk profits and a burgeoning Arabic press in the 1870s. Henry and Bahiyyah—a son of London, and the Girl of Egypt—are to be engaged: "That night the home of Wāṣif Bey was lit up and in its garden was placed a large tent for which plants were pulled up from the thickets and exchanged for luxurious carpets and in it were placed gilded chairs and seats and from it were hung large chandeliers, its candles exchanged for electric lights."[49] It is a celebration of the fiction of finance, of an age of industrialization, of a globally imagined *nahḍah* of electric-lit material progress, uprooting the idylls of the past. In attendance are

> men and women from all the nations residing [*al-qāṭinah*] in Egypt and the tourists who flock to it in the winter among them Copts,

> Arabs, Syrians [*Shawām*], Turks, Circassians, Persians, Greeks, Italians, Englishmen, Frenchmen, and Germans, from all classes of people from government ministers to their advisors and important employees, agents of European governments, major religious *imāms*, heads of trade, directors of companies, property holders and newspaper owners, most of whom are in foreign or Turkish dress, and a few in local attire, while all of them are wearing their best especially the Syrian, European and American women . . . with bouquets of flowers in their hands.[50]

In this imaginary garden of the *Nahḍah*, the anxieties born of the stock market's volatility, of Egypt's or Syria's penetration by imperial European capital, of investing in irrigation or real estate, and the threat more profitable venues for investment pose in this first age of finance capital are for a moment suspended. "The moon is full, the heavens are clear and there are neither clouds nor dust in the Cairo sky";[51] it is the eve of the 1907 crash. On this still night in a garden of Cairo's *Nahḍah*, one haunted from its beginning by the markets of Beirut, like a butterfly stirring from its chrysalis, capital is already in flight.

Coda

The novels studied in *Fictitious Capital* enact fictions of capital in Arabic in the late nineteenth and early twentieth centuries, as French and British empire intensifies in the region through the industrializing silk and cotton markets, securities exchanges, real estate speculation, and the stock market. Often urban tales of Damascus, Beirut, Cairo, and Alexandria, connected like the Arabic press by carriage, steamship, train, the telegraph, commodities, empires, and the desire to be in a garden, these early Arabic novels tap a geography of storytelling, trade, and world economy across the Mediterranean and Red Seas, the Suez Canal, the Nile River, and the Indian, Pacific, and Atlantic Oceans.

In *Freaks of Fortune*, Levy notes that nineteenth-century American discourse on risk "abounded with storm-tossed marine imagery, with one clear message: do not look to markets, which are perilous, for protection from the perils of markets."[1] A maritime trade geography persisted from merchant days, but with the late nineteenth century and the advent of the telegraph, the rules changed, Levy argues, along the axis of time: "The telegraph had made it so that merchants knew prices in markets at the port of destination before they shipped their goods. The only 'blind venture' now left was a futures transaction across time."[2] Serialized Arabic novels from 1859 with Khalīl al-Khūrī's *Way idhan lastu bi-ifranjī* (Alas, I am not a foreigner), Yūsuf al-Shalfūn's 1870 *al-Shābb al-maghrūr* (The conceited or tempted youth); Salīm al-Bustānī's 1870 *al-Huyām fī jinān al-Shām* (Love in the gardens of Damascus), 1871 *Zanūbiyyā* (Zanubiyya), 1872

Budūr (Budur), 1875 *Bint al-ʿaṣr* (Daughter of the age), and 1882–84 *Sāmiyyah* (Samiyyah); and Yaʿqūb Ṣarrūf's *Fatāt Miṣr* (Girl of Egypt) held readers, perhaps paid-up subscribers, in suspense, enacting this sense of "blind venture" into "the perils of markets." Of neither the nation nor the village, these early Arabic novels are fictions of capital in an age of competing empires, dreaming of *Nahḍah* in a garden of Damascus, afraid the silk moths are all about to rend their cocoons and take flight.

The Arabic novel of the late nineteenth century performed a technology of time, hope, and fear subtending fictions of capital meted out on the installment plan. But whereas Salīm al-Bustānī's just-in-time installments were caught up in the market's ups and downs, Jurjī Zaydān's bound editions of the novels of the history of Islam made an industry of extricating the novel from the perils of Beirut's silk futures, Cairo's stock exchange, and the fictions of global finance, the better to capitalize on its potential to be marketed and sold. Arabic literary critics, including ʿAbd al-Muḥsin Ṭāhā Badr and, much more recently, Samah Selim and Ghenwa Hayek, bring nation-centered questions to the history of the Arabic novel. *Fictitious Capital* looks instead to al-Bustānī's and Zaydān's Beirut years, and the thick nexus of global finance and Arabic fiction that has proven "hard to see," as Arrighi writes, "because of the actual invisibility or the complexity of the activities that constitute it."

As Hayek searches in her book *Beirut, Imagining the City* for a nationalist narrative archetype, she finds not the gardens of Damascus and fears of capital flight wracking a Beirut newly ratcheted to the global economy but rather what will become a persistent village/city geography for the Lebanese novel, first worked out by Jesuit priest Henri Lammens's 1898 Arabic novel *Kharīṭat Lubnān*, serialized in Beirut's Jesuit journal, *Al-Mashriq*.[3] Samah Selim's *The Novel and the Rural Imaginary in Egypt* traces a history of Egyptian fiction that, while it shares *Fictitious Capital*'s materialist impulse, looks not to finance and the high seas but inland, to the rural and its authors, for a literary history bound by nation. Rather than the transcontinental bourgeois reading public of al-Bustānī's *Al-Jinān*, Nimr and Ṣarrūf's *Al-Muqtaṭaf*, and Zaydān's *Al-Hilāl* that Khuri-Makdisi gestures toward in *The Eastern Mediterranean and the Making of Global Radicalism, 1860–1914*, Lucie Ryzova and Wilson Chacko Jacobs limn the rise of the *effendiya* class in Egypt from the 1920s, a nationalist reading public of Arabic to come. In the process, Arabic literary history becomes bound by nations, part of anticolonial struggles that, in a predictable ruse of capital, threaten to obscure how very much changes wrought in the countryside of Egypt are connected through a global web of textiles futures, real estate markets, and commodities trades to those remaking Mount Lebanon, Japan, California, Manchester, and the American South.

Fictitious Capital reads from what came before a will to find in Arabic novels tales of nation, looking instead to novels that remembered a time of *Sindbad*, knew risk's long history at sea, and could play fiction to the capital flight apace. Looking back from Cairo to Beirut, from Beirut to Damascus, from Damascus to al-Andalus, al-Andalus to Baghdad, crisscrossing the Mediterranean, the Atlantic, the Pacific, the Indian Ocean, the Red Sea to what is to come, these novels, like the American texts Levy studies, speculate in the "future that capitalism is constantly seeking to generate, manage, and exploit."[4] Finance capital in Egypt and Beirut as in the United States and elsewhere in the world economy would continue, of course, to "generate, manage, and exploit" our past, present, and future through precarious, elaborately sustained, multiply collateralized games of risk in real estate, stocks, and commodities futures, mortgaging land through interconnected local and international banks, a global fabric of speculation in "fictitious value" that the novels of *Fictitious Capital* animated and critiqued and that the 1907 financial crisis rendered broadly legible, if only for a moment.

The terrain that the Arabic novel of the nation inherits from al-Khūrī, al-Bustānī, al-Shalfūn, Zaydān, and Ṣarrūf as the First World War threatened was a heavily mortgaged one: it is the feared future at the horizon of late nineteenth-century Beirut and Cairo, arrived. When Zaydān died in 1914 at his desk, amid his papers and the last issue of that year's *Al-Hilāl*, those distant Damascus gardens would soon be under French mandate, and the British were still in Cairo. But the Arabic novel was finally on the rise.

NOTES

INTRODUCTION

1. Elliott Colla, "How *Zaynab* Became the First Arabic Novel," *History Compass* 6 (2007). Speaking of ʿAbd al-Muḥsin Ṭāhā Badr's *Taṭawwur al-riwāyah al-ʿarabiyyah al-ḥadīthah fī Miṣr (1860–1938)* (Cairo: Dār al-Maʿārif, 1976), Colla writes: "One cannot help but marvel at the way Badr's study attempted to lay down the groundwork for the critical acceptance of a national canon of novels. As such, we should see it as part of the wider process by which Egyptian universities were being remade in the image of Nasser" (7).

2. Giovanni Arrighi, *The Long Twentieth Century: Money, Power and the Origins of Our Times* (New York: Verso, 1994), 25, 24.

3. Ibid., 24, 113.

4. The list is long indeed. Some of the most important and widely cited works include Samah Selim, *The Novel and the Rural Imaginary in Egypt, 1880–1985* (London: RoutledgeCurzon, 2004), and her essays "The People's Entertainments: Translation, Popular Fiction, and the Nahdah in Egypt," in *Other Renaissances: A New Approach to World Literature*, ed. Brenda Deen Schildgen, Gang Zhou, and Sander Gilman, 35–58 (New York: Palgrave-Macmillan, 2007), and "Fiction and Colonial Identities: Arsène Lupin in Arabic," *Middle Eastern Literatures* 13, no. 2 (August 2010); Shaden Tageldin, *Disarming Words: Empire and the Seductions of Translation in Egypt* (Berkeley: University of California Press, 2011); Elliott Colla, *Conflicted Antiquities: Egyptology, Egyptomania, Egyptian Modernity* (Durham, NC: Duke University Press, 2007); Timothy Mitchell, *Colonising Egypt* (Berkeley: University of California Press, 1991), and his *Rule of Experts: Egypt, Techno-Politics, Modernity* (Berkeley: University of California Press, 2002); Raouf Abbas and Assem El-Dessouky, *The Large Landowning Class and the Peasantry in Egypt, 1837–1952*, trans. Amer Mohsen with Mona Zirki (Syracuse: Syracuse University Press, 2012); Marylin Booth, *May Her Likes Be Multiplied: Biography and Gender Politics in Egypt* (Berkeley: University of California Press, 2001); Beth Baron, *Egypt as a Woman: Nationalism, Gender and Politics* (Berkeley: University of California Press, 2005), and *The Women's Awakening in Egypt: Culture, Society, and the Press* (New Haven:

Yale University Press, 1994). On Barak, *On Time: Technology and Temporality in Modern Egypt* (Berkeley: University of California Press, 2013); Ziad Fahmy, *Ordinary Egyptians: Creating the Modern Nation through Popular Culture* (Stanford: Stanford University Press, 2011). There are others.

5. While many critics of Arabic literature make reference to 1870s and 1880s Beirut in their histories of the Arabic novel, there is a strong tendency to relegate this tremendously rich and yet seldom read body of journals to a passing comment about a Syrian émigré's past. A superficial glance is cast at 1870s and 1880s Beirut as critics rush on to Egypt at the turn of the century, which in the process crystallizes as the literary epicenter of early modern narrative fiction in Arabic. (In English, the work of Sabry Hafez, John A. Haywood, Matti Moosa, Shmuel Moreh, and Stephen Sheehi represents notable departures. In Arabic, the work of Shākir Muṣṭafā, Muḥammad Yūsuf Najm, Ibrāhīm al-Saʿāfīn, and ʿAbd al-Raḥmān Yāghī concerns itself with the literary history of late nineteenth-century Beirut.) Paul Starkey writes: "The period covered by the present chapter, 1880–1933, represents a crucial one in the emergence of modern Arabic narrative in the form of the novel and short story as usually understood in the West. Perhaps more than any other chapter, it will be dominated by developments in Egypt—though . . . Syrian émigrés also played a crucial, contributory role" (Starkey, *Modern Arabic Literature* [Edinburgh: Edinburgh University Press, 2006], 97). Often these pivotal decades are distilled down to a brief mention of Salīm al-Bustānī without sustained attention to the literary forms or intellectual atmosphere of 1870s and 1880s Beirut. Even Hamdi Sakkut's monumental bilingual, six-volume bibliography of the Arabic novel, despite its careful documentation of late nineteenth-century Syrian literary production, follows in this critical trend when he discusses the place of *Zaynab* in Arabic literary production (see Sakkut, *The Arabic Novel: Bibliography and Critical Introduction, 1865–1995* [Cairo: American University in Cairo Press, 2000]). This phenomenon is evinced (though later revised) by Roger Allen when he explains that Egypt, "quickened by the new arrivals from Syria, became the fullest and most often cited example of intellectual developments in the early decades of the twentieth century. Our concentration in what follows on trends in Egypt reflects this tendency" (Allen, *The Arabic Literary Heritage* [Cambridge: Cambridge University Press, 1998], 72). We see a similar critical bent in the work of M. M. Badawi, particularly in his overwhelming focus on Egypt as he locates the origins of the Arabic novel and *A Short History of Modern Arabic Literature* (Oxford: Oxford University Press, 1993). A trademark in this literary-critical trend is a discrete focus on Jurjī Zaydān as the example par excellence of the Syrian émigré and his contributions to the history of the Arabic novel, to be discussed at length in chapters 4 and 5.

6. In *Men of Capital: Scarcity and Economy in Mandate Palestine*, Sherene Seikaly reads a utopia of economic *nahḍah* in the Palestinian press from the 1930s, noting in passing the importance of journals such as *Al-Jinān*, *Al-Muqtaṭaf*, and *Al-Hilāl* to this utopian discourse (30). Seikaly bemoans "a resounding [critical] silence on Arab capitalist practices," arguing for "economic thought as a formative component of the *nahda*" (8, 24). *Ficitious*

Capital, too, takes the economic to be central to thinking *nahḍah*, but insists this must be understood historically within the context of speculation since at least 1860, when finance capital and the novel emerged in the region as mutually imbricated processes (Seikaly, *Men of Capital: Scarcity and Econony in Mandate Palestine* [Palo Alto: Stanford University Press, 2016]).

7. Mitchell, *Rule of Experts*, 95.

8. Aaron Jakes, "Review Essay: A New Materialism? Globalization and Technology in an Age of Empire," *International Journal of Middle East Studies* 47 (2015): 379. See also Jakes, "Boom, Bugs, Bust: Egypt's Ecology of Interest, 1882–1914," *Antipode* (2016).

9. Khalīl al-Khūrī, *Way—idhan lastu bi-ifranjī: Al-Riwāyah al-ʿarabiyyah al-ūlā wa-l-rāʾidah*, ed. Shirbil Dāghir (Beirut: Dār al-Fārābī, 2009), 88. The novel was originally published serially in *Ḥadīqat al-Akhbār* 93 (October 1859)–153 (March 1860), and immediately announced as available for purchase as a stand-alone book in March 1860.

10. Ibid., 87.

11. Ibid., 88.

12. Peter Gran identifies the mid-1860s through at least World War I (though in the case of Egypt as late as 1952) as the "first age of finance capitalism," a history of finance in the region to which al-Khūrī's equivocal rendering of Aleppo in 1859 and 1860 versions of his novel lends credence (Gran, *Islamic Roots of Capitalism: Egypt, 1760–1840* [Syracuse: Syracuse University Press, 1998], xxxvi).

13. See Ellis Goldberg, *Trade, Reputation, and Child Labor in Twentieth-Century Egypt* (New York: Palgrave Macmillan, 2004), esp. chap. 2, "Reputation, Regulation, and Trade."

14. al-Khūrī, *Way—idhan lastu bi-ifranjī*, 73. I thank Rebecca Johnson for pointing this out at a panel on translation and the *Nahḍah* for the 2013 annual meeting of the American Comparative Literature Association. See also Rebecca C. Johnson, "Importing the Novel: The Arabic Novel in and as Translation," *Novel: A Forum on Fiction* 48, no. 2 (2015).

15. Stephen Sheehi, "Towards a Critical Theory of *al-Nahḍah*: Epistemology, Ideology and Capital," *Journal of Arabic Literature* 43, no. 2–3 (2012): 269–70.

16. *Al-Hilāl* 5, no. 14 (March 15, 1897): 530.

17. I am extremely grateful to the staff of the Ministère des Affaires Étrangères at the Centre des Archives Diplomatiques in Nantes, France, for their research guidance, and to Bard College for generously funding my time in the French archives. The correspondence regarding the threat of *papillonnage* is from 166PO/D11 Cote 22 (Ambassade de France à Constantinople, Série D [correspondance consulaire], Répertoire Numérique de la Sous-Série Beyrouth, 1755–1914). The mention of scandal and fraud comes on the second page of letter no. 67, dated January 19, 1872.

18. Letter no. 16 (October 21, 1872).

19. Letter no. 83 (May 17, 1872), 1.

20. Ibid., 3.

21. Letter no. 67 (January 19, 1872), 2–3.

22. Letter no. 4 (April 3, 1873), 2.

23. Letter no. 12 (September 8, 1873), 16–17.

24. The confounding of local dreams of financial prosperity would persistently appear in the colonial archives of the region. Consider a British advisor to the Ministry of Finance in 1909: "Suggestions, again, are sometimes made that it rests with the Government to restore confidence and prosperity by some stroke of policy or financial operation. This is a delusion. There is no royal road, short and infallible, to prosperity" (from *Reports by His Majesty's Agent and Consul-General on the Finances, Administration, and Condition of Egypt and the Soudan in 1908* [London: Harrison and Sons, 1909], 10, qtd. in Jakes, "Boom, Bugs, Bust").

25. Letter no. 4 of November 8, 1871, regarding the weighing of raw cocoons. He writes of "les plus grands précautions aux transports par terres qu'ils [the cocoons] doivent subir pour arriver aux filatures. On les fait voyager de nuit et aussi rapidement que possible et souvent malgré tous ces soins on ne parvient pas à éviter le *papillonnage*" (4). He goes on to speculate as to what the doubling of the passage of cocoons from twelve to twenty-four hours might mean for the future of the silk industry around Beirut.

26. Caught between empires, as Jens Hanssen has noted, "the city of Beirut was at once the product, the object and the project of imperial and urban politics of difference [in which . . . o]verlapping European, Ottoman, and local civilizing missions competed" (Hanssen, *Fin-de-Siècle Beirut: The Making of an Ottoman Provincial Capital* [New York: Oxford University Press, 2005], 4).

27. Fredric Jameson, "Culture and Finance Capital," *Critical Inquiry* 24 (Autumn 1997): 254, 259.

28. Ian Baucom, *Specters of the Atlantic: Finance Capital, Slavery, and the Philosophy of History* (Durham, NC: Duke University Press, 2005), 143.

29. Jameson, "Culture and Finance Capital," 251, my italics.

30. "Muhājirat dūd al-qazz" [The migration of the silkworm], *Al-Mushīr* 3, no. 121 (February 12, 1897): 1027. The newspaper was founded in 1894 by Salīm Sarkīs and had repeated encounters with censors. It contained satirical articles, serialized narratives, true stories from the region, as well as the occasional utterly fake spoof.

Salīm Sarkīs [S.S.] also wrote under the name Maryam Maẓhar [M.M.], editor of one of the first women's Arabic journals *Mir'āt al-Ḥasnā'*, founded in Cairo in 1896 (see Beth Baron, *The Women's Awakening in Egypt: Culture, Society, and the Press* [New Haven: Yale University Press, 1994], 17, and the article she cites there: Salīm Sarkīs, "Man hiya Ānisah Maryam Maẓhar?," *Majallat Sarkīs* 2, no. 21 [1907]: 645–51).

31. "Muhājirat dūd al-qazz," 1027.

32. Ibid.

33. Ibid.

34. For more on *ta'ajjub* in the context of *The Thousand and One Nights*, see Roy Mottahedeh, "*'Aja'ib* in The Thousand and One Nights," in *The Thousand and One Nights in Arabic Literature and Society*, ed. Richard G. Hovannisian and Georges Sabagh (Cambridge: Cambridge University Press, 1997), 29–39.

35. In addition to those texts mentioned elsewhere in the introduction and its notes, I should also add Ilham Khuri-Makdisi, *The Eastern Mediterranean and the Making of Global Radicalism* 1860–1914 (Berkeley: University of California Press, 2010); Marwa ElShakry, *Reading Darwin in Arabic, 1860–1950* (Chicago: University of Chicago Press, 2013); Tarek El-Ariss, *Trials of Arab Modernity: Literary Affects and the New Political* (New York: Fordham University Press, 2013); Dana Sajdi, *The Barber of Damascus: Nouveau Literacy in the Eighteenth-Century Ottoman Levant* (Stanford: Stanford University Press, 2013); Stephen Sheehi, *Foundations of Modern Arab Identity* (Gainesville: University Press of Florida, 2004); and Thomas Philipp, *The Syrians in Egypt: 1725–1975* (Stuttgart: Franz Steiner Verlag, 1985). While not at all recent, this book would have been much harder to write without the scholarship of Fīlīp dī Ṭarrāzi, *Tārīkh al-ṣiḥāfah al-ʿarabiyyah* (Beirut: al-Maṭbaʿah al-adabiyyah, 1913), vols. 1–4.

36. Joseph Massad, *Desiring Arabs* (Chicago: University of Chicago Press, 2007).

37. Michael Allan, "How *Adab* Became Literary: Formalism, Orientalism and the Institutions of World Literature," *Journal of Arabic Literature* 43, no. 2–3 (2012); Jeffrey Sacks, *Iterations of Loss: Mutilation and Aesthetic Form, al-Shidyaq to Darwish* (New York: Fordham University Press, 2015).

38. Sheehi, *Foundations of Modern Arab Identity.*

39. Rastegar, *Literary Modernity between the Middle East and Europe* (London: Routledge, 2007).

40. Muhsin al-Musawi, *Scheherazade in England: A Study of the Nineteenth-Century Criticism of the Arabian Nights* (Washington, DC: Three Continents, 1981).

41. In addition to the work of Badr already discussed, see al-Saʿāfīn, *Taṭawwur al-riwāyah al-ʿarabiyyah al-ḥadīthah fī bilād al-Shām: 1870–1967* (Beirut: Dār al-Minâhil, 1987); Matti Moosa, *The Origins of Modern Arabic Fiction* (Boulder, CO: Lynne Rienner, 1997); Jurjī Zaydān, *Tarīkh ādāb al-lughah al-ʿArabiyyah*, vol. 4 (Cairo: Dār al-Hilāl, 1957); Allen, *The Arabic Literary Heritage* and *The Arabic Novel: An Historical and Critical Introduction* (Syracuse: Syracuse University Press, 1995); Muḥsin Jāsim al-Mūsawī, *al-Riwāyah al-ʿarabiyyah: al-nashaʾah wa-l-taḥawwul* (Cairo: Al-Hayʾah al-Miṣriyyah al-ʿĀmmah li-l-Kitāb, 1988); M. M. Badawi, *Modern Arabic Literature and the West* and *A Short History of Modern Arabic Literature*; ʿAbd al-Raḥmān Yāghī, *Al-Juhūd al-riwāʾiyyah min Salīm al-Bustānī ilā Najīb Maḥfūẓ* (Beirut: Dār al-fārābī, 1999); and the tremendously valuable study by Muḥammad Yūsuf Najm, *Al-Qissah fi-l-adab al-ʿarabī al-ḥadīth* (Cairo: Dār Miṣr li-l-Ṭibāʿah, 1952).

42. Rastegar, *Literary Modernity between the Middle East and Europe,* 30, 7.

43. Raymond Williams, *Marxism and Literature* (New York: Oxford University Press, 1977), 94.

44. Ibid., 92.

45. Elliott Colla, "Field Construction," *International Journal of Middle Eastern Studies* 43 (2011): 722.

46. Samah Selim, "Toward a New Literary History," *International Journal of Middle Eastern Studies* 43 (2011): 735.

47. Williams, *Marxism and Literature*, 114.

48. Clifford Siskin, "Epilogue: The Rise of Novelism," in *Cultural Institutions of the Novel*, ed. Deirdre Lynch and William Beatty Warner (Durham, NC: Duke University Press, 1996), 436.

49. Ibid., 425.

50. See Goldberg, *Trade, Reputation, and Child Labor.*

51. Jameson, "Culture and Finance Capital," 261.

52. Jakes, "Boom, Bugs, Bust."

53. Walter Benjamin, "Paris: Capital of the Nineteenth Century," *Perspecta* 12 (1969): 163–72, 72.

54. *Nahḍah*'s corollary is of course *inḥiṭāṭ*, decline. If the *Nahḍah* can be characterized as a dream impelled toward an awakening, even at a moment of colonization and financial crisis, there is a concomitant parallel hazard for critics of—as Dana Sajdi has argued of the Ottoman rhetoric of decline—"falling into the trap of their myths," rightly observing that "the 'decline consciousness' found in Ottoman *texts* was not immediately to be translated into *real* Ottoman decline" (Sajdi, "Decline, Its Discontents, and Ottoman Cultural History: By Way of Introduction," in *Ottoman Tulips, Ottoman Coffee: Leisure and Lifestyle in the Eighteenth Century*, ed. Sajdi [London: I. B. Tauris, 2007], 8, 25).

CHAPTER 1: IN THE GARDEN: SERIALIZED ARABIC FICTION AND ITS READING PUBLIC—BEIRUT, 1870

1. The term in this period is decisively *riwāyah*, offering further evidence of the limits of Charles Pellat's claims to the novel being *qiṣṣah* and only *qiṣṣah* in Arabic (see, on this point, Allen, "Narrative Genre and Nomenclature: A Comparative Study," *Journal of Arabic Literature* 23, no. 3 [1992]: 213). In a recent article on Jurjī Zaydān (who would begin publishing Arabic *riwāyāt* in the 1890s) and his translation into Persian, Kamran Rastegar hesitates to render *riwāyāt* as "novels," concerned that in so doing we risk importing into our literary criticism "a framework of value derived from criticism of the novel [. . . r]ather than evaluating texts of the period in question by using criteria that can be validly ascribed to the sites of their production." Writing from the 1890s, Zaydān is at times quite explicit—both in the authors to whom he traces inspiration in *Tarīkh ādāb al-lughah al-ʿarabiyyah* (portions of this four-volume work were serialized in *Al-Hilāl* beginning in its second year [1893–94]), as well as in his self-conscious modeling of a European-styled literary criticism for his uninducted readers in the pages of *Al-Hilāl*—that he *is* writing novels, and that they are like European ones. The precedent of European historical novels is cited in Arabic literary critical debates in 1890s Cairo journals such as *Al-Hilāl* and *Al-Muqtaṭaf* (cf. "Ta'līf al-riwāyāt wa-intiqādihā," *Al-Muqtaṭaf* 16, no. 5 [February 1892]: 345). For Zaydān, the question is not whether these are two different genres (European novels and Arabic *riwāyāt*) but rather one of inflection: history appears ascendent over plot in Arabic's historical novels, in contradistinction to their inverse roles in European fiction

(see Jurjī Zaydān's response to the inquisitive reader Rafīq al-ʿAẓm of Cairo under "Riwāyāt tārīkh al-Islām," *Al-Hilāl* 7, no. 16 [May 15, 1899]: 489–94). Announcements in *Al-Hilāl* for Riwāyāt al-Hilāl inform audiences of the future that the series will include both translations of European novels as well as original ones written in Arabic (see, for instance, "Riwāyāt al-Hilāl," *Al-Hilāl* 2, no. 20 [June 15, 1894]: 640—this was a recurring announcement). For more on Salīm al-Bustānī and Jurjī Zaydān as early Arabic novelists, see Sheehi, *Foundations of Modern Arab Identity* (Gainesville: University Press of Florida, 2004); Moosa, *Origins of Modern Arabic Fiction* (Boulder, CO: Lynne Rienner, 1997); and Elizabeth M. Holt, "From Gardens of Knowledge to Ezbekiyya after Midnight: The Novel and the Arabic Press from Beirut to Cairo, 1870–1892," *Middle Eastern Literatures* 16, no. 3 (December 2013): 232–48, and chapter 6 of this volume.

2. I am grateful to Jens Hanssen for sharing with me his thoughts on the "botanical imaginary" of late nineteenth-century Beirut.

3. See some of the titles listed in Bilal Orfali, "A Sketch Map of Arabic Poetry Anthologies up to the Fall of Baghdad," *Journal of Arabic Literature* 43, no. 1 (2012): 29–59. I am indebted to Bilal Orfali for his research and guidance on an earlier Arabic tradition of cultivating gardens of knowledge. See also Bilal Orfali and Nada Saab, eds., *Sufism, Black and White: A Critical Edition of "al-Bayāḍ wa-l-Sawād" by Abū Ḥasan al-Sīrjānī (d. ca. 470/1077)* (Boston: Brill, 2012); and Bilal Orfali, "The Art of the *Muqaddimma* in the Works of Abū Manṣūr al-Thaʿālibī (d. 429/1039)," in *The Weaving of Words: Approaches to Classical Arabic Prose*, ed. Lale Behzadi and Vahid Behmardi (Beirut: Orient Institut Beirut, 2009): 181–202.

4. Allen, "Narrative Genre and Nomenclature," 211.

5. I thank Timothy Mitchell for pointing this out to me.

6. On the changing status of *adab* from at least the 1890s, and in particular the role of Jurjī Zaydān in marking its changing meanings for Arabic literary history, see Michael Allan, "How *Adab* Became Literary."

7. Profuse thanks is due to Christine Boustany, Nora Boustany, Kamran Rastegar, and Christine Lindner for their help in locating biographical information regarding Adelaide and other members of the Bustānī family. In "Narrative and the Reading Public in 1870s Beirut," I suggested that Adelaide may have been a pen name used by Salīm al-Bustānī to encourage women readers to write. Adelaide was in fact real, "Hanrī wa Amīliyā" standing as her only published *riwāyah* (Holt, "Narrative and the Reading Public in 1870s Beirut," *Journal of Arabic Literature* 40, no. 1 [2009]: 37–70). Ghenwa Hayek offers a comparative reading of Adelaide's short story and its figuring of gender and narration in "Experimental Female Fictions; or, the Brief Wondrous Life of the *Nahḍa* Sensation Story," *Middle Eastern Literatures* 16, no. 3 (2013): 249–65. For more on gender in late nineteenth-century Syria, see Fruma Zachs and Sharon Halevi, *Gendering Culture in Greater Syria: Intellectuals and Ideology in the Late Ottoman Period* (New York: I. B. Tauris, 2015).

8. *Al-Jinān* 13 (1870): 407. For a translation of the complete story, see Adelaide al-Bustani, "Henry and Amelia," trans. Elizabeth M. Holt, in *The*

Arab Renaissance: Anthology of Nahda Thought, Literature, and Language, ed. Tarek El-Ariss (New York: Modern Language Association, 2016).

9. Translation from Henry Harris Jessup, *The Women of the Arabs* (New York: Dodd and Mead, 1873), 163.

10. See "Selected Anecdotes and Announcements from the 1870s Beirut Press," trans. Elizabeth M. Holt, in *The Arab Renaissance: Anthology of Nahda Thought, Literature, and Language.*

11. See Abū al-Ḥasan ʿAlī b. al-Ḥasan al-Kirmānī al-Sīrjānī (d. ca. 470/1077)'s *Kitāb al-Bayāḍ wa-l-sawād min khaṣāʾiṣ ḥikam al-ʿibād fī naʿt al-murīd wa-l-murād*, an anthology of Sufi anecdotes that includes the following: "Some of the poor said: If you see a poor [man] leave his food know that he has succumbed to thought, and if you see him return to it know that he is in the garden of knowledge [*ḥadīqat al-maʿrifah*]" (Orfali and Saab, eds. *Sufism, Black and White*, 154). On al-Andalus, see Yaseen Noorani, "The Lost Garden of Al-Andalus: Islamic Spain and the Poetic Inversion of Colonialism," *International Journal of Middle East Studies* 31, no. 2 (1999).

12. Qtd. in Orfali, "Art of the *Muqaddima*," 189.

13. Ibid., 194.

14. Qtd. ibid., 193–94.

15. Buṭrus al-Bustānī, *Dāʾirat al-maʿārif*, vol. 6 (Beirut: al-Maṭbaʿah al-Adabiyyah, 1876), 559.

16. "*Dāʾirat al-maʿārif* li-l-Bustānī," *Al-Hilāl* 7, no. 1 (October 1, 1898): 24. Jurjī Zaydān would include *Dāʾirat al-maʿārif* among his footnoted sources in historical novels such as *Fatāt Ghassān* (serialized in *Al-Hilāl*'s fifth year [1896–97]).

17. Ibn Jubayr, a Muslim traveler from al-Andalus visiting the gardens of Damascus in the late twelfth century, is quoted as having said, "By Allah, they spoke truth who said, 'If Paradise be on earth it is Damascus without a doubt; and if it be in Heaven, Damascus is its earthly counterpart and equivalent'" (qtd. in Jonas Benzion Lehrman, *Earthly Paradise: Garden and Courtyard in Early Islam* [Berkeley: University of California Press, 1980], 190).

18. Credit is due to Stephen Sheehi for bringing the importance of this *khuṭbah* to the attention of contemporary scholars in his recent study *Foundations of Modern Arab Identity.*

19. Buṭrus al-Bustānī, "Khuṭbah fī ādāb al-ʿarab," in *al-Jamʿiyah al-sūriyyah li-l-ʿulūm wa-l-funūn 1847–1852*, ed. Yūsuf Qizmā Khūrī (Beirut: Dār al-Ḥamrāʾ, 1990), 115. (Lecture originally published in Beirut by al-Maṭbaʿah al-Amīrkāniyyah in 1859. Lecture given on February 15, 1859.)

20. Ibid.

21. *Al-Nashrah al-Usbūʿiyyah* 1, no. 29 (1871): 2–3.

22. On educational and scholarly institutions during this period, see Jens Hanssen, "Chapter IV: The Birth of an Educational Quarter: Zokak el-Blat as a Cradle of Cultural Revival in the Arab World," in *History, Space and Social Conflict in Beirut: The Quarter of Zokak el-Blat*, ed. Hans Gebhardt, Dorothée Sack, Ralph Bodenstein, Andreas Fritz, Jens Hanssen, Bernhard Hillenkamp, Oliver Kögler, Anne Mollenhauer, and Friederike Stolleis

(Beirut: Orient Institute, 2005): 143–74; and Fīlīp dī Ṭarrāzi, *Tārīkh al-ṣiḥafah al-ʿarabiyyah*, vol. 2 (Beirut: al-Maṭbaʿah al-Adabiyyah, 1913), 1–8.

23. See Yūsuf Qizmā Khūrī, ed., *Aʿmāl al-jamʿīyah al-ʿilmiyyah al-sūriyyah* (Beirut: Dār al-Ḥamrāʾ, 1990), 5–6.

24. Ibid., 192.

25. *Al-Jinān* 1, no. 9 (1870): 277.

26. Ibid.

27. Ibid., 278.

28. Ibid.

29. Ibid.

30. Compare this with Richard Altick's depicition of Victorian reading habits, and the reversal of terms in the economic equation—it was, of course, money that bought the time to read, and not the other way around:

> "Cards, of course, were forbidden, and, while a game of bagatelle might be allowed, billiards, even in the home, were never mentioned." In so scrupulous an atmosphere, the reading habit flourished. The place of the evening reading circle in Victorian middle-class family life is so well known that it need be merely mentioned here. How widespread the institution was, and how deeply it influenced the tastes of the children who grew up in such homes, is attested in countless memoirs. However, only the relatively well-to-do minority of the middle class, the merchants, bankers, professional men, manufacturers, and so on, could spend full evenings with their families and their books.

(Altick, *The English Common Reader: A Social History of the Mass Reading Public 1800–1900* [Chicago: University of Chicago Press, 1957], 86).

31. *Al-Jinān* 1, no. 22 (1870): 686–87.

32. Nada Sehnaoui, *L'occidentalisation de la vie quotidienne à Beyrouth: 1860–1914* (Beirut: Éditions Dar an-Nahar, 2002); Leila Tarazi Fawaz, *Merchants and Migrants in Nineteenth-Century Beirut* (Cambridge: Harvard University Press, 1983).

33. *Al-Jinān* 1, no. 2 (January 1870): 59.

34. Ibid., 56.

35. See Sheehi's *Foundations of Modern Arab Identity* on smoking in the works of Salīm al-Bustānī.

36. *Al-Jinān* 1, no. 2 (January 1870): 60.

37. Sheehi, *Foundations of Modern Arab Identity*, esp. chap. 3, "Desiring Selves, Desiring Others."

38. *Al-Jinān* 1, no. 2 (January 1870): 61.

39. *Al-Jinān* 1, no. 3 (1870): 91.

40. For more on the dynamics of epistolarity in intellectual circles of the *Nahḍah*, see Boutheina Khaldi, "Epistolarity in a Nahḍah Climate: The Role of Mayy Ziyādah's Letter Writing," *Journal of Arabic Literature* 40, no. 1 (2009): 1–36, which addresses Mayy Ziyādah's letter writing as an extension of her salon in early twentieth-century Egypt.

41. *Al-Jinān* 1, no. 23 (1870): 732.

42. *Al-Zahrah* 1, no. 2 (1870): 16.

43. *Al-Zahrah* 1, no. 10 (1870): 80.
44. Ibid.
45. *Al-Zahrah* 1, no. 11 (1870): 88.
46. Ibid.
47. *Al-Zahrah* 1, no. 17 (1870):136.
48. *Al-Zahrah* 1, no. 19 (1870): 156.
49. Ibid.
50. Ibid.
51. *Al-Jinān* 16 (1870): 510.
52. *Al-Jinān* 21 (1870): 666.
53. Linda K. Hughes and Michael Lund, *The Victorian Serial* (Charlottesville: University Press of Virginia, 1991), 6.
54. For more on the multiple Ottoman and European discourses of reform informing narratives of progress in late nineteenth-century Beirut and Mount Lebanon, see esp. chap. 2, "The Gentle Crusade," and chap. 5, "Reinventing Mount Lebanon" in Ussama Makdisi, *The Culture of Sectarianism: Community, History, and Violence in Nineteenth-Century Ottoman Lebanon* (Berkeley: University of California Press, 2000).
55. Hughes and Lund, *The Victorian Serial*, 4.
56. Caroline Levine, *The Serious Pleasures of Suspense: Victorian Realism and Narrative Doubt* (Charlottesville: University of Virginia Press, 2003), 2.
57. Ibrāhīm al-Saʿāfīn, *Taṭawwur al-riwāyah al-ʿarabiyyah al-ḥadīthah fī bilād al-Shām: 1870–1967* (Beirut: Dār al-Minähil, 1987), 26, 25.
58. For a comparative perspective on the relationship of *A Thousand and One Nights* to the novel in the nineteenth century, and to Aḥmad Fāris al-Shidyāq in particular, see Rebecca Carol Johnson, Richard Maxwell, and Katie Trumpener, "*The Arabian Nights*, Arab-European Literary Influence, and the Lineages of the Novel," *Modern Language Quarterly* 68, no. 2 (June 2007): 243–79. See also Muhsin Jassim al-Musawi, *Scheherazade in England: A Study of the Nineteenth-Century Criticism of the Arabian Nights* (Washingston, DC: Three Continents, 1981).
59. *Al-Zahrah* 1, no. 35 (1870): 275.
60. Ibid.
61. Ibid.
62. Ibid.
63. I thank Dwight Reynolds for pointing this out to me.
64. B. al-Bustānī, *Khuṭbah*, 114.
65. Ferial J. Ghazoul, *Nocturnal Poetics: The Arabian Nights in Comparative Context* (Cairo: American University in Cairo Press, 1996), 85.
66. Husain Haddawy, trans. *The Arabian Nights* (New York: Norton, 1990), 18.
67. *Al-Zahrah* 1, no. 43 (1870): 314.
68. *Al-Bashīr* 1, no. 51 (August 19, 1871), inside front cover.
69. ʿAbd al-Raḥmān Yāghī, *Al-Juhūd al-riwā'iyyah min Salīm al-Bustānī ilā Najīb Maḥfūẓ* (Beirut: Dār al-fārābī, 1999), 38.

70. Ami Ayalon, *The Press in the Arab Middle East: A History* (New York: Oxford University Press, 1995), 37; see also Ayalon, "Private Publishing in the *Nahḍah*," *International Journal of Middle East Studies* 40 (2008): 561–77.

CHAPTER 2: LIKE A BUTTERFLY STIRRING WITHIN A CHRYSALIS: SALĪM AL-BUSTĀNĪ, YŪSUF AL-SHALFŪN, AND THE REMAINDER TO COME

1. Jens Hanssen, *Fin de Siècle Beirut: The Making of an Ottoman Provincial Capital* (Oxford: Clarendon, 2005), 28–30. See also Thomas Philipp, *Acre: The Rise and Fall of a Palestinian City—World Economy and Local Politics* (New York: Columbia University Press, 2002).

2. Hanssen, *Fin de Siècle Beirut*, 31.

3. Ibid., 32, 36.

4. Boutros Labaki, *Introduction à l'histoire économique du Liban: Soie et commerce extérieur en fin de période ottomane (1840–1914)* (Beirut: Publications de l'Université Libanaise, 1984), 20.

5. Khalīl al-Khūrī, *Way—idhan lastu bi-ifranjī: Al-Riwāyah al-ʿarabiyyah al-ūlā wa-l-rāʾidah,* ed. Shirbil Dāghir (Beirut: Dār al-Fārābī, 2009), 88. The novel was originally published serially in *Ḥadīqat al-Akhbār* 93 (October 1859)–153 (March 1860), and immediately announced as available for purchase as a stand-alone book in March 1860.

6. Ibid., 58.

7. Shākir al-Khūrī, *Majmaʿ al-masarrāt*, ed. Ilyās Qaṭṭār (1908; Beirut: Dār Laḥd Khāṭir, 1985), 142.

8. Akram Fouad Khater, *Inventing Home: Emigration, Gender, and the Middle Class in Lebanon, 1870–1920* (Berkeley: University of California Press, 2001), 26.

9. Ibid., 28.

10. Giovanni Arrighi, *The Long Twentieth Century: Money, Power and the Origins of Our Times* (New York: Verso, 1994), 24.

11. Boutros Labaki, *Introduction à l'histoire économique du Liban: Soie et commerce extérieur en fin de période ottomane (1840–1914)* (Beirut: Publications de l'Université Libanaise, 1984), 23.

12. Ibid., 51.

13. Ibid., 52.

14. Leila Tarazi Fawaz, *Merchants and Migrants in Nineteenth-Century Beirut* (Cambridge: Harvard University Press, 1983), 66–67.

15. For an analysis of the crumbling of local social structures between 1831 and 1860 that focuses on the emergence of a culture of sectarianism in the wake of the 1831–40 Egyptian occupation of Syria and the resulting Ottoman *Tanzimat* reforms, see Ussama Makdisi, *The Culture of Sectarianism: Community, History, and Violence in Nineteenth-Century Ottoman Lebanon* (Berkeley: University of California Press, 2000).

16. Fawaz, *Merchants and Migrants in Nineteenth-Century Beirut*, 40, 41.

17. Jürgen Habermas, *The Structural Transformation of the Public Sphere: An Inquiry into a Category of Bourgeois Society*, trans. Thomas Burger with the assistance of Frederick Lawrence (1962; Cambridge: MIT Press, 1989), 16.

18. In 1870, as On Barak notes in his book *On Time: Technology and Temporality in Modern Egypt*, the official Egyptian newspaper *Wādī al-Nīl* ran a description of the newly opened Cairo bourse, to be discussed in chapter 6. Lamenting the lack of attention to cotton for a history of the Arabic press (and completely overlooking the pivotal role of Beirut's silk industry to that history), Barak points out that "daily telegraphic news from Britian and Alexandria were hung on the bourse walls," arguing that "the first Egyptian daily newspaper was actually [not *Al-Ahrām* but] a posting (or wallpaper)" inside the bourse (see Barak, *On Time: Technology and Temporality in Modern Egypt* [Berkeley: University of California Press, 2013], 130).

19. The exception to the poor crop and prices seen for silk in 1870 was the silk produced in the Bekaa, which, in light of the poor quality elsewhere in the region, was sold for 80 *ghirsh* per *uqqah* (see Gaston Ducousso, *L'industrie de la soie en Syrie et au Liban* [Beirut: Imprimerie Catholique and Paris: Librairie Maritime et Coloniale Augustin Challamel, 1918]; Labaki, *Introduction à l'histoire économique du Liban*; and also Maurice H. Chéhab, *Rôle du Liban dans l'histoire de la soie* [Beirut: Publications de l'Université Libanaise, 1967], 42–43).

20. The year 1875 was a particularly bad one for Beirut, as a cold and rainy May destroyed hopes for the silk harvest that year.

21. *Al-Jinān* 1, no. 9 (1870): 261.

22. Ibid., 285.

23. *Al-Jinān* 1, no. 10 (1870): 300.

24. Ibid., 313.

25. *Al-Jinān* 1, no. 11 (1870): 326.

26. *Al-Jinān* 1, no. 15 (1870): 479–1, no. 16 (1870): 506.

27. Ducousso, *L'industrie de la soie en Syrie et au Liban*, 106.

28. Caroline Levine, *The Serious Pleasures of Suspense: Victorian Realism and Narrative Doubt* (Charlottesville: University of Virginia Press, 2003), 2.

29. *Al-Zahrah* 1, no. 21 (1870): 168.

30. *Al-Jinān* 1, no. 10 (1870): 315.

31. Ibid., 319.

32. *Al-Zahrah* 1, no. 24 (1870): 192.

33. *Al-Jinān* 1, no. 11 (1870): 348.

34. *Al-Zahrah* 1:25 (1870), 200. Three years later, in 1873, Daniel Bliss, then president of the Syrian Protestant College, would write a letter to his wife in Amherst, Massachusetts, from a Beirut still fettered by the soldiers of worry: "There was quite an excitement downtown today. Frangia, the man who had a shop near Yousuf Matta's—killed himself this morning. He had lost his property in some way" (Bliss, *Letters from a New Campus, 1873–74* [Beirut: American University in Beirut Press, 1994], 68).

35. *Al-Jinān* 1, no. 13 (1870): 414.

36. Adelaide Bustānī, "Henry and Amelia," trans. Elizabeth M. Holt, in *The Arab Renaissance: Anthology of Nahda Thought, Literature, and Language*, ed. Tarek El-Ariss (New York: Modern Language Association, 2016). This story originally appeared in *Al-Jinān* 1, no. 12–1, no. 13 (late June–early July 1870).

37. *Al-Najāḥ* 1, no. 39 (1871): 621.

38. Bliss, *Letters from a New Campus*, 51.

39. Ibid., 54.

40. *Al-Jinān* 1, no. 8 (1870): 253.

41. Ibid.

42. *Al-Zahrah* 1, no. 42 (1870): 336 (marked p. 306 in the journal, but the numbering falls behind by thirty pages with issue 37).

43. *Al-Jinān* 1, no. 16 (1870): 510.

44. Ibid.

45. Ibid.

46. Ian Baucom, *Specters of the Atlantic: Finance Capital, Slavery, and the Philosophy of History* (Durham, NC: Duke University Press, 2005), 17.

47. Shākir al-Khūrī tells a memorable anecdote of the highly successful French entrepreneur Antoine-Fortuné Portalis's own dissimulations in the years prior to *Al-Jinān*'s publication (see al-Khūrī, *Majmaʿ al-masarrāt*, ed. Ilyās Qaṭṭār [1908; Beirut: Dār Laḥd Khāṭir, 1985], 139):

> [Portalis] did not advance *dirhams* for the [silk] season by means of a promissory note or a certificate of exchange, but rather on faith. It occurred sometimes that some of the landlords or property owners would deny the amount, and in that event he would be content with only an oath from them by placing their hand on the Bible that he had on his table, having them swear that they had not taken the *dirhams*.
>
> The denier upon swearing with his right hand and placing it upon the table would feel a great trembling and would immediately confess, and the reason for that was that Fortuné was smart and had discovered that complaining and allegations were tiresome and prolonged and incurred losses more often and since he had a lot of business and did not have time for these sorts of matters and in the end was obligated to advance [money] for the silk cocoons, he prepared an electric device and placed it under the table and ran the current into the Bible such that all who touched it felt the electric current and trembled without knowing the reason save for his denial of the *dirhams* and so confessed and in this manner the faith of the deniers in the Bible increased and Fortuné got back his *dirhams*.

48. *Al-Jinān* 1, no. 2 (1870): 64.

49. Ibid.

50. Ibid.

51. Ibid., 36.

52. Books and journals during the period could be purchased at the printer's, while periodicals and some books were available through subscription via post, the most popular means of distribution (and the subject of many a journal's apologies to readers over postal delays). While books, as seen in Zaydān's memory of purchasing *Majmaʿ al-baḥrayn*, could be bought from merchants or individuals, Buṭrus al-Bustānī noted in 1869 that there were "no stores that contain what is delightful to read in the way of books

and trade journals" (al-Būstanī, "Khiṭāb fī al-hay'ah al-ijtimāʿiyyah wa-l-muqābilah bayn al-ʿawā'id al-ʿarabiyyah wa-l-ifranjiyyah" [A speech on the social environment and the encounter betwen Arab and foreign customs], in *Aʿmāl al-jamʿīyah al-ʿilmiyyah al-sūriyyah*, ed. Khūrī, 207.

53. All figures for workers' salaries from Labaki, *Introduction à l'histoire économique du Liban*, 121. See also Khater, *Inventing Home*, for a discussion of working conditions across the silk industry for both men and women.

54. *Al-Nashrah al-Usbūʿiyyah* 1, no. 38 (1871): 2.

55. Based on the August 1871 price of *baladī* silk (260–90 *ghirsh* per *uqqah*), printed in *Al-Najāḥ* 63 (1871): 1013.

56. In 1871, *Al-Nashrah al-Usbūʿiyyah* printed on the back page of issue 44 a lesson in capitalism with the title "Qīmat al-shughl" (The value of work). The short article asked what was the most lucrative thing that one could make out of a 100 *ghirsh* piece of iron, revealing that "if one made from it buttons for shirts, its value would exceed 58,960 *ghirsh*" (*Al-Nashrah al-Usbūʿiyyah* 1, no. 44 [1871]).

57. *Al-Najāḥ* 1, no. 63 (1871): 1013–14.

58. Ibid., 1014.

59. Salīm Kassab, "Al-Ṣināʿah [Industry]" in *Aʿmāl al-jamʿīyah al-ʿilmiyyah al-sūriyyah*, ed. Khūrī, 174.

60. Ibid.

61. Ibid.

62. *Al-Zahrah* 1, no. 23 (1870): 178.

63. *Al-Zahrah* 1, no. 12 (1870): 90.

64. Ibid.

65. For more on Egyptian department stores during this period, see Uri M. Kupferschmidt, "Who Needed Department Stores in Egypt? From Orosdi-Back to Omar Effendi," *Middle Eastern Studies* 43, no. 2 (2007): 175–92; and Nancy Reynolds, *A City Consumed: Commerce, the Cairo Fire, and the Politics of Decolonization in Egypt* (Palo Alto: Stanford University Press, 2012).

66. *Al-Zahrah* 1, no. 12 (1870): 91.

67. Kassab, "Al-Ṣināʿah [Industry]," 175.

68. *Al-Zahrah* 1, no. 34 (1870): 266.

69. *Al-Jinān* 1, no. 4 (1870): 123.

70. Kassab, "Al-Ṣināʿah [Industry]," 177.

71. Ibid.

72. *Al-Jinān* 2, no. 1 (1871): 30.

73. Ibid., 26. On the ruins motif, see Jaroslav Stetkevych, *The Zephyrs of Najd: The Poetics of Nostalgia in the Classical Arabic Nasib* (Chicago: University of Chicago Press, 1993).

74. *Al-Jinan* 2, no. 24 (1871): 860.

75. Williams, *Marxism and Literature*, 114.

76. *Al-Jinān* 2, no. 23 (1871): 820–21.

77. Even less remains now, after the destruction wrought by ISIS.

78. *Al-Jinān* 2, no. 24 (1871): 854.

79. Elliott Colla, *Conflicted Antiquities: Egyptology, Egyptomania, Egyptian Modernity* (Durham, NC: Duke University Press, 2007), 89.

80. *Al-Jinān* 2, no. 6 (1871): 205.
81. *Al-Jinān* 2, no. 1 (1871): 26.
82. *Al-Jinān* 2, no. 3 (1871): 101.

CHAPTER 3: FICTIONS OF CAPITAL IN 1870S AND 1880S BEIRUT

1. The title of this chapter borrows from George L. Henderson's *California and the Fictions of Capital* (New York: Oxford University Press, 1999).
2. See the introductions to Samah Selim, *The Novel and the Rural Imaginary in Egypt, 1880–1985* (New York: RoutledgeCurzon 2004); and Elisabeth Kendall, *Literature, Journalism, and the Avant-Garde: Intersection in Egypt* (New York: Routledge, 2006).
3. Jens Hanssen, *Fin-de-Siècle Beirut: The Making of an Ottoman Provincial Capital* (New York: Oxford University Press, 2005), 85.
4. Ibid.
5. *Al-Jinān* 6, no. 6 (1875): 212.
6. Fīlīp dī Ṭarrāzi, *Tārīkh al-ṣiḥāfah al-'arabiyyah*, vol. 2 (Beirut: al-Maṭba'ah al-adabiyyah, 1913), 54.
7. Ibid.
8. *Al-Muqtaṭaf* 1, no. 8 (1877): 206–7.
9. *Al-Zahrah* 23 (1870): 178.
10. *Al-Muqtaṭaf* 1, no. 1 (1876): 24.
11. Ibid., 27–29.
12. *Al-Muqtaṭaf* 1, no. 2 (1876): 37.
13. *Al-Muqtaṭaf* 1, no. 9 (1877): 213.
14. *Al-Muqtaṭaf* 1, no. 1 (1876): 3–7.
15. *Al-Muqtaṭaf* 1, no. 9 (1877): 240.
16. *Al-Muqtaṭaf* 1, no. 4 (1876): 98.
17. See, for instance, *Al-Muqtaṭaf* 1, no. 6 (1877): 166; *Al-Muqtaṭaf* 1, no. 8 (1877): 203; and *Al-Muqtaṭaf* 1, no. 9 (1877): 223.
18. *Al-Muqtaṭaf* 1, no. 1 (1876): 24.
19. *Al-Jinān* 13, no. 20 (1882): 633.
20. *Al-Muqtaṭaf* 2, no. 7 (1877): 186.
21. *Al-Muqtaṭaf* 2, no. 4 (1877): 93.
22. *Al-Muqtaṭaf* 2, no. 7 (1877): 186–87.
23. *Al-Jinān* 3, no. 7 (1872): 251.
24. *Al-Jinān* 3, no. 8 (1872): 281.
25. Sabry Hafez, *The Genesis of Arabic Narrative Discourse: A Study in the Sociology of Modern Arabic Literature* (London: Saqi, 1993), 113. Hafez is by no means alone in this condemnation of Salīm al-Bustānī. For more on the responses of recent literary critics to the work of al-Bustānī and others writing in Beirut during this period, see chapter 1.
26. See, for instance, *al-Jinān* 3, no. 18 (1872): 641, when the narrator explains that Budūr is speaking ambiguously in an attempt to attain her freedom, leading her captor, the pirate captain, to mistake her meaning for the one he wishes to hear.
27. *Al-Jinān* 3, no. 16 (1872): 571.

28. Stephen Best and Sharon Marcus, "Surface Reading: An Introduction," *Representations* 108, no. 1 (Fall 2009): 14.

29. *Al-Jinān* 3, no. 7 (1872): 249.

30. Bruce Robbins, *The Servant's Hand: English Fiction from Below* (Durham, NC: Duke University Press, 1993), 22.

31. Ibid., xi.

32. *Al-Jinān* 3, no. 4 (1872): 142.

33. *Al-Jinān* 3, no. 8 (1872): 283.

34. Akram Fouad Khater, *Inventing Home: Emigration, Gender, and the Middle Class in Lebanon, 1870–1920* (Berkeley: University of California Press, 2001).

35. This switching around of names occurs a number of times (see, for instance, *Al-Jinān* 3, no. 8 [1872]: 284).

36. Ibid., 286.

37. Matti Moosa, *The Origins of Modern Arabic Fiction* (Boulder, CO: Lynne Rienner, 1997), 177.

38. *Al-Bashīr* 1, no. 45 (September 8, 1871): 400.

39. Ilham Khuri-Makdisi, *The Eastern Mediterranean and the Making of Global Radicalism, 1860–1914* (Berkeley: University of California Press, 2010), 35.

40. *Al-Najāḥ* 1, no. 74 (1871); *Al-Najāḥ* 1, no. 75 (1871). See also *Al-Najāḥ* 1, no. 36 (1871); *Al-Najāḥ* 1, no. 37(1871); and *Al-Najāḥ* 1, no. 47 (1871).

41. *Al-Bashīr* 1, no. 41 (June 10, 1871): 358.

42. *Al-Bashīr* 1, no 35 (April 29, 1871): 300.

43. Moosa, *The Origins of Modern Arabic Fiction*, 176, 177.

44. *Al-Jinān* 13, no. 13 (1882): 411.

45. Ibid.

46. *Al-Jinān* 14, no. 10 (1883): 316.

47. *Al-Jinān* 13, no. 13 (1882): 413.

48. *Al-Jinān* 13, no. 16 (1882): 510.

49. *Al-Jinān* 13, no. 18 (1882): 574.

50. *Al-Jinān* 13, no. 13 (1882): 412.

51. Ibid., 415.

52. *Al-Jinān* 14, no. 22 (1883): 683.

53. *Al-Jinān* 14, no. 23 (1883): 713.

54. *Al-Jinān* 13, no. 13 (1882): 415.

55. For more on the telegraph station in Beirut, see Hanssen, *Fin de Siècle Beirut*, 39.

56. *Al-Jinān* 13, no. 17 (1882): 538.

57. *Al-Jinān* 13, no. 16 (1882): 509.

58. *Al-Jinān* 6, no. 1 (1875): 31.

59. *Al-Jinān* 6, no. 2 (1875): 71.

60. *Al-Jinān* 6, no. 1 (1875): 34.

61. Ibid.

62. *Al-Jinān* 6, no. 3 (1875): 105.

63. *Al-Jinān* 6, no. 1 (1875): 32.

64. *Al-Jinān* 6, no. 4 (1875): 140.
65. Ibid., 143.
66. *Al-Jinān* 6, no. 5 (1875): 177.
67. Ibid., 175.
68. Ibid., 176–77.
69. Ibid., 177.
70. Ibid.
71. Ibid.
72. Ibid.
73. Ibid., 177–78.
74. *Al-Jinān* 6, no. 6 (1875): 210.
75. Ibid.
76. Ibid., 214.
77. *Al-Jinān* 6, no. 7 (1875): 250.
78. *Al-Jinān* 6, no. 8 (1875): 285.
79. Ibid., 285–86.

CHAPTER 4: MOURNING THE *NAHḌAH*:
FROM BEIRUT TO CAIRO, AFTER MIDNIGHT

1. In her chapter on the emergence and development of literary journalism in Egypt, Elisabeth Kendall notes that "in the decade before the British occupation, only 9 percent of newspapers, journals, and periodicals were scientific, literary or satirical; the rest were political. In the first decade of the occupation, this rose to 75 per cent." She relies here on the work of Sāmī ʿAzīz in *al-Ṣiḥāfah al-Miṣriyyah wa-mawqifuhā min al-iḥtilāl al-Inglīzī* [The Egyptian press and its position on the British occupation] (1968) (see Kendall, *Literature, Journalism and the Avant-Garde: Intersection in Egypt* [New York: Routledge, 2006], 20).

2. *Lisān al-Ḥāl* (September 25 1884): 1.

3. Ibid.

4. Ibid.

5. Ibid.

6. Ibid.

7. Ibid.

8. Shafik Jeha, *Darwin and the Crisis of 1882 in the Medical Department and the First Student Protest in the Arab World in the Syrian Protestant College (Now the American University of Beirut)*, trans. Sally Kaya (Beirut: American University of Beirut Press, 2004); Marwa ElShakry, *Reading Darwin in Arabic, 1860–1950* (Chicago: University of Chicago Press, 2014); Michael Allan, *In the Shadow of World Literature: Sites of Reading in Colonial Egypt* (Princeton: Princeton University Press, 2016).

9. Ibid., 99.

10. Ibid., 102.

11. Fāris Nimr and Yaʿqūb Ṣarrūf were also evidently members of a secret anti-Ottoman, nationalist society. Jeha charts his debate (see 127), with Asad Rustum "reveal[ing] decisive evidence" of Nimr's and Ṣarrūf's involvement in the secret society in his 1973 study. Jeha points also to George Antonius's

corroboration of their involvement (see George Antonius, *The Arab Awakening: The Story of the Arab National Movement* [Beirut: Librairie du Liban, 1969], esp. 81, where Antonius writes: "I am greatly indebted, for the narrative [of the secret society] that I have just given, to one of its original founders, Dr. Faris Nimr Pasha who, at the ripe age of eighty and in the fullest enjoyment of his faculties, remembered the main facts and the names of twenty-two members. I spent several sittings with him . . . until I had the narrative complete, save in one important respect: the texts of the placards" that the group had anonymously posted on walls throughout Beirut in the mid-1870s and into the early 1880s. Antonius discovered the text of these placards while he was "in the Public Record Office in London," when he "came upon a telegram from the British Consul-General in Bairut, dated June 28, 1880" [82]). The telegram announced the appearances of placards in Beirut and others in Damascus and transmitted the text of the placards. One stated the goals of the secret society, which were:

> (1). the grant of independence to Syria in union with the Lebanon;
>
> (2). the recognition of Arabic as an official language in the country;
>
> (3). the removal of the censorship and other restrictions on the freedom of expression and the diffusion of knowledge;
>
> (4). the employment of locally-recruited units of local military service only. (84)

12. "Risālat al-Duktūr Van Dyck," *Al-Muqtaṭaf* 9, no. 6 (March 1885): 322.

13. This saying is ascribed to al-Ṣāḥib bin ʿAbbād (d. 995) upon intercepting the Andalusian Ibn ʿAbd Rabīh (d. 940)'s *al-ʿIqd al-farīd*. "Risālat al-Duktūr Van Dyck," *Al-Muqtaṭaf* 9, no. 6 (March 1885): 322.

14. *Al-Muqtaṭaf*'s arrival in Cairo was met with great pomp (in letters from Sharīf Pasha and Riyāḍ Pasha [ibid., 321–22]) and some regret (in a letter from Dr. Van Dyck [ibid., 322]). A brief announcement of the move appears in the final page of the February 1885 issue as well (320). It would appear that Nimr and Ṣarrūf traveled separately to Cairo, perhaps accounting for the varied years (1884 and 1885) given for *Al-Muqtaṭaf*'s move to Cairo from Beirut. In a letter dated January 26, 1885, one Mrs. Porter "wrote . . . to a friend in the Syria Mission" in the aftermath of the Lewis affair and Nimr's and Ṣarrūf's dismissal from the Syrian Protestant College faculty: "Do you see the Arabic Scientific Journal? I do not know how to write the name in English, but you know what I mean, the one published by our late tutors. You have doubtless read the articles full of spite which have been published in it lately. Is it not too bad that young men of so many excellent qualities should show such a mean spirit? I believe it is the married one, who still remains here in Beirut, more than it is the other one, who has gone to Egypt" (qtd. in Nadia Farag, "The Lewis Affair and the Fortunes of al-Muqtataf," *Middle Eastern Studies* 8, no. 1 [January 1972]: 81).

15. Fīlīp dī Ṭarrāzi, *Tārīkh al-ṣiḥāfah al-ʿarabiyyah*, vol. 2 (Beirut: al-Maṭbaʿah al-adabiyyah, 1913), 54.

16. Donald J. Cioeta, "Ottoman Censorship in Lebanon and Syria, 1876–1908," *International Journal of Middle East Studies* 10, no. 2 (May 1979): 178.

17. Cioeta lists some of the most important Syrian émigrés to the future of the Arabic press in Egypt, including the Taqlā brothers, Salīm ʿAntūrī, Salīm Fāris al-Shidyāq, Amīn Shumayyil, Shahīn Makārīyūs, Salīm al-Naqqāsh, and Adīb Isḥāq before the watershed year of 1889, and Salīm Sarkīs, Ibrahīm Yāzijī, Farāh Anṭūn, and Rashīd Riḍā emigrating after 1889 in the wake of stricter Ottoman censorship (ibid., 179).

18. Ibid., 180.

19. Ami Ayalon, *The Press in the Arab Middle East: A History* (New York: Oxford University Press, 1995), 37.

20. Ibid., 39.

21. *Lisān al-Ḥāl* (September 25, 1884): 2.

22. *Al-Jinān* 13, no. 15 (1882): 459–64.

23. Ibid., 459.

24. Ibid.

25. Ibid., 460.

26. Ibid., 459.

27. The following Arabic literary critical works all specifically emphasize the importance of Syrian émigrés in Egypt to the early Arabic press and the history of the Arabic novel yet overlook the Beirut scene of the 1870s and early 1880s entirely or ascribe to it an extremely limited role, a critical aporia that the early chapters of this book seek to redress: Paul Starkey, *Modern Arabic Literature*; Elisabeth Kendall, *Literature, Journalism and the Avant-Garde: Intersection in Egypt*; Roger Allen, *The Arabic Literary Heritage*; M. M. Badawi, *Modern Arabic Literature and the West* and *A Short History of Modern Arabic Literature*; and ʿAbd al-Badr, *Taṭawwur al-riwāyah al-ʿarabiyyah al-ḥadīthah fī Miṣr.*

28. See also Muḥammad Yūsuf Najm, *Al-Qissah fi-l-adab al-ʿarabī al-ḥadīth* (Cairo: Dār Miṣr li-l-Ṭibāʿah, 1952). Najm argues that the reasons for emigration were largely economic, citing August Adīb Pasha's *Lubnān baʿd al-ḥarb*, as well as Mīshāl Shiblī's *al-Muhājirah al-Lubnāniyyah*, who also points to the draw of tales of Syrian entrepreneurial success for those who left Beirut and Mount Lebanon.

29. Kendall, *Literature, Journalism and the Avant-Garde*, 13.

30. For more on the history of Egyptian department stores, see Uri M. Kupferschmidt, "Who Needed Department Stores in Egypt? From Orosdi-Back to Omar Effendi," *Middle Eastern Studies* 43, no. 2 (2007). See also Thomas Philipp, *The Syrians in Egypt: 1725–1975* (Stuttgart: Franz Steiner Verlag, 1985).

31. "Al-Jarāʾid al-ʿarabiyyah fi-l-ʿālam," *Al-Hilāl* 1, no. 1 (September 1892): 9.

32. Ibid.

33. Ibid., 10.

34. Ibid., 11. The section heading in Arabic reads "Al-Jarāʾid allatī ẓaharat thumma tawārat amā taʿlīqan ilā ajal wa-amā ilghāʾan muʾabbadan."

35. Ibid., 12.

36. Jurjī Zaydān, *Mudhākirāt Jurjī Zaydān*, ed. Ṣalāḥ al-Dīn al-Munajjid (Beirut: Dār al-Kitāb al-Jadīd, 1968). See also Jeha, *Darwin and the Crisis of 1882*, 77.

37. Jurjī Zaydān, *Mudhākirāt Jurjī Zaydān*, ed, Ṣalāḥ al-Dīn al-Munajjid (Beirut: Dār al-Kitāb al-Jadīd, 1968), 36.

38. Ibid., 39.

39. Ibid., 41.

40. Ibid., 42.

41. Ibid., 42–43.

42. "Tidhkārāt al-madrasah wa-fīhā tārīkh awal thawrah madrasiyyah fī al-ʿālam al-ʿarabī: Ṣafaḥāt min mudhakkirāt muʾassis *Al-Hilāl*" (*Al-Hilāl* 33, no. 1 [October 1, 1924]: 17–20).

43. Ibid., 19.

44. The Lebanese novelist Rashīd al-Ḍaʿīf has capitalized on these scenes of grave robbing and dissection in his recently published *Tablīṭ al-baḥr* (which could politely translate as "Go Pave the Sea"), a historical novel set in part in late nineteenth-century Beirut with none other than Jurjī Zaydān as one of its main characters (Rashīd al-Ḍaʿīf, *Tablīṭ al-baḥr* [Beirut, Riad El-Rayyes Books, 2011]). Sections of the novel closely limn Zaydān's memoirs. See, for instance, the bouquet of flowers in the coffin of a corpse stolen for dissection (ibid., 47; Zaydān, *Mudhakirrāt*, 58).

45. Zaydān, *Mudhakirrāt*, 96–97.

46. Matti Moosa, *The Origins of Modern Arabic Fiction* (Boulder, CO: Lynne Rienner, 1997), 197.

47. "Jurjī Bey Zaydān," *Al-Muqtaṭaf* 45, no. 2 (September 1914): 285.

48. Jurjī Zaydān, *Tarīkh adāb al-lughah al-ʿarabiyyah*, vol. 4 (Cairo: Dār al-Hilāl, 1957), written in 1914, 208–9.

49. Thomas Philipp, "The Role of Jurji Zaydan in the Intellectual Development of the Arab Nahdah from the Beginning of the British Occupation of Egypt to the Outbreak of WWI" (Ph.D. diss., University of California, Los Angeles, 1971), 113.

50. Muḥammad ʿAbd al-Ghanī Ḥasan, *Jurjī Zaydān* (Cairo: Al-Hayʾah al-Miṣriyyah al-ʿĀmmah li-l-Tāʾlīf wa-l-Nashr, 1970), 99.

51. Zaydān, *Tārīkh ādāb*, vol. 4, 208–9.

52. "Jurjī Bey Zaydān," *Al-Muqtaṭaf* 45, no. 2 (September 1914): 285.

53. Ḥasan, *Jurjī Zaydān*, 11.

54. Zaydān, *Tārīkh adāb*, vol. 4, 73.

55. Jurjī Zaydān, *Yawmiyyāt riḥlah baḥriyyah: Makhṭūṭah tunshir li-l-marrah al-ūlā*, ed. Jān Dāyh (Beirut: Fajr al-Nahḍah, 2010), 51.

56. Ibid., 68.

57. Ibid.

58. "Jurjī Bey Zaydān," *Al-Muqtaṭaf* 45, no. 2 (September 1914): 285.

59. Ibid.

60. *Al-Hilāl* 1, no. 4 (December 1892 [1st ed.]): 192.

61. Jurjī Zaydān, *Asīr al-Mutamahdī* (Beirut: Dār Maktabat al-Ḥayāt, 2002–03), originally published by Maṭbaʿat al-Hilāl and advertised for sale in *Al-Hilāl*.

62. Ibid.

63. Zaydān, *Asīr al-Mutamahdī*, 9.

64. Ibid.

65. Ibid., 11.
66. Ibid., 12.
67. Ibid., 14.
68. Ibid., 12.
69. Ibid., 20.
70. "Shajarat Ādam," *Al-Hilāl* 4, no. 9 (January 1, 1896): 341.
71. Ibid.
72. Zaydān, *Yawmiyyāt riḥlah baḥriyyah*, 68–69.
73. Janet Abu Lughod, "Tale of Two Cities: The Origins of Modern Cairo," *Comparative Studies in Society and History* 7, no. 4 (July 1965): 444.
74. Ibid., 449.
75. This is the street on which Zaydān lived beginning in October 1886, having moved there from the apartment in Bayt al-Zuhār, in the same building in which Fāris Nimr, Yaʿqūb Ṣarrūf, and Shāhīn Makāriyūs lived (Zaydān, *Riḥlah baḥriyyah*, 68–69).
76. *Al-Hilāl* 5, no. 20 (June 15, 1897): 800.
77. Zaydān, *Asīr al-Mutamahdī*, 14.

CHAPTER 5: OF LITERARY SUPPLEMENTS, SECOND EDITIONS, AND THE LOTTERY: THE RISE OF JURJĪ ZAYDĀN

1. "Khātimat al-sanah al-tāsiʿah," *Al-Muqtaṭaf* 9, no. 12 (September 1885): 860.
2. "Ujrat muḥarrirī al-jarāʾid, "*Al-Muqtaṭaf* 13, no. 6 (March 1, 1889): 464.
3. *Al-Muqtaṭaf* 32, no. 11 (November 1907): 945.
4. Samah Selim, "The People's Entertainment: Translation, Popular Fiction, and the Nahdah in Egypt," in *Other Renaissances: A New Approach to World Literature*, ed. Brenda Deen Schildgen (New York: Palgrave Macmillan, 2006), 44.
5. *Al-Muqtaṭaf* 30, no. 5 (May 1905): 414.
6. Walter Benjamin, "The Storyteller," in *The Novel: An Anthology of Criticism and Theory 1900–2000*, ed. Dorothy J. Hale (Malden, MA: Blackwell, 2006), 363, 367.
7. See his introduction to his third serialized novel, *Fatāt Ghassān* (1896–97), in *Al-Hilāl* 5, no. 1 (September 1, 1896).
8. Ibid.
9. Jacques Derrida, *Given Time: I. Counterfeit Money*, trans. Peggy Kamuf (Chicago: University of Chicago Press, 1992), 101. Derrida here is very much in agreement with Clifford Siskin's observation regarding the British periodicals of the eighteenth century, with "the flow of contributions [to the periodicals] inducing the flow of capital, for this was the appropriation of surplus value in its purest form: almost all of the material was provided (and could be reprinted) for free" (Siskin, "Epilogue: The Rise of Novelism," in *Cultural Institutions of the Novel*, ed. Deirdre Lynch and William Beatty Warner [Durham, NC: Duke University Press, 1996], 427).
10. ʿAbd al-Muḥsin Ṭāhā Badr, *Taṭawwur al-riwāyah al-ʿarabiyyah al-ḥadīthah fī Miṣr*, 5th. ed. (Cairo: Dār al-Maʿārif, 1992), 43.

11. See Samah Selim, *The Novel and the Rural Imaginary in Egypt, 1880–1985* (New York: RoutledgeCurzon 2004); Samah Selim, "The People's Entertainment: Translation, Popular Fiction, and the Nahdah in Egypt," in *Other Renaissances: A New Approach to World Literature*, ed. Brenda Deen Schildgen (New York: Palgrave Macmillan, 2006); and Shaden Tageldin, *Disarming Words: Empire and the Seductions of Translation in Egypt* (Berkeley: University of California Press, 2011).

12. Samah Selim, in *The Novel and the Rural Imaginary*, analyzes the disdain surrounding Badr's *riwāyat al-tasliyah wa-l-tarfīh* in the context of popular translated fiction in turn-of-the-century Egypt, noting that these translated novels claimed a large share of the market (44).

13. ʿAbd al-Muḥsin Ṭāhā Badr, *Taṭawwur al-riwāyah al-ʿarabiyyah al-ḥadīthah fī Miṣr*, 5th. ed. (Cairo: Dār al-Maʿārif, 1992), 98.

14. Ibid., 114n6.

15. Ibid., 116n2.

16. Ibid., 142.

17. *Al-Hilāl* 8, no. 23–24 (September 15, 1900): 726.

18. Ibid., 726–27.

19. In 1893, the Cairo-based journal *Al-Ustādh* published figures it had received from the post office in Cairo for periodicals passing through its post. Though *Al-Ustādh* notes that journals were also sold by the issue, the postal figures for subscribers provide some measure of the extent to which *Al-Hilāl*'s distribution may have increased over the course of five years (or of the extent to which Zaydān may have been trumpeting his wares):

Al-Muʾayyad. 1,200
Al-Ahrām. 2,775
Al-Hilāl. 740
Al-Zirāʿah. 600
Al-Maḥrūsah. 443
Al-Fallāḥ. 545
Al-Muqaṭṭam. 1,455
Al-Muqtaṭaf. 1,300
Al-Ustādh. 1,345

See *Al-Ustādh* 1, no. 20 (January 3, 1893): 477.

20. *Al-Hilāl* 7, no. 1 (October 1, 1898): 32.

21. *Al-Hilāl* 5, no. 17 (May 1, 1897): 664

22. *Iʿlānāt al-Hilāl*, published as a supplement to *Al-Hilāl* in the fall of 1897, 1.

23. Ibid., 2.

24. Ibid.

25. Ibid., 3.

26. Ibid.

27. Ibid., 4.

28. Ibid.

29. Ibid., 5.

30. Ibid., 6.

31. Ibid.

32. Ibid., 7.
33. Ibid.
34. "Muhājirat dūd al-qazz" [The migration of the silk worm], *Al-Mushīr* 3, no. 121 (February 12, 1897): 1027.
35. *Al-Hilāl* 5, no. 15 (April 1, 1897): 595.
36. *Al-Mushīr* 4, no. 2 (November 6, 1897): 15.
37. *Al-Hilāl* 5, no. 9 (January 1, 1897): 330. An earlier announcement detailing the plans for a new reading room and bookstore appeared in *Al-Hilāl* 5, no. 3 (October 1, 1896): 119–20.
38. *Al-Hilāl* 6, no. 5 (November 1, 1897): 192.
39. *Al-Hilāl* 8, no. 6 (December 15, 1899):182.
40. "Al-Sūriyyūn fī-Miṣr," 271.
41. Ibid., 273.
42. See the long bar scenes and the endless search for a prostitute in the *ʿumdah* sections of al-Muwaylīḥī's *Ḥadīth ʿĪsā ibn Hishām.*
43. "The destructive habit (*al-ʿādah al-muḍirrah*)"—see *Al-Hilāl* 4, no. 2 (September 15, 1895): 50; as well as Jurjī Zaydān, *Asīr al-Mutamahdī* (Beirut: Dār Maktabat al-Ḥayāt, 2002–03), 19; and Joseph Massad's discussion of the discourse surrounding masturbation in *Desiring Arabs* (Chicago: Chicago University Press, 2007). This scene from Zaydān's memoirs also appears as a lesson in how "a man milks himself" in Rashīd al-Ḍaʿīf's *Tablīṭ al-bahr* (Beirut, Riad El-Rayyes, 2011), 37–38.
44. On the dangers of drinking beer, frequenting cafés (a habit that from Zaydān's observations eventually leads to the bars and clubs around Ezbekiyyah), and of the inevitability of gambling in all these establishments, see "Sāʿāt al-farāgh" (Free time), *Al-Hilāl* 2, no. 21 (July 1, 1894): 648–50.
45. Ibid., 651.
46. "Yā-naṣīb *Al-Hilāl*," *Al-Hilāl* 7, no. 6 (December 15, 1898): 176
47. "Jāʾizat *Al-Hilāl*," *Al-Hilāl* 7, no. 9 (February 1, 1899): 285.
48. Ibid.
49. Ibid.
50. Offers listed in section entitled "Imtiyāzāt mushtarikī *Al-Hilāl*," *Al-Hilāl* 8, no. 23–24 (September 15, 1900): 736.
51. *Al-Hilāl* 5, no. 14 (March 15, 1897): 530.

CHAPTER 6: IT WAS COTTON MONEY NOW: NOVEL MATERIAL IN YAʿQŪB ṢARRŪF'S TURN-OF-THE-TWENTIETH-CENTURY CAIRO

1. Fīlīp dī Ṭarrāzī, *Tārīkh al-ṣiḥāfah al-ʿarabiyyah*, vol. 2 (Beirut: al-Maṭbaʿah al-adabiyyah, 1913), 54.
2. Consider Peter Gran's accounts of the late nineteenth-century rise of finance capital in Arabic, Gran, *Islamic Roots of Capitalism: Egypt, 1760–1840* (Syracuse: Syracuse University Press, 1998), xxxvi.
3. See Karl Marx, *Capital, Vol. III* (1894; London: Penguin, 1991). Chapter 25 is entitled "Credit and Fictitious Capital."
4. M. Roustan le Gerant (le Consulat Genèral de France à Beyrouth) to Ambassador M. le Vogüé in Constantinople, April 3, 1873, Box 22, Letter

no. 4 (2), Série D (correspondance consulaire), Répertoire Numérique de la Sous-Série Beyrouth 1755–1914 (41 articles) 166PO/D11, Ministère des Affaires Étrangères, Centre des Archives Diplomatiques de Nantes.

5. M. Roustan le Gerant (le Consulat Genèral de France à Beyrouth) to Ambassador M. le Vogüé in Constantinople, September 8, 1873, Box 22, Letter no. 12, Série D (correspondance consulaire), Répertoire Numérique de la Sous-Série Beyrouth 1755–1914 (41 articles) 166PO/D11, Ministère des Affaires Étrangères, Centre des Archives Diplomatiques de Nantes.

6. ʿAbd al-Muḥsin Ṭāhā Badr, *Taṭawwur al-riwāyah al-ʿarabiyyah al-ḥadīthah fī Miṣr, 1870–1938*, 5th. ed. (Cairo: Dār al-Maʿārif, 1992), 46.

7. Samah Selim, *The Novel and the Rural Imaginary in Egypt, 1880–1985* (New York: RoutledgeCurzon, 2004).

8. Benedict Anderson, *Imagined Communities: Reflections on the Origin and Spread of Nationalism* (New York: Verso, 1983), 25–26, 35.

9. For more on Mayy Ziyādah's Cairo salon and its contributions to the *Nahḍah*, see Boutheina Khaldi, *Egypt Awakening in the Early Twentieth Century: Mayy Ziyadah's Intellectual Circles* (New York: Palgrave Macmillan, 2012).

10. Yaʿqūb Ṣarrūf, *Fatāt Miṣr*, 4th ed. (Cairo: Maṭbaʿat al-Muqtaṭaf, 1922), d–h.

11. See chapter 5 on the Cairo journal *Al-Rāwī*, and the discussions in *Al-Muqtaṭaf* as to its financial viability.

12. For more on the antinovel debates in *Al-Muqtaṭaf*, see the first chapter of Elisabeth Kendall, *Literature, Journalism and the Avant-Garde: Intersection in Egypt* (New York: Routledge, 2006). Selim's *Novel and the Rural Imaginary* also touches on this discussion of "household management" in *Al-Muqtaṭaf*.

13. *Al-Muqtaṭaf* 30, no. 1 (January 1905): 87.

14. Jabr Ḍūmiṭ, "Intiqād *Fatāt Miṣr*," *Al-Muqtaṭaf*, 31, no. 7 (July 1906): 545.

15. Ibid., 553.

16. Ibid., 548. This excerpt is from pp. 52–53 of the novel in its fourth edition, in the voice of the character Henry.

17. Ibid., 545.

18. Ibid., 554.

19. Ibid., 548.

20. *Al-Muqtaṭaf* 30, no. 8 (August 1905): 664–65 (under the section on *Tadbīr al-manāzil*, or "Household Management").

21. Ibid.

22. ʿAbd al-Muḥsin Ṭāhā Badr, *Taṭawwur al-riwāyah al-ʿarabiyyah al-ḥadīthah fī Miṣr, 1870–1938*, 5th. ed. (Cairo: Dār al-Maʿārif, 1992), 43.

23. Ibid., 46.

24. Ibid., 94, my italics.

25. "Āfat al-quṭn fī al-quṭr al-Miṣrī [The plague upon cotton in Egypt]," *al-Mu'ayyad* (January 31, 1905), qtd. in Aaron Jakes, "Boom, Bugs, Bust: Egypt's Ecology of Interest, 1882–1914," *Antipode* (2016): 1.

26. Pierre Arminjon, "Les Enseignements de la crise financière Égyptienne actuelle et le bilan économique de l'Égypte," *Revue Économique Internationale* (February 1909): 265.

27. Anna Kornbluh's discussion of Victorian realism and real estate in the introduction to *Realizing Capital: Financial and Psychic Economies in Victorian Form* (New York: Fordham University Press, 2013) provides a helpful counterpoint from the center of the British Empire.

28. Fredric Jameson, "Culture and Finance Capital," *Critical Inquiry* 24 (Autumn 1997): 251, my italics.

29. Yaʿqūb Ṣarrūf, *Fatāt Miṣr*, 4th ed. (Cairo: Maṭbaʿat al-Muqtaṭaf, 1922), 88.

30. Ibid., 90.

31. Ibid., 104.

32. Ibid.

33. Ibid., 1.

34. Ibid., 5.

35. Ibid., 4.

36. Ibid., 13.

37. Ibid.

38. Ibid.

39. I am grateful to Bilal Orfali for his research and guidance on an earlier Arabic tradition of cultivating gardens of knowledge. See Holt, "From Gardens of Knowledge to Ezbekiyya after Midnight: The Novel and the Arabic Press from Beirut to Cairo, 1870–1892," in "Authoring the *Nahḍa*: Writing the Arabic 19th Century," special issue, *Middle Eastern Literatures* 16, no. 3 (December 2013): 232–48.

40. Ṣarrūf, *Fatāt Miṣr*, 174.

41. Ibid., 110.

42. Ibid., 111.

43. See esp. chap. 2, "The *Nahḍa*, the Press, and the Construction and Dissemination of a Radical Worldview," in Ilham Khuri-Makdisi, *The Eastern Mediterranean and the Making of Global Radicalism, 1860–1914* (Berkeley: University of California Press, 2010).

44. Thomas Philipp, *The Syrians in Egypt: 1725–1975* (Stuttgart: Franz Steiner Verlag: 1985), 93n33.

45. Walter Benjamin, "The Storyteller," in *The Novel: An Anthology of Criticism and Theory 1900–2000*, ed. Dorothy J. Hale (Malden, MA: Blackwell, 2006), 363, 367.

46. Ṣarrūf, *Fatāt Miṣr*, 112.

47. Ibid., 123.

48. Ibid., 133.

49. Ibid., 173.

50. Ibid.

51. Ibid., 172.

CODA

1. Jonathan Levy, *Freaks of Fortune: The Emerging World of Capitalism and Risk in America* (Cambridge: Harvard University Press, 2012), 13.

2. Ibid., 240.

3. Ghenwa Hayek, *Beirut, Imagining the City: Space and Place in Lebanese Literature* (London: I. B. Tauris, 2014).

4. Levy, *Freaks of Fortune*, 14.

BIBLIOGRAPHY

JOURNALS

Al-Bashīr
Ḥadīqat al-Akhbār
Al-Hilāl
Al-Jannah
Al-Jinān
Lisān al-Ḥāl
Majallat Sarkīs
Al-Muʾayyad
Al-Muqtaṭaf
Al-Mushīr
Al-Naḥlah
Al-NajāḥAl-Nashrah al-Usbūʿiyyah
Al-Nashrah al-Usbuʿiyyah
Al-Rāwī
Thamarāt al-Funūn
Al-Ustādh
Al-Zahrah

ARCHIVES

Répertoire Numérique de la Sous-Série Beyrouth 1755–1914 (41 articles). 166PO/D11. Ministère des Affaires Étrangères, Centre des Archives Diplomatiques de Nantes.

SECONDARY SOURCES

Abbas, Raouf, and Assem El-Dessouky. *The Large Landowning Class and the Peasantry in Egypt, 1837–1952*. Translated by Amer Mohsen with Mona Zirki. Syracuse: Syracuse University Press, 2012.

Abu Lughod, Janet. "Tale of Two Cities: The Origins of Modern Cairo." *Comparative Studies in Society and History* 7, no. 4 (July 1965): 429–57.

Allan, Michael. "How *Adab* Became Literary." *Journal of Arabic Literature* 43, no. 2–3 (2012): 172–96.

———. *In the Shadow of World Literature: Sites of Reading in Colonial Egypt*. Princeton: Princeton University Press, 2016.

Allen, Roger. *The Arabic Literary Heritage*. Cambridge: Cambridge University Press, 1998.

———. *The Arabic Novel: An Historical and Critical Introduction*. Syracuse: Syracuse University Press, 1995.

———. "Narrative Genres and Nomenclature: A Comparative Study." *Journal of Arabic Literature* 23, no. 3 (1992): 208–14.

Althusser, Louis. "Ideology and the Ideological State Apparatus." In *Lenin and Philosophy, and Other Essays*, 127–86. New York: Monthly Review Press, 1971.

Altick, Richard D. *The English Common Reader: A Social History of the Mass Reading Public 1800–1900*. Chicago: University of Chicago Press, 1957.

Anderson, Benedict. *Imagined Communities: Reflections on the Origin and Spread of Nationalism*. New York: Verso, 1983.

Antonius, George. *The Arab Awakening: The Story of the Arab National Movement*. Beirut: Librairie du Liban, 1969.

Arrighi, Giovanni. *The Long Twentieth Century: Money, Power and the Origins of Our Times*. New York: Verso, 1994.

Ayalon, Ami. *The Press in the Arab Middle East: A History*. New York: Oxford University Press, 1995.

———. "Private Publishing in the *Nahḍa*." *International Journal of Middle East Studies* 40 (2008): 561–77.

Badawi, M. M. *Modern Arabic Literature and the West*. London: Ithaca Press, 1985.

———. *A Short History of Modern Arabic Literature*. Oxford: Oxford University Press, 1993.

Badr, ʿAbd al-Muḥsin Ṭāhā. *Taṭawwur al-riwāyah al-ʿarabiyyah al-ḥadīthah fī Miṣr, 1870–1938*. 5th. ed. Cairo: Dār al-Maʿārif, 1992.

Barak, On. *On Time: Technology and Temporality in Modern Egypt*. Berkeley: University of California Press, 2013.

Baron, Beth. *Egypt as a Woman: Nationalism, Gender and Politics*. Berkeley: University of California Press, 2005.

———. *The Women's Awakening in Egypt: Culture, Society, and the Press.* New Haven: Yale University Press, 1994.

Baucom, Ian. *Specters of the Atlantic: Finance Capital, Slavery, and the Philosophy of History.* Durham, NC: Duke University Press, 2005.

Benjamin, Walter. "Paris: Capital of the Nineteenth Century." *Perspecta* 12 (1969): 163–72.

———. "The Storyteller." In *The Novel: An Anthology of Criticism and Theory 1900–2000*, edited by Dorothy J. Hale, 361–78, Malden, MA: Blackwell, 2006.

Best, Stephen, and Sharon Marcus. "Surface Reading: An Introduction." *Representations* 108, no. 1 (Fall 2009): 1–21.

Bliss, Daniel. *Letters from a New Campus, 1873–74.* Beirut: American University in Beirut Press, 1994.

Booth, Marilyn. *May Her Likes Be Multiplied: Biography and Gender Politics in Egypt.* Berkeley: University of California Press, 2001.

Bourdieu, Pierre. *The Field of Cultural Production: Essays on Art and Literature.* New York: Columbia University Press, 1993.

Bustānī, Adelaide. "Henry and Amelia." Translated by Elizabeth M. Holt. In *The Arab Renaissance: Anthology of Nahda Thought, Literature, and Language*, edited by Tarek El-Aris. New York: Modern Language Association, 2016.

al-Būstānī, Buṭrus. *Dā'irat al-ma'ārif.* Vol. 6. Beirut: al-Maṭba'ah al-Adabiyyah, 1876.

———. "Khiṭāb fī al-hay'ah al-ijtimā'iyyah wa-l-muqābilah bayn al-'awā'id al-'arabiyyah wa-l-ifranjiyyah" [a speech on the social environment and the encounter between Arab and foreign customs]. In *A'māl al-jam'īyah al-'ilmiyyah al-sūriyyah*, edited by Yūsuf Qizmā Khūrī, Beirut: Dār al-ḥamrā', 1990.

———. "Khuṭbah fī Ādāb al-'Arab." In *al-Jam'iyah al-sūriyyah li-l-'ulūm wa-l-funūn 1847–1852*, edited by Yūsuf Qizmā Khūrī, Beirut: Dār al-Ḥamrā', 1990. (Lecture originally published in Beirut by al-Maṭba'ah al-Amīrkāniyyah in 1859.)

al-Bustānī, Salīm. *Al-Huyām fī futūḥ al-Shām.* New York: Idārat al-Mir'āt, 1874.

Chéhab, Maurice H. *Rôle du Liban dans l'histoire de la soie.* Beirut: Publications de l'Université Libanaise, 1967.

Cioeta, Donald J. "Ottoman Censorship in Lebanon and Syria, 1876–1908." *International Journal of Middle East Studies* 10, no. 2 (May 1979): 167–86.

Colla, Elliott. *Conflicted Antiquities: Egyptology, Egyptomania, Egyptian Modernity.* Durham, NC: Duke University Press, 2007.

———. "Field Construction." *International Journal of Middle Eastern Studies* 43 (2011): 722–24.

———. "How *Zaynab* Became the First Arabic Novel." *History Compass* 6 (2007): 1–12.

al-Ḍaʿīf, Rashīd. *Tablīṭ al-bahr*. Beirut: Riad El-Rayyes, 2011.

Derrida, Jacques. *Given Time: I. Counterfeit Money*. Translated by Peggy Kamuf. Chicago: University of Chicago Press, 1992).

dī Ṭarrāzi, Fīlīp. *Tārīkh al-ṣiḥāfah al-ʿarabiyyah*. Vols. 1–4. Beirut: al-Maṭbaʿah al-Adabiyyah, 1913.

Ducousso, Gaston. *L'industrie de la soie en Syrie et au Liban*. Beirut: Imprimerie Catholique; Paris: Librairie Maritime et Coloniale Augustin Challamel, 1918.

El-Ariss, Tarek, ed. *The Arab Renaissance: Anthology of Nahda Thought, Literature, and Language*. New York: Modern Language Association, 2016.

———. *Trials of Arab Modernity: Literary Affects and the New Political*. New York: Fordham University Press, 2013.

ElShakry, Marwa. *Reading Darwin in Arabic, 1860–1950*. Chicago: University of Chicago Press, 2014.

Fahmy, Ziad. *Ordinary Egyptians: Creating the Modern Nation through Popular Culture*. Stanford: Stanford University Press, 2011.

Farag, Nadia. "The Lewis Affair and the Fortunes of *al-Muqtataf*." *Middle Eastern Studies* 8, no. 1 (January 1972): 73–83.

Fawaz, Leila Tarazi. *Merchants and Migrants in Nineteenth-Century Beirut*. Cambridge: Harvard University Press, 1983.

Ghazoul, Ferial J. *Nocturnal Poetics: The Arabian Nights in Comparative Context*. Cairo: American University in Cairo Press, 1996.

Goldberg, Ellis. *Trade, Reputation, and Child Labor in Twentieth-Century Egypt*. New York: Palgrave Macmillan, 2004.

Gran, Peter. *Islamic Roots of Capitalism: Egypt, 1760–1840*. Syracuse: Syracuse University Press, 1998.

Habermas, Jürgen. *The Structural Transformation of the Public Sphere: An Inquiry into a Category of Bourgeois Society*. Translated by Thomas Burger with the assistance of Frederick Lawrence. 1962; Cambridge: MIT Press, 1989.

Haddawy, Husain, trans. *The Arabian Nights*. New York: Norton, 1990.

Hafez, Sabry. *The Genesis of Arabic Narrative Discourse: A Study in the Sociology of Modern Arabic Literature*. London: Saqi, 1993.

Hanssen, Jens. "The Birth of an Educational Quarter: Zokak el-Blat as a Cradle of Cultural Revival in the Arab World." In *History, Space and*

Social Conflict in Beirut: The Quarter of Zokak el-Blat, edited by Hans Gebhardt, Dorothée Sack, Ralph Bodenstein, Andreas Fritz, Jens Hanssen, Bernhard Hillenkamp, Oliver Kögler, Anne Mollenhauer, and Friederike Stolleis. Beirut: Orient Institute, 2005.

———. *Fin de Siècle Beirut: The Making of an Ottoman Provincial Capital.* Oxford: Clarendon Press, 2005.

Ḥasan, Muḥammad ʿAbd al-Ghanī. *Jurjī Zaydān.* Cairo: Al-Hayʾah al-Miṣriyyah al-ʿĀmmah li-l-Tāʾlīf wa-l-Nashr, 1970.

Hayek, Ghenwa. *Beirut, Imagining the City: Space and Place in Lebanese Literature.* London: I. B. Tauris, 2014.

———. "Experimental Female Fictions; or, the Brief Wondrous Life of the *Nahḍa* Sensation Story." *Middle Eastern Literatures* 16, no. 3 (2013): 249–65.

Henderson, George L. *California and the Fictions of Capital.* New York: Oxford University Press, 1999.

Holt, Elizabeth M. "From Gardens of Knowledge to Ezbekiyya after Midnight: The Novel and the Arabic Press from Beirut to Cairo, 1870–1892." In "Authoring the *Nahḍa*: Writing the Arabic 19th Century," special issue, *Middle Eastern Literatures* 16, no. 3 (December 2013): 1–17.

———, trans. "Henry and Amelia" and "Selected Anecdotes and Announcements from the 1870s Beirut Press." In *The Arab Renaissance: Anthology of Nahda Thought, Literature, and Language*, edited by Tarek El-Ariss. New York: Modern Language Association, 2016.

———. "Narrative and the Reading Public in 1870s Beirut." *Journal of Arabic Literature* 40, no. 1 (2009): 37–70.

———. "Speculating in Egypt: Yaʿqūb Ṣarrūf's 1905 Novel Fatāt Miṣr." Abhath (2016).

Hughes, Linda K., and Michael Lund. *The Victorian Serial.* Charlottesville: University Press of Virginia, 1991.

Jakes, Aaron. "Boom, Bugs, Bust: Egypt's Ecology of Interest, 1882–1914." *Antipode* (2016): 1–25. Online.

———. "Review Essay: A New Materialism? Globalization and Technology in an Age of Empire." *International Journal of Middle East Studies* 47 (2015): 369–81.

Jameson, Fredric. "Culture and Finance Capital." *Critical Inquiry* 24 (Autumn 1997): 246–65.

Jeha, Shafik. *Darwin and the Crisis of 1882 in the Medical Department and the First Student Protest in the Arab World in the Syrian Protestant College (Now the American University of Beirut).* Translated by Sally Kaya. Beirut: American University of Beirut Press, 2004.

Jessup, Henry Harris. *The Women of the Arabs*. New York: Dodd and Mead, 1873.

Johnson, Rebecca C. "Importing the Novel: The Arabic Novel in and as Translation." *Novel: A Forum for Fiction* 48, no. 2 (2015): 243–60.

Johnson, Rebecca Carol, Richard Maxwell, and Katie Trumpener. "*The Arabian Nights*, Arab-European Literary Influence, and the Lineages of the Novel." *Modern Language Quarterly* 68, no. 2 (June 2007): 243–60.

Kendall, Elisabeth. *Literature, Journalism and the Avant-Garde: Intersection in Egypt*. New York: Routledge, 2006.

Khaldi, Boutheina. *Egypt Awakening in the Early Twentieth Century: Mayy Ziyadah's Intellectual Circles*. New York: Palgrave Macmillan, 2012.

———. "Epistolarity in a Nahḍah Climate: The Role of Mayy Ziyādah's Letter Writing." *Journal of Arabic Literature* 40, no. 1 (2009): 1–36.

Khater, Akram Fouad. *Inventing Home: Emigration, Gender, and the Middle Class in Lebanon, 1870–1920*. Berkeley: University of California Press, 2001.

al-Khūrī, Khalīl. *Way—idhan lastu bi-ifranjī: Al-Riwāyah al-ʿarabiyyah al-ūlā wa-l-rāʾidah*. Edited by Shirbil Dāghir. Beirut: Dār al-Fārābī, 2009.

al-Khūrī, Shākir. *Majmaʿ al-masarrāt*. Edited by Ilyās Qaṭṭār. 1908. Beirut: Dār Laḥd Khāṭir, 1985.

Khūrī, Yūsuf Qizmā, ed. *Aʿmāl al-jamʿīyah al-ʿilmiyyah al-sūriyyah*. Beirut: Dār al-Ḥamrāʾ, 1990.

———. *al-Jamʿiyah al-sūriyyah li-l-ʿulūm wa-l-funūn 1847–1852*. Beirut: Dār al-Ḥamrāʾ, 1990.

Khuri-Makdisi, Ilham. *The Eastern Mediterranean and the Making of Global Radicalism, 1860–1914*. Berkeley: University of California Press, 2010.

Kornbluh, Anna. *Realizing Capital: Financial and Psychic Economies in Victorian Form*. New York: Fordham University Press, 2013.

Kupferschmidt, Uri M. "Who Needed Department Stores in Egypt? From Orosdi-Back to Omar Effendi." *Middle Eastern Studies* 43, no. 2 (2007): 175–92.

Labaki, Boutros. *Introduction à l'histoire économique du Liban: Soie et commerce extérieur en fin de période ottomane (1840–1914)*. Beirut: Publications de l'Université Libanaise, 1984.

Lehrman, Jonas Benzion. *Earthly Paradise: Garden and Courtyard in Early Islam*. Berkeley: University of California Press, 1980.

Levine, Caroline. *The Serious Pleasures of Suspense: Victorian Realism and Narrative Doubt*. Charlottesville: University of Virginia Press, 2003.

Levy, Jonathan. *Freaks of Fortune: The Emerging World of Capitalism and Risk in America*. Cambridge: Harvard University Press, 2012.

Makdisi, Ussama. *The Culture of Sectarianism: Community, History, and Violence in Nineteenth-Century Ottoman Lebanon*. Berkeley: University of California Press, 2000.

Marx, Karl. *Capital*. Vols. 1–3. London: Penguin, 1991.

Massad, Joseph. *Desiring Arabs*. Chicago: University of Chicago Press, 2007.

Mitchell, Timothy *Colonising Egypt*. Berkeley: University of California Press, 1991.

———. *Rule of Experts: Egypt, Techno-Politics, Modernity*. Berkeley: University of California Press, 2002.

Moosa, Matti. *The Origins of Modern Arabic Fiction*. Boulder, CO: Lynne Rienner, 1997.

Mottahedeh, Roy. "*'Aja'ib* in *The Thousand and One Nights*." In "*The Thousand and One Nights" in Arabic Literature and Society*, edited by Richard G. Hovannisian and Georges Sabagh. Cambridge: Cambridge University Press, 1997.

Mūsā, Salāma. *The Education of Salāma Mūsā*. Translated by L. O. Schuman. Leiden: Brill, 1961.

al-Mūsawī, Muḥsin Jāsim. *al-Riwāyah al-ʿarabiyyah: al-nashaʾah wa-l-taḥawwul*. Cairo: Al-Hayʾah al-Miṣriyyah al-ʿĀmmah li-l-Kitāb, 1988.

al-Musawi, Muhsin Jassim. *The Medieval Islamic Republic of Letters: Arabic Knowledge Construction*. Notre Dame: University of Notre Dame Press, 2015.

———. *Scheherazade in England: A Study of the Nineteenth-Century Criticism of the Arabian Nights*. Washington, DC: Three Continents, 1981.

al-Muwayliḥī, Muḥammad. *Ḥadīth ʿĪsā ibn Hishām, aw fatrah min al-zaman*. Translated by Roger Allen in a bilingual edition, *What 'Isa ibn Hisham Told Us: or, A Period of Time, Volume One*. New York: Library of Arabic Literature, New York University Press, 2015.

Najm, Muḥammad Yūsuf. *Al-Qissah fi-l-adab al-ʿarabī al-ḥadīth*. Cairo: Dār Miṣr li-l-Ṭibāʿah, 1952.

Noorani, Yaseen. "The Lost Garden of Al-Andalus: Islamic Spain and the Poetic Inversion of Colonialism." *International Journal of Middle East Studies* 31, no. 2 (1999): 237–54.

Orfali, Bilal. "The Art of the *Muqadimma* in the Works of Abū Manṣūr al-Thaʿālibī (d. 429/1039)." In *The Weaving of Words: Approaches to Classical Arabic Prose*, edited by Lale Behzadi and Vahid Behmardi, 181–202. Beirut: Orient Institut Beirut, 2009.

———. "A Sketch Map of Arabic Poetry Anthologies up to the Fall of Baghdad." *Journal of Arabic Literature* 43, no. 1 (2012): 29–59.

Orfali, Bilal, and Nada Saab, eds. *Sufism, Black and White: A Critical Edition of "al-Bayāḍ wa-l-Sawād" by Abū Ḥasan al-Sīrjānī (d. ca. 470/1077).* Boston: Brill, 2012.

Philipp, Thomas. *Acre: The Rise and Fall of a Palestinian City—World Economy and Local Politics.* New York: Columbia University Press, 2002.

———. "The Role of Jurji Zaydan in the Intellectual Development of the Arab Nahdah from the Beginning of the British Occupation of Egypt to the Outbreak of WWI." Ph.D. diss., University of California, Los Angeles, 1971.

———. *The Syrians in Egypt: 1725–1975.* Stuttgart: Franz Steiner Verlag, 1985.

Rastegar, Kamran. "Literary Modernity between Arabic and Persian Prose: Jurji Zaydan's Riwayat in Persian Translation." *Comparative Critical Studies* 4, no. 3 (2007): 359–78.

———. *Literary Modernity between the Middle East and Europe.* London: Routledge, 2007.

Reports by His Majesty's Agent and Consul-General on the Finances, Administration, and Condition of Egypt and the Soudan in 1908. London: Harrison and Sons, 1909.

Reynolds, Nancy. *A City Consumed: Commerce, the Cairo Fire, and the Politics of Decolonization in Egypt.* Palo Alto: Stanford University Press, 2012.

Robbins, Bruce. *The Servant's Hand: English Fiction from Below.* Durham, NC: Duke University Press, 1993.

Ryzova, Lucie. *The Age of the Efendiyya: Passage to Modernity in National-Colonial Egypt.* Oxford: Oxford University Press, 2014.

———. "The Good, the Bad and the Ugly: Collector, Dealer and Academic in the Informal Old-Paper Markets of Cairo." In *Archives, Museums and Collecting Practices in the Modern Arab World*, edited by Sonja Mejcher-Atassi and John Pedro Schwartz, 98–120. Burlington, VT: Ashgate, 2012.

al-Saʿāfīn, Ibrāhīm. *Taṭawwur al-riwāyah al-ʿarabiyyah al-ḥadīthah fī bilād al-Shām: 1870–1967.* Beirut: Dār al-Mināhil, 1987.

Sacks, Jeffrey. "Futures of Literature: *Inhitat, Adab, Naqd.*" *diacritics* 37, no. 4 (Winter 2007): 32–55.

———. *Iterations of Loss: Mutilation and Aesthetic Form, al-Shidyaq to Darwish.* New York: Fordham University Press, 2015.

Sajdi, Dana. *The Barber of Damascus: Nouveau Literacy in the Eighteenth-Century Ottoman Levant.* Palo Alto: Stanford University Press, 2013.

———. "Decline, Its Discontents, and Ottoman Cultural History: By Way of Introduction." In *Ottoman Tulips, Ottoman Coffee: Leisure and*

Lifestyle in the Eighteenth Century, edited by Dana Sajdi. London: I. B. Tauris, 2007.

———. "Print and Its Discontents: A Case for Pre-Print Journalism and Other Sundry Print Matters." *Translator* 15, no. 1 (2009): 105–38.

Sakkut, Hamdi. *The Arabic Novel: Bibliography and Critical Introduction, 1865–1995*. Cairo: American University in Cairo Press, 2000.

Ṣarrūf, Yaʿqūb. *Fatāt Miṣr*. 4th ed. Cairo: Maṭbaʿat al-Muqtaṭaf, 1922.

Sartori, Andrew. *Bengal in Global Concept History: Culturalism in the Age of Capital*. Chicago: University of Chicago Press, 2008.

Sehnaoui, Nada. *L'occidentalisation de la vie quotidienne à Beyrouth: 1860–1914*. Beirut: Éditions Dar an-Nahar, 2002.

Seikaly, Sherene. *Men of Capital: Scarcity and Economy in Mandate Palestine*. Palo Alto: Stanford University Press, 2016.

Selim, Samah. "Fiction and Colonial Identities: Arsène Lupin in Arabic." *Middle Eastern Literatures* 13, no. 2 (August 2010): 191–210.

———. *The Novel and the Rural Imaginary in Egypt, 1880–1985*. New York: RoutledgeCurzon 2004.

———. "The People's Entertainment: Translation, Popular Fiction, and the Nahdah in Egypt." In *Other Renaissances: A New Approach to World Literature*, edited by Brenda Deen Schildgen, 35–88. New York: Palgrave Macmillan, 2006.

———. "Toward a New Literary History." *International Journal of Middle Eastern Studies* 43 (2011): 734–36.

Sheehi, Stephen. *Foundations of Modern Arab Identity*. Gainesville: University Press of Florida, 2004.

———. "A Social History of Early Arab Photography, or a Prolegomenon to an Archaeology of the Lebanese Imago." *International Journal of Middle East Studies* 39 (2007).

———. "Towards a Critical Theory of *al-Nahḍah*: Epistemology, Ideology and Capital." *Journal of Arabic Literature* 43, no. 2–3 (2012): 269–98.

Siskin, Clifford. "Epilogue: The Rise of Novelism." In *Cultural Institutions of the Novel*, edited by Deirdre Lynch and William Beatty Warner, 399–422. Durham, NC: Duke University Press, 1996.

Starkey, Paul. *Modern Arabic Literature*. Edinburgh: Edinburgh University Press, 2006.

Tageldin, Shaden. *Disarming Words: Empire and the Seductions of Translation in Egypt*. Berkeley: University of California Press, 2011.

Watt, Ian. *The Rise of the Novel*. Berkeley: University of California Press, 2001.

Williams, Raymond. *Marxism and Literature*. New York: Oxford University Press, 1977.

Yāghī, ʿAbd al-Raḥmān. *al-Juhūd al-riwā'iyyah min Salīm al-Bustānī ilā Najīb Maḥfūẓ*. Beirut: Dār al-fārābī, 1999.

Zachs, Fruma, and Sharon Halevi. *Gendering Culture in Greater Syria: Intellectuals and Ideology in the Late Ottoman Period*. New York: I. B. Tauris, 2015.

Zaydān, Jurjī. *Asīr al-Mutamahdī*. Beirut: Dār Maktabat al-Ḥayāt, 2002–3.

———. *Mudhākirāt Jurjī Zaydān*. Edited by Ṣalāḥ al-Dīn al-Munajjid. Beirut: Dār al-Kitāb al-Jadīd, 1968.

———. *Tarīkh ādāb al-lughah al-ʿarabiyyah*. Vol. 4. 1914. Cairo: Dār al-Hilāl, 1957.

———. *Yawmiyyāt riḥlah baḥriyyah: Makhṭūṭah tunshir li-l-marrah al-ūlā*. Edited by Jān Dāyh. Beirut: Fajr al-Nahḍah, 2010.

INDEX